Arnold Suppan, Maximilian Graf (Eds.)

From the Austrian Empire to Communist East Central Europe

EUROPA ORIENTALIS

herausgegeben vom

Institut für Osteuropäische Geschichte
an der Universität Wien

Band 10

LIT

From the Austrian Empire to Communist East Central Europe

edited by

Arnold Suppan and Maximilian Graf

LIT

Cover Picture: Österreichisches Hospiz Jerusalem
Photo: www.hudelist.com

Layout: Richard Lein

Gedruckt mit Unterstützung des Bundesministeriums
für Wissenschaft und Forschung in Wien

Bibliographic information published by the Deutsche Nationalbibliothek
The Deutsche Nationalbibliothek lists this publication in the Deutsche Nationalbibliografie; detailed bibliographic data are available in the Internet at http://dnb.d-nb.de.

ISBN 978-3-643-50235-3

A catalogue record for this book is available from the British Library

Krotenthallergasse 10/8
A-1080 Wien
Tel. +43 (0) 1-409 56 61
Fax +43 (0) 1-409 56 97
e-Mail: wien@lit-verlag.at
http://www.lit-verlag.at

LIT VERLAG Dr. W. Hopf
Berlin 2010
Fresnostr. 2
D-48159 Münster
Tel. +49 (0) 2 51-620 320
Fax +49 (0) 2 51-922 60 99
e-Mail: lit@lit-verlag.de
http://www.lit-verlag.de

Distribution:
In Germany: LIT Verlag Fresnostr. 2, D-48159 Münster
Tel. +49 (0) 2 51-620 32 22, Fax +49 (0) 2 51-922 60 99, e-mail: vertrieb@lit-verlag.de
In Austria: Medienlogistik Pichler-ÖBZ, e-mail: mlo@medien-logistik.at
In Switzerland: B + M Buch- und Medienvertrieb, e-mail: order@buch-medien.ch

In the UK: Global Book Marketing, e-mail: mo@centralbooks.com

In North America by:

Transaction Publishers
New Brunswick (U.S.A.) and London (U.K.)

Transaction Publishers
Rutgers University
35 Berrue Circle
Piscataway, NJ 08854

Phone: +1 (732) 445 - 2280
Fax: + 1 (732) 445 - 3138
for orders (U. S. only):
toll free (888) 999 - 6778
e-mail: orders@transactionpub.com

Index of contents

Preface

It is a great pleasure to present to the scientific community the third special volume of the series Europa Orientalis regularly published by the Institute for East European History at the University of Vienna. It contains a compilation of papers and reports from the Annual Convention of the Centers for Austrian and Central European Studies held in November 2009 at the Hebrew University of Jerusalem. Like its predecessors, this volume covers a wide range of topics in modern central European history prepared by young scholars of the Centers for Austrian and Central European Studies. Their contributions, as well as the introductory reports by the Centers' directors, provide an excellent overview of the activities of these institutions during the academic year 2009/2010.

When the Austrian Federal Ministry for Science and Research started its ambitious program to promote Austrian and Central European studies in other parts of the world in the 1970s with the foundation of the "Center for Austrian Studies" at the University of Minnesota and the Austrian chair at Stanford University, nobody could foresee the exceptional success of this initiative. Today six institutions of this kind exist in four different countries (Canada, Hungary, Israel, U.S.A), which have proven to be of great significance not only for students of the host nations who want to learn about Austrian and Central European history, but also for young scholars who are eager to study in foreign countries and get in touch with the local scientific community. These colleagues conduct valuable research not only on the history of the former Austro–Hungarian Empire and its successor states, but also on the contemporary history of Central Europe.

In this context, it has become one of the aims of the Austrian Federal Ministry for Science and Research not only to supply Austrian students with scholarships, but also to help them establish themselves in the international scientific community. While experienced scholars are usually well–connected with partners all over the world, students and young scientists often experience difficulties in trying to get in touch with colleagues abroad. Therefore in 2007 the Austrian Federal Ministry for Science and Research decided to bring together the best young scholars conducting their research at the Centers for Austrian and Central European Studies. As the first meeting in Minneapolis was such an outstanding success, the Austrian Federal Ministry for Science and Research decided to carry forward this initiative and to bring together scholars and students of the Centers on a regular basis. The present volume clearly documents the success and importance of this initiative, not only for the participating colleagues, but for the whole scientific community as well.

Dr. Beatrix Karl
Austrian Federal Minister of Science and Research

Centers

Marija Wakounig

The Department of East European History University of Vienna

The Department of East European History in Vienna has continued its wide-ranging activities in the academic year 2009/10. Owing to the Bologna process, which was introduced in Austria last fall, the University of Vienna has fundamentally reformed its study programs, introducing a new Bachelor (BA) and several Master (MA) programs in the field of historical sciences. On the basis to this development, our Department started its own MA study program "East European History", which is quite popular among the students. The last academic year has, however, shown quite clearly that some aspects of the BA program as well as of the MA program need to be modified since the increasing number of students at the University of Vienna, which couldn't be foreseen during the planning process, lead to overcrowded lecture halls and booked up courses. During the past academic year, the Department organized a large-scale lecture series one on the topic of *Women in East-, Central- and Southeast Europe in the Twentieth Century*. A second lecture series on the topic of *The Political Song in East- and Southeast Europe* was co-organized by the Department of East European history and the Department of Slavonic Studies in context with the Research Platform "Wiener Osteuropaforum". Both events were attended by about 100 students every week, coming from nearly all departments of our faculty.

It is furthermore our sad duty to announce that a long-standing member of our academic staff, emer. Univ. Prof. Dr. Walter Leitsch has died on February 22, 2010. Leitsch had held the chair for East European history at our Department from 1965 until 1996 and was a well-known expert on the history of East Central Europe. At his funeral, Univ. Prof. Dr. Arnold Suppan, Secretary General of the Austrian Academy of Sciences, and ao. Univ. Prof. Mag. Dr. Marija Wakounig praised the deceased as an outstanding scientist and colleague, whom we will all miss gravely. Walter Leitsch's last major work, a four-volume monograph abut life at the court of king Sigismund III of Poland, was published posthumous and presented to the scientific community in a ceremony at our Department in April 2010. We also have to report that Univ. Prof. Dr. Horst Haselsteiner, likewise a long-standing member of our staff, is retiring at the end of September 2010. Haselsteiner, an expert on Hungarian history from ancient up to present times, will be succeeded by Univ. Prof. Dr. Philipp Ther, who has recently joined our team. It is furthermore our pleasure to announce that two of our younger colleagues, Armina Galijas and Richard Lein, have completed their studies and earned a doctorate by completing their PhD theses and passing the final exams during the past academic year. We wish both young scholars the best for their future and their promising scientific careers. Our staff was furthermore joined by two young scientists, Mag. Paul Worster and Mag. Andreas Rathberger, who will complete their doctoral studies within the next two years.

For the upcoming academic year the Department of East European History plans to continue its program of organizing guest lectures, conferences and other scientifically relevant events, which have proven to be quite popular among the local scientific community. Due to the fact that two more members of our academic staff are going to retire within the next twelve months, the Department is expected to experience some radical changes in the near future. Despite this fact and despite the still challenging economic situation, which fortunately hasn't hit us quite as hard as other Universities all over the World, we are looking forward to the academic year 2010/11 with great confidence.

Basic Facts

Personnel: 14 scholars (four full professors, four associate professors, four assistant professors, two assistants), five general employees, three part-time instructors;

Academia: approximately 2.000 students per semester, 30 PhD candidates, 50 diploma candidates;

Regular events: International Seminar for Students of the Historical Department of the University of Ljubljana, held every spring;

Regular publications: Europa Orientalis; Prague Papers on the History of International Relations (published together with the Department of World History, Charles University Prague);

Library: 120,000 volumes; two librarians, one part-time employee;

Fields of research: Soviet Union, Russia, East Central Europe, Southeast Europe, CIS.

Current Activities

Research Platform „Wiener Osteuropaforum“

The interdisciplinary Research Platform "Wiener Osteuropaforum", sponsored by the University of Vienna, has been established in 2009 and is based at the Department for East European History. In accordance with its aim – bringing together researchers from different fields of study to enable them to share their knowledge on Eastern

Europe and initiate interdisciplinary research projects – the Platform has carried out a number of activities.

In March 2010 the "Wiener Osteuropaforum" on the occasion of its public presentation was honoured to host a public lecture with HE Fürst Karl Schwarzenberg in the presence of 200 participants from the fields of science, media, culture and politics as well as the interested public on the topic "Return to Europe? What remains open after 20 years of European East–West–Integration?" On behalf of the Platform, Prof. Oliver J. Schmitt and Prof. Dieter Segert from the Department for Political Sciences at the University of Vienna inter alia announced the launch of the new website „www.osteuropaforum.at", which provides researchers of the University of Vienna with the possibility to present their skills and activities online while getting into contact with colleagues working on related fields of study. The website, which also documents the various activities organized by the Platform, thus has set up a unique, continuously growing network of professionals at the University of Vienna from a wide range of subject areas.

Senior and junior researchers since winter semester 2009/10 have furthermore worked together to establish two new important forums for interdisciplinary exchange. The "Interdisciplinary Colloquium" and the "Jour fixe" aim at enhancing interdisciplinary dialogue, touching upon all the different fields of study that come together in the context of the Platform.

In April 2010, the Platform hosted the twenty–fifth Romanistic Colloquium, bringing together under the lead of the Department for Romanistic Studies an international group of most distinguished researchers from the fields of Linguistics, Balkanology, Byzantine Studies, Ethnology, Geography, History, Greek studies, Romanistic Studies and Slavonic Studies. The event, which sets its focus on the issue of "Settlements and Migration in South Eastern Europe", was co–organized by the Department of East European History at the University of Vienna, the Balkans Commission at the Austrian Academy of Sciences and the Department of Linguistics at the University of Vienna.

In summer semester 2009, the Research Platform under the lead of the Department of East European History at the University of Vienna and the Department for Slavonic Studies at the University of Vienna hosted an interdisciplinary lecture series on "The Political Song in East and South Eastern Europe". The results of this lecture series, which brought together experts from the disciplines of History and Slavonic and Byzantine Studies, will be published in the series "Europa Orientalis" by the Department of East European History in 2010.

The Platform has furthermore announced a second lecture series for the winter semester 2010/11 focusing on the topic of

"Saints in East and South Eastern Europe" and including perspectives from the fields of History, Theology, Romanistic Studies, Byzantine Studies and Archaeology. Under the lead of the Department of Classical Archaeology at the University of Vienna and the Department for Theology and History of the Eastern Churches at the University of Vienna, this series particularly called upon junior researchers to participate as lecturers and thus actively contribute to the research process. It is also very much in accordance with a central aim of the Platform – the support of young researchers – that an initiative group of PhD students from the fields of Classical Archaeology, Slavonic Studies, History and History of Art has organized an interdisciplinary symposium to be held in October 2010. The event has the organisational and financial support of the research platform and focuses on the topic of "Everyday life in East and South Eastern Europe from late antiquity to the present time".

"Galicia" doctoral college (interdisciplinary)

The Department of East European History and the Department of Slavonic Studies are the leading institutions of the interdisciplinary „Galicia" doctoral college, sponsored by the Austrian Science Fund (FWF). It consists of nine collegiates from six different countries, studying Slavic studies, German studies, East European History, Economic and Social History. The college was set up in November 2006 and has been recently renewed for another five years. Due to the upcoming retirement of Univ. Prof. Dr. Andreas Kappeler, who had been the head of the doctoral college since its establishment, his responsibilities as leader of the research team have been taken over by Univ. Prof. Mag. Dr. Alois Woldan from the Department of Slavonic Studies of the University of Vienna and our colleague ao. Univ. Prof. Dr. Christoph Augustynowicz. They will continue the work of Andreas Kappeler and lead the college, which has recently been provided with state-of the-art facilities on the University's Campus, to its future tasks.

Guest Lectures

- „Die Turksprachen: Ein Überblick" (Prof. Claus Schönig, Germany), April 23, 2009
- „Ideology and Alliance Politics: Reflections on the Rise and Demise of the Sino-Soviet Alliance" (Prof. Chen Jian, USA), May 13, 2009.
- „Kulturelle Begegnungen" (Prof. Ingeborg Baldauf, Germany), May 28, 2009.
- „Die Deutsche (Karls-)Universität vom Münchener Abkommen bis zum Ende des Zweiten Weltkrieges. Universitätsleitung und

Wandel des Professorenkollegiums" (Doz. Alena Míšková, Czech Republic), May 4, 2009.

- „Ukrainian History as Family History“ (Prof. Timothy Snyder, USA), November 3 2009.
- „Die Ukraine nach der Präsidentenwahl” (Dr. Tatjana Zhurzhenko, Ukraine), January 26, 2010.
- „Österreich-Ungarn, die Botschafterkonferenz von Konstantinopel und die Kretakrise 1896–1898“ (Mag. Andreas Rathberger), March 4, 2010.
- „Kosovo als Region. Raumbegriffe, Identitäten und Diskurse in der Vergangenheit und heute (Eva Frantz, M.A.), March 4, 2010.
- „Das Konzept des Neuen Menschen im kommunistischen Albanien (1961–1971“ (Idrit Idrizi), March 11, 2010.
- „Der siebenbürgische Wald als Habitat am Rande des Habsburgischen Reiches” (Dorin Rus, Romania), March 11, 2010.
- „Chiliastische Strömungen der 2. Hälfte des 15. Jhs und Strategien des Überlebens orthodoxer Christen im Zeitalter der osmanischen Eroberungen in Südosteuropa. Der Umgang des Patriarchen Gennadios mit der neuen Herrschaft“ (St. Bulasikis), March 11, 2010.
- „Der Modernisierungsdiskurs der albanischen Gesellschaft der Zwischenkriegszeit“ (Mag. Lindita Sina), March 18, 2010.
- „Von Alba Iulia nach Bukarest. Siebenbürgen und der rumänische Zentralstaat (1918–1940)“ (Mag. Florian Kührer), March 18, 2010.
- „Polnische Frauenbewegung im 19. und zu Beginn des 20. Jahrhunderts“ (Univ. Doz. Dr. Almut Bues, Poland), April 13, 2010.
- „Der Seehandel der Städte Korčula, Split und Trogir – Ein Blick auf Wirtschafts-, Sozial- und Umweltgeschichte Dalmatiens zwischen 1480 und 1573” (Sascha Attia), April 15, 2010.
- „Protektorate der Großmächte im Südosteuropa des 19. Jahrhunderts: ein Vergleich der Beispiele Griechenland, Donaufürstentümer und Bulgarien“ (Rosa Engl) April 15, 2010.
- „Nationale Identität und Sport in Kroatien nach 1991 – eine theoretisch-methodologische Annäherung“ (Dario Brentin), April 15, 2010.
- „Screening socialism: The everyday life of Bulgarian cinema in the 1970–1980s (Dr. Nadige Ragaru, France), April 22, 2010.
- „Die Entstehung des Mythos von Peter dem Großen” (Dr. Francine-Dominique Liechten, France), April 26, 2010.

- „Lage der Frau in der modernen slowakischen Gesellschaft“ (Zuzaná Kicková, Slovakia), April 27, 2010.
- „Zur Situation der Frauen in der slowakischen Gesellschaft“ (Univ. Prof. Dr. Etela Farkašova, Slovakia), April 27, 2010.
- „The collectivization of agriculture in Rumania 1949 – 1962 (Dr. Dorin Dobrincu, Romania), April 29, 2010.
- „Frauen in Bulgarien im 20. Jahrundert" (Ass. Prof. Dr. Kristina Popov, Bulgaria), May 11, 2010.
- „Die Lieder der Eisernen Garde, eine inhaltliche und funktionelle Analyse“ (Andra Drăghiciu), June 24, 2010.
- „Konkurrieren um den öffentlichen Raum in Ioanna“ (Theodora Danek), June 24, 2010.

Conferences

- „Prozesse ukrainischer Nationsbildung“ (Prof. Andreas Kappeler together with the Department of East European History), October 1 - October 3, 2009.
- "The Revolutions of 1989" (Prof. Arnold Suppan together with the Austrian Academy of Sciences) October 1 – October 3, 2009.

Other major events

- Book presentation: „Rumänien. Geschichte und Geographie“ by Kurt Scharr and Rudolf Gräf, February 4, 2009.
- Book presentation: „Humanismus bei den Slovenen. Slovenische Humanisten bis zur Mitte des 16. Jahrhunderts“, ed. by Marija Wakounig, June 6, 2009.
- Book presentation: „Imperienvergleich. Beispiele und Ansätze aus osteuropäischer Perspektive“, ed. by Guido Hausmann and Angela Rustemeyer, September 29, 2009.
- Book presentation: „Galizien – Fragmente eines diskursiven Raums“, ed. By Doktoratskolleg Galizien, March 4, 2010.
- Book presentation: „Das Leben am Hof König Sigismunds III. von Polen“, by Walter Leitsch (†), April 26, 2010.

Current research projects

- „The Forest as Habitat in Transylcania of the eighteenth century: Society, Economy and Environment in the Edge of the Habsburg Empire" (Project leader: Univ. Prof. Mag. Dr. Oliver Jens Schmitt).
- „Politics and Society in Late Ottoman Kosovo 1870–1913" (Project leader: Univ. Prof. Mag. Dr. Oliver Jens Schmitt).

Main Publications 2009/2010

- Arnold Suppan, Wolfgang Mueller (Eds.), Peaceful Coexistence or Iron Curtain? Austria, Neutrality, and Eastern Europe in the Cold War and Détente, 1955–1989, Europa Orientalis 7, Wien/Berlin 2009.
- Oliver Jens Schmitt, Gherardo Ortalli (Eds.), Balcani occidentali, Adriatico e Venezia fra XIII e XVIII secolo. Der westliche Balkan, der Adriaraum und Venedig (13.–18. Jahrhundert), Österreichische Akdemie der Wissenschaften – Schriften der Balkan-Kommission 50, Venezia/Wien 2009.
- Klaus Koch, Walter Rauscher, Arnold Suppan, Elisabeth Vyslonzil (Eds.), Außenpolitische Dokumente der Republik Österreich 1918–1938 (ADÖ), Band 8: Österreich im Zentrum der Mitteleuropapläne. 12. September 1931 bis 23. Februar 1933, Wien 2009.
- Oliver Jens Schmitt, Eva Anne Frantz (Eds.) Albanische Geschichte. Stand und Perspektiven der Forschung, Südosteuropäische Arbeiten 140, Regensburg 2009.
- Doktoratskolleg Galizien (Ed.), Galizien – Fragmente eines diskursiven Raums, Innsbruck/Wien/Bozen 2009.
- Oliver Jens Schmitt, Skanderbeg. Der neue Alexander auf dem Balkan, Regensburg 2009.
- Guido Hausmann, Angela Rustemeyer (Eds.), Imperienvergleich. Beispiele und Ansätze aus osteuropäischer Perspektive. Festschrift für Andreas Kappeler, Forschungen zur osteuropäischen Geschichte 75, Wiesbaden 2009.
- Arnold Suppan, Richard Lein (Eds.), East European Identities in the 19th and 20th Century, Europa Orientalis 8, Wien/Berlin 2009.
- Georg Kastner, Ungarn 1956 vor der UNO, Innsbruck/Wien/Bozen 2010.

Gary Cohen

The Center for Austrian Studies University of Minnesota

Programs and Initiatives in 2009

In 2009 governments in the United States and throughout the world continued to face challenging economic conditions. All universities and research institutes had to endure budgetary cuts. In addition, the Center for Austrian Studies (CAS) at the University of Minnesota saw the market value of its endowment, and therefore its income, decline. As a result, we aggressively and successfully sought outside funding. This enabled us both to enhance the best elements in our established programs and to add new initiatives which broadened the work of the Center.

Ongoing programs and collaborations

As in the past, Center offered a diverse range of lectures, literary readings, and musical performances open to the campus and Twin Cities communities, with fourteen events in addition to the 25th Annual Robert A. Kann Memorial Lecture, delivered by David Luft. The richly varied subjects included music education, cultural studies, Jewish studies, social and political history, sociology, and international relations. The presentations demonstrated clearly the vitality of the research being devoted at present to Austrian and Central European questions as well as the high levels of current artistic endeavors in that part of the world. The Center's close cooperation with many other departments, centers, and individual colleagues in the College of Liberal Arts as well as other segments of the University of Minnesota contributed to the high intellectual interest of our programs and to the diverse audiences which they attracted.

The Center's long history of collaborations with Austrian and Central European universities and individual scholars bore fruit in the return of distinguished figures who are old friends of the Center as well as the participation of individuals new to the Center and the University of Minnesota. Ruth Wodak (applied linguistics), Hanspeter Neuhold (international law), and Monika Oebelsberger (music education) are examples of renowned Austrian scholars and past collaborators who returned to participate in the CAS lecture series. On the other hand, Klaus Hödl (Jewish studies) and Harald Rohracher (sociology), among other scholars, visited the University of Minnesota campus for the first time, bringing fascinating new perspectives and drawing new audiences.

The Center for Austrian Studies had two Austrian Fulbright Visiting Professors during the calendar year 2009. In the spring semester, art and architectural historian Anselm Wagner (Technische Universität Graz) taught a class in the Department of Art History, and presented two lectures, one for CAS and one for Art History. In the fall semester, Franz Kernic, a political scientist (University of Innsbruck and the Institute for Strategy and Security Policy, Vienna) taught a course in the Department of Political Science and delivered a lecture in the CAS series. Both scholars were welcomed into their host departments, making new scholarly contacts and enriching the education of both undergraduate and graduate students. The Center sponsored other kinds of events as well. In February, musicians Florian Kitt (cello) and Rita Medjimorec (piano), from the University of Music and Dramatic Arts in Graz, gave a recital.

Thanks in large part to the efforts of the Center's administrative manager, Linda Andrean, we have increased in recent years our programming for public audiences outside the immediate University of Minnesota campus community. Professional development workshops for teachers in middle and high schools have become a regular feature of the Center schedule. In February 2009, Linda Andrean, together with colleagues from the Department of Geography at Macalester College (St. Paul, MN), the University of Wisconsin–River Falls, and secondary schools in the Twin Cities area, organized a successful workshop entitled "The Spatial Dynamics of Austria and Central Europe in the 21st Century." It was supported by CAS, the Institute for Global Studies at the University of Minnesota, and the Department of Geography and the Minnesota Alliance for Geographic Education at Macalester College.

Publications

The Center's publications in 2009 also demonstrated the strength of our continuing activities. Daniel Pinkerton produced two issues of the *Austrian Studies Newsletter* with the wide range and freshness of content that have become a hallmark of this internationally circulated publication. Pieter Judson, whose tenure as editor of the *Austrian History Yearbook* began in 2005, agreed to extend his term to 2015. Volume 40 of the *AHY* appeared in the spring and offered a rich array of new scholarship on subjects ranging from a forum in honor of R. J. W. Evans to eugenics in Hungary during World War I.

The Center currently has three new volumes in preparation for its book series, Austrian and Habsburg Studies (Berghahn Books). *Diversity and Dissent: Negotiating Religious Difference in Central Europe, 1500–1800*, edited by Howard Louthan, Franz A. J. Szabo, and Gary B. Cohen, should be published by late 2010. *Social Policy in the Smaller European Union States*, edited by Gary B. Cohen, Ben W. Ansell, Jane Gingrich, and Robert Henry Cox; and *Understanding Multiculturalism and the Central European Experience*, edited by Johannes Feichtinger and Gary B. Cohen, have been submitted to Berghahn Books.

Central European Studies, a book series at Purdue University Press for which Center director Gary Cohen serves as associate editor, published four new books in 2009: two on the collapse of socialist Yugoslavia and its aftermath, a monograph on public architecture in Habsburg Lemberg, and a book by the Austrian historian Peter Thaler on nationality issues in the German–Danish borderlands.

Conferences and new initiatives

Since the Center held an international scholarly symposium, "Social Policy in the New Europe: The Experience of Austria and the Smaller EU Members," *and* a major public forum, "Climate Change, Sustainable Agriculture, and Bioresources," in 2008, we did not host a conference at the University of Minnesota in 2009. The public forum continued to reach a larger audience than any previous CAS event as Twin Cities Public Television (TPT) aired a thirty–minute television program based on interviews with presenters entitled, "Food, Fuel, and Climate Change: An Austrian–American Forum" thirty–six times between February and December of 2009. In the fall, it became available for streaming on the internet from the websites of The Minnesota Project and TPT. By taking advantage of multiple media outlets, CAS has made tens of thousands of people aware of what Austrians and Americans are doing in this vital field.

In 2009 the Center did cosponsor an international conference, "Sex in the Cities: Prostitution, White Slaving, and Sexual Minorities in Eastern and Central Europe," held in L'viv, Ukraine. The other partners were the Wirth Institute for Austrian and Central European Studies and the Center for Urban History of East Central Europe.

The Center's new initiatives during 2009 also included preparations for a new multi–year team research project entitled "Understanding the Migration Experience: The AustrianAmerican Connection." Funded by a generous gift from the Dietrich W. Botstiber Foundation, the research, data collection, and analysis phase were scheduled to begin in January 2010, with a team of researchers including Dr. Annemarie Steidl and Dr. Wladimir Fischer from Vienna and Prof. James Oberly from the University of Wisconsin, Eau Claire. Steidl arrived in late December, Fischer and Oberly followed in January 2010.

Finally, also thanks to the generosity of the Dietrich W. Botstiber Foundation, the first-ever Botstiber Graduate Fellowship was awarded to Adelia Chrysler for the 2009–10 academic year. Chrysler, a former Fulbright English Teaching Assistant in Upper Austria, is a graduate student in German studies. The Botstiber Foundation paid for the first year of her graduate studies, and the university guarantees four more years of funding in the form of fellowships or assistantships.

Franz A.J. Szabo

The Wirth Institute for Austrian and Central European Studies University of Alberta

The 2009–2010 academic year continued to be a busy one for the Wirth Institute for Austrian and Central European Studies despite the challenging economic conditions that saw the Institute forced to take a 23% cut in its endowment income. Continuing support by the Central European ethnic communities of Edmonton and the Austrian Federal Ministry of Science and Research and a major $1.25 million donation by the Austrian Canadian Council helped offset some of the financial difficulties and ensured a full academic and cultural program over the course of the year.

Even before the beginning of the academic year the Wirth Institute was able to persuade the Provost and Vice-President Academic of the University of Alberta, Dr. Carl Amrhein, to undertake a mission to Central Europe on its behalf, accompanied by the Institute Director. In addition to launching a number of promising initiatives, the outcomes of this mission included the signing of the renewal of the agreement with the Hungarian Ministry of Education that provides for an annual Hungarian Doctoral Research Fellow at the Institute, and the conclusion of a partnership agreement with the Franz Schubert Institute of Baden bei Wien. By virtue of the latter agreement participants at this, Europe's leading training centre for the German *Lied,* will now have official University of Alberta credit, which will be transferable to all other North American universities. In addition a special relationship between the staff of the Schubert Institute and the University of Alberta Department of Music was established, with the Director of the former now giving regular master classes at the latter.

As in the past, over the past academic year the Wirth Institute continued the tradition of mounting conferences on Central European themes both at the University of Alberta, and, in fulfillment of its national mandate, in cooperation with other universities in Canada. Chief among the latter was a major scholarly conference on the life and work of Franz Joseph Haydn, mounted together with York University in Toronto on the occasion of the two-hundredth anniversary of Haydn's death, bringing together 38 prominent Haydn scholars from around the world. The conference, held on 6–9 August 2009 and entitled "Celebrating Haydn: His Times and His Legacy," also included recitals by Malcolm Bilson and by the Penderecki String Quartet.

The Institute continued its commemoration of the great Austrian composer's death by sponsoring a series of concerts in Edmonton. It hosted the Lafayette String Quartet in an all-Haydn concert at the University of Alberta on November 15 and co-operated with some of its usual partners – the Alberta Baroque Ensemble for an all-Haydn concert on October 25, and the University of Alberta Symphony Orchestra and Chorus for a performance of Haydn's Oratorio, "The Creation," on November 5. Other musical events included a recital by the famous Czech saxophonist, Felix Slovaček, accompanied by Boris Krajný on the piano, in cooperation with the local chapter of the Czech and Slovak Society for the Arts and Sciences (SVU), the Institute's annual Christmas concert, "Silent Night," which features soloists and Central European community choirs from Edmonton and Calgary, and was rounded out by a March 28 concert "The Art Song of Central Europe," with Elizabeth Turnbull, John Tessier and Michael McMahon with songs by Mozart, Schubert, Wolf, Beethoven, Mahler, Bartók, Kodály, and Lehár. In addition, the Institute cultural program included an exhibition of photographs by the renowned Czech photographer, Přemysl Hněvkovský, "Czech Students at the Turning Point, 1968 and 1989," and a retrospective film festival devoted to the works of the Austrian-born director, Joseph von Sternberg.

On track with its ambitious program of academic conferences, the Institute mounted two major international conferences at the University of Alberta this past fall. On September 11–12 scholars from Canada, the U.S., Britain, Germany, Ukraine, Hungary, Romania and Serbia gathered to take an interdisciplinary look at "Eastern Christians in the Habsburg Monarchy." The conference included papers on all aspects of sacral culture, including architecture, music, painting, embroidery, carving, and metalworking, as well as on confessional politics and the politics of confession. While scholarly work on the Habsburg empire has tended to focus either on individual crown lands, such as Bohemia or Galicia, or on politics as viewed from the centers, Vienna and Budapest, this conference sought to address the large middle ground between the center and the local. Papers dealt with both Orthodox and Greek Catholics within the Monarchy during the entire Habsburg period, and brought together scholars working on a large swath of territory from Galicia through Bukovina and Transylvania to Voivodina, Slavonia and Bosnia. The conference included a special concert of Ukrainian ecclesiastical music, mounted by the Institute at St. George's Ukrainian Catholic Church in Edmonton, featuring the parish choir of that church.

Three weeks later, on October 2–3, the Institute in cooperation with the University of Innsbruck mounted a conference entitled "Emperor Maximilian I. (1459–1519): Perceptions, Transfers, Comparisons," which marked the 550th anniversary of the birth and 490th anniversary of the death of this famous Habsburg emperor. Participants from Canada, the U.S., Austria, Germany and Russia attempted to shed new light on various aspects of the emperor's reign. The conference was part of a larger Maximilian I. research project, which will be published in cooperation with the Wirth Institute shortly.

The Fall of 2009 marked the expansion of the Wirth Institute's regular lecture series. Joining the endowed Holocaust Lecture series, established in 2004, Brandeis University's Antony Polonski formally launched the Institute's new "Tova Yedlin Lecture Series" on the history of Central and East European Jewry prior to the Holocaust with a lecture entitled "The Failure of Jewish Assimilation in the Polish Lands in the Nineteenth Century and its Consequences" on 11 September 2009. The second lecture in this new series was held on 14 March 2010 with a lecture by Marsha L. Rozenblit, Harvey M. Meyerhoff Professor of Jewish History at the University of Maryland, entitled "Assimilation or Jewish Identity: The Dilemmas of Jews in Habsburg Austria." The Institute's annual 'Toby and Saul Reichert Holocaust Lecture' was held on 11 April 2010 and featured Omer Bartov, John P. Birkelund Distinguished Professor of European History at Brown University, speaking on "Genocide in a Multiethnic Town: Event, Origins, Aftermath."

The Institute has also committed to sponsor an annual art history lecture series on Central European themes in the University of Alberta's Department of Art and Design from its own Wirth Endowment. This year's lecturer on 2 November 2009 was Tag Gronberg of the University of London, speaking on "The Viennese Café and fin-de-siècle Culture." In addition, on 30 March Pál Tamás, Director of the Institute of Sociology at the Hungarian Academy of Sciences gave a guest lecture entitled "European Identities in Central Europe: Hopes and disappointments." Finally, the Institute was honoured by a return visit by Salzburg's distinguished professor emeritus, Ernst Wangermann. His two lectures, held on 9 March 2010, "From Joseph II to the Jacobin Trails in the Austrian Empire" and "Public Opinion and Bourgeois Culture in the Habsburg Monarchy on the Eve of the French Revolution" elicited the usual lively discussions we have come to expect.

Finally the Institute's publication program continued with three new collections. A joint publication project with the Canadian Institute of Ukrainian Studies was completed with the publication of an English translation of Vasyl Kuchabsy, *Western Ukraine in Conflict with Poland and Bolshevism, 1918–1923*, translated by Gus Fagan (Edmonton & Toronto: Canadian Institute of Ukrainian Studies Press, 2009). An independent publication project of the Wirth Institute was completed with the publication of Hans Schulte and

Gerald Chapple, eds., *Shadows of the Past: Austrian Literature of the Twentieth Century* (New York: Peter Lang, 2009). And, finally, the proceedings of our Institute's May 2008 conference in cooperation with the University of Ottawa were published this past year as Agatha Schwartz, ed., Gender and Modernity in Central Europe: The Austro-Hungarian Monarchy and its Legacy (Ottawa: University of Ottawa Press, 2010).

Günter Bischof

CenterAustria
University of New Orleans

As a result of the economic downturn and diminishing state revenues, American public universities have been under siege. In the state of Louisiana this is coupled by Governor Bobby Jindal's presidential ambitions who wants to be perceived as a tax-slashing staunch conservative. During this time of diminishing public support for public universities, Austrian Centers probably will need to be even more active in raising private funds to justify their survival and maintain their activities (Franz Szabo's success in raising an endowment for his "Wirth Center" stands as a shining paragon to follow). We will need to be even more active in programming and publishing to demonstrate our utility as Austrian and European Studies centers in the North American landscape of higher education under siege by the budget cutters in our state legislatures and our universities. Whatever we do academically, they only will take note of the bottom line. In spite of such a dire opening statement, at University of New Orleans' (UNO's) CenterAustria we can report a banner year of activities.

UNO's CenterAustria premier contribution to our university's well-being and to our international partnership activities again has been bringing (fee-paying!) students from the University of Innsbruck to UNO, mentoring them and taking care of each and every one of them. 38 (fee-paying students) studied at UNO during the fall and 29 in the spring semester. The majority of them were international business and business administration majors, with psychology running a strong second. Alexander Smith, our Ministry of Science fellow, worked on a dissertation in political science on the politics of oil pipelines in Europe; Manfred Kohler, also a political science PhD candidate and the Nick Mueller fellow, did research on European identity; Philipp Strobl, a Botstiber fellow, worked on the emigration of the Burgenländer in the 1920/30s and will graduate with an MA in History in the fall of 2010; Thomas Maier, another Botstiber fellow, was enrolled in electrical engineering and computer courses. Judith Kopf, who started out as a Fulbright lecturer in German, completed her Master's Degree in French in the Department of Foreign Languages. In February 2010 we had our one-month "Austrian Student Program" with 30 students from many Austrian universities – a "*Schnupperstudium*" in American Studies. All in all, we took care of a whopping 100 Austrian students at UNO in the academic year of 2009/10. There is no American university with a larger turn-over of Austrian students than UNO.

We welcomed Peter Moser, Austria's Ambassador to the United States from 1999 to 2001, as our tenth Marshall Plan Chair in Austrian and European Studies. He was the first diplomat-in-residence at UNO ever. Moser taught courses in European Diplomatic History and on the Practice of Diplomacy. Students greatly appreciated his rich repertoire of colorful stories and pertinent examples of practical diplomacy from a 40+ year career in Austria's Foreign Service. Moser also took this time to finish a first draft of his memoirs. They will be particularly rich on his years as general consul in Los Angeles in the 1980s and Ambassador in Washington during the crisis surrounding the formation of the Schüssel coalition government with the FPÖ. The entire CenterAustria team got involved in typing, proof-reading and commenting on the manuscript; we were greatly enriched by this unique experience. Moser also prepped our "Model UN-Team" going to New York, gave lectures, visited area schools and was engaged in the local community.

"*1989 – Year of Miracles: The End of the Cold War from an Austrian Perspective*" – was a travelling exhibit I curated (with Lorenz Mikoletzky from the Austrian State Archives) for the Austrian Cultural Forum in New York (with generous financial support from the Botstiber Institute of Austrian-American Studies). The exhibit showed at the Austrian Embassy in Washington, D.C. in September/October, at the National World War II Museum in New Orleans in late October/early November, at the Harriman Institute at Columbia University in November/December 2010, and at the Michigan State School of Law in February/March 2010. 20 panels covered much of the history of Austria during the Cold War from Yalta to the crises in the Communist Bloc (1956, 1968, 1980/1) on Austria's borders, as well as the collapse of communism in Eastern Europe in 1989 and beyond to the Balkan Wars of the 1990s. It concluded with EU Eastern expansion in the past ten years. Austria opens an interesting window into the Cold War era as major events unfolded in Austria and beyond its immediate borders. Vienna was a favorite venue for East West summitry (1961, 1979). Austria opened its gates to refugees from neighboring countries after failed attempts to dislodge communist regimes (1956, 1968, 1981). The first major breaches in the iron curtain on the Austro-Hungarian border opened in the summer of 1989, toppling the rest of the falling dominoes. Hundreds of visitors saw this exhibit in these various venues; the Austrian Studies scholarly community had an opportunity to visit it during the "German Studies Association" annual meeting in Arlington, VA, in early October.

On October 1–3, 2009, the Science Division of the Austrian Embassy in Washington, D.C., organized the annual *Austrian Science Talks* under the general theme "*Under Crisis Conditions: Mit Forschung und Technologie aus der Krise*" in New Orleans. CenterAustria worked with Philipp Marxgut from the Embassy on local contacts and logistics. Christian Prosl, Austria's Ambassador to the United States, opened the Science Talks and reminded the 100 or so attendees: "Time is not standing still, not even in Austria." He called on them to "engage proactively and get yourselves informed and involved." It was the sixth time that the Austrian Science Talk – the major annual networking event for US-based Austrian scientists – had been hosted by the Austrian Federal Ministry for Transport, Innovation and Technology (BMVIT) along with the "brainpower austria" initiative. Friedrich Faulhammer, director general at the Austrian Ministry of Science and Research (BMWF), and Getraud Oberzaucher from BMVIT, who is in charge of the "brainpower austria" initiative within BMVIT, provided firsthand information to the attentive audience at the Austrian Science Talk about what's happening in the Austrian research landscape. They pointed out the importance of initially encouraging interest in research among a broad base of people, in order to end up later with an elite group of excellent researchers. UNO researchers briefed the visiting delegation on Louisiana's environmental challenges with annual threats of hurricane and subsiding marches that are supposed to act as coastal barriers to hurricanes.

Norbert Bischofberger, the research director of Gilead Science in Foster City, CA, delivered a riveting keynote address. Twenty-two years ago he was involved in founding a small start-up enterprise in the San Francisco Bay area. It took Gilead 15 years of intense research and development, along with venture capital of more than $1 billion, to develop marketable drugs. Today, Gilead is a 4000-employee multinational company, with a turnover on sales that exceeds five billion dollars. *Tamiflu* and *Atripla* are notable examples of their product range. As Bischofberger observed, not only research activities but, more importantly, the entrepreneurial spirit of the Bay Area led to this success. Gilead is in good company with enterprises such as Intel, Google, and Genentech also based in the Bay Area or nearby. Having access to a well-established venture capital financiers, not being averse to risk-taking, and having the ability to accept failure are major differences between the entrepreneurial spirit found in the Bay Area and in Europe, averred Bischofberger. However, he also had to pay a price for the better business environment in California. A native of Vorarlberg, Bischofberger used his preferred language – which, after more than two decades, is now English – to make his presentation to the bemused Austrian ex-pat community who well understood the language issue.

While UNO fine arts students Jeff Rinehart and Natalie Scorvino exhibited their art in July at the Andechs Gallerie in Innsbruck's old city, in November 2009, Tyrolese artists Ursula Groser and Elisabeth Schutting exhibited their new work at the University of New Orleans St. Claude Gallery. This is part of the annual art exchange between the Cultural Office of the City of Innsbruck and the UNO Fine Arts Department.

In late October 2009, the International Marshall Plan Center at Dodona Manor in Lynchburg, Virginia, organized a one-week teachers' workshop to study the principal Marshall Plan sites in Austria. Günter Bischof consulted with Dodona Manor in conceptualizing the program in Austria and helped arrange for Austria Marshall Plan experts to give guest lectures to a group of 20 American and Austrian social studies teachers.

As part of UNO's faculty exchanges with the University of Innsbruck, University Research Professor Emeritus of Political Science and former Chair of UNO's Department of Political Science Charles D. Hadley taught the block seminar "American Political Institutions" to 38 students at the University of Innsbruck, December 4–18, 2009. He also gave a well attended public presentation on "President Obama: First Year Review", sponsored by the Department of Political Science and the American Corner of the University of Innsbruck.

UNO's CenterAustria also had an unusually busy year with its publications program. In October The Schüssel Era in Austria, volume 18 of our flagship series Contemporary Austrian Studies (hereafter CAS) was published. This is the first CAS volume jointly published by UNO and innsbruck university press (iup). In this unique cooperation within the UNO - University of Innsbruck partnership arrangements, UNO Press is producing the CAS volumes and iup will be their distributor in Europe. Vol. 19

From Empire to Republic: Post-World War I Austria, with Peter Berger from the *Wirtschaftsuniversität Wien* as guest editor, was copy-edited and produced at UNO in the spring and published in the fall of 2010. *Global Austria*, our twentieth volume, is in the planning stages, with Anton Pelinka and Alexander Smith serving as guest editors. Günter Bischof and Fritz Plasser continue to serve as the editors of CAS. Fritz Plasser and Anton Pelinka presented *The Schüssel Era* to a Viennese audience in April 2010 with considerable interest from the print media.

In November 2009 Günter Bischof and Dieter Stiefel, along with digital editor Hannes Richter, presented their new volume *Images of the Marshall Plan: Film, Photographs, Exhibits, Posters* in Vienna. This volume appeared in the CenterAustria series TRANSATLANTICA with the StudienVerlag in Innsbruck. A DVD with Marshall Plan documentaries and pictures is attached in a back pocket of the book; an expanded complimentary archive of Marshall Plan documentaries and pictures is now also available under http://www.marshallplanimages.com/. In December *The Prague Spring and the Warsaw Pact Invasion of Czechoslovakia in 1968*, Günter Bischof, Stefan Karner, and Peter Ruggenthaler, eds., appeared in the Harvard Cold War Studies Book Series edited by Mark Kramer. This volume of essays by an international group of scholars was based on an April 2008 conference in New Orleans organized by CenterAustria with the *Boltzmann Institut für Kriegsfolgen-Forschung* in Graz. Günter Bischof presented it at the Czech Embassy in Washington in June 2010.

In February 2010 CenterAustria organized with the University of Innsbruck a workshop as part of its annual conference series on "*International Student Mobility in the Global Age- Best Practices in Europe and the United States.*" Lonnie Johnson from the Austrian Fulbright Commission served as a keynoter and summarized the many exchanges that have been going on between the U.S. and Austria since the end of World War II, demonstrating that the UNO – Innsbruck students exchanges have been in the lead in volume in past years. Key insights from the workshop presentations by Roberta Maierhofer (Graz) and Erich Thöni (Innsbruck) are that internationalization came later in Austria (1990s) than in the United States and has benefitted from university reforms by the federal Ministry of Science giving Austrian universities more autonomy. Austrian universities and students participating in European Union programs such as *Erasmus* (Austria participated before joining the EU in 1995) has dramatically increased international student mobility in Austria (with over 2 million exchanges [162,000 annually]), *Erasmus* is the largest exchange network in the world promoting international student mobility). As a result of the professionalization of international student mobility programs, Austrian universities have moved from traditional overseas programs in the U.S. (often launched by American Studies departments) towards global student mobility; many of the recent partnerships and short-term program initiatives launched have occurred in Asia (Innsbruck) and Latin America (Graz), eg. the globalizing trend of international education initiatives – American exchanges are less popular (the Bush Presidency and American visa restrictions have done a lot of damage). The European Union and its promotion of international student exchanges has moved from intra-European to global too; joint degree programs within Europe and by way of trans-Atlantic partnerships are a popular trend as well; both Innsbruck and Graz maintain some 500 partnership with universities worldwide; intercultural awareness is a high goal; Austrian universities are struggling with a nativist national sentiment in the U.S. of "closing the doors" with a growing number of visa restrictions for foreign students from certain areas.

CenterAustria welcomed regular visitors from Austrians for "lunch talks" throughout the year:

Gregor Thuswaldner, Gordon College, MA:
How Austrian is Austrian Literature?

Christian Stadler, Tusk School of Business, Dartmouth College, and Innsbruck:
The Secrets of Leading Firms: How You Achieve Enduring Success

Dr. Christina Antenhofer & Dr. Andreas Oberhofer, University of Innsbruck:
Tyrol as Historical Landscape: Dynamics of a Multicultural Region

Dr. Lonnie Johnson, Fulbright – Austrian-American Educational Commission:
Looking back on Central Europe: Twenty Years after 1989
Presentation of his book *Central Europe: Enemies, Neighbors, Friends*, 3rd. ed. (Oxford University Press, 2010)

Erhard Busek, Vienna – Forum Alpbach:
European Identity – How to Combine Unity and Variety?

Peter Moser, University of New Orleans,
Tenth Annual Marshall Plan Chair Lecture:
E Pluribus Unum – A Road Map for a New Global Order?

Eduard Fuehr, Brandenburg Technical University, Cottbus, and Visiting Professor UNO:
The Wall – A Battle Cry Against Communism

Gillian Sorenson, United Nations Foundation, New York:
Facing the Crises of Our Times: The US and the UN in 21st Century

Annual CenterAustria Fellows' Presentation:

Alexander Smith, Austrian Ministry of Science Fellow, UNO:
Values and Imperatives: EU's Foreign Energy Policies between Ethics and Interests

Manfred Kohler, Nick Mueller Fellow, UNO:
The Historic Battle for Civic Ideals in the United States? Which Ideals Prevail in Today's America?

Dr. Hans Petschar, Director, Picture Archives, Austrian National Library:
History and Photography. Historical Sources at the Picture Archives of the Austrian National Library

When the budget cutters go to work, how do they assess the elevation of the discourse environment on a university campus by international visitors? What are publications that add to the scholarly reputation of an institution worth to them? How do they value the edification and humanity and artistic creativity derived from an art exhibit or classical concert? What kind of value does a university attach to the international students exchanges that not only benefit the students directly involved but also those who attend classes and interact with these students? How important is it to the budget cutters that international student exchanges rip young minds mired in deep provincialism out of their comfort zone and educate them to become global citizens? We know that the network of Austrian studies centers in the world are an important tool for the Austrian government to project Austrian scholarship, science and culture into the global community. But how important are these Austrian studies centers to the institutions that host them?

Dieter Binder

Faculty of Central European Studies
Andrássy University Budapest

Dean's Report

The new master's degree course in history was approved by the Hungarian Accreditation Committee in the 2008/09 session and introduced at the beginning of the 2009 summer semester.

In August 2009, the Federal Ministry of Science and Research in Vienna approved a doctoral colloquium. An agreement was concluded concerning its installation at the Andrássy University in autumn 2009. Embedded in the doctoral school of AUB, this organisational unit will be headed by Dieter A. Binder, Georg Kastner and Arnold Suppan. The first year will begin with four work places on 1 January 2010, the second year will begin on 1 September 2010, and the third year will begin on 1 September 2011. The scholarships will be published internationally and each work place lasts three years.

In January 2009, the habilitation procedure was completed successfully by Dr. Georg Kastner for "Central European History", and Mr Kastner as Dr.phil.habil was appointed to head the History II course. The post-doctoral thesis, analysing the events in Hungary in 1956 within the UN, will be published by Studienverlag Innsbruck in 2010.

In autumn 2008, in co-operation with the Austrian Cultural Forum (director: Minister Dr. Elke Atzler) and the Università di Messina (Italy) and with the co-operation of Georg Kastner and extensive international participation, a Euro Lab was held on the topic of "The Future of the Humanities in the European Union". The Faculty organised a panel at the conference of the German Studies Association in Minneapolis, in which Ms Hermannova, who had won a competition published internally at the university, took part along with Binder and Kastner.

The following monographs were published by Faculty members in the report period:

- Oplatka, Andreas: Dr erste Riss in der Mauer. September 1989 – Ungarn öffnet die Grenze. Vienna: Zsolnay 2009.
- Dieter A. Binder: Die Freimaurer. Geschichte, Mythos und Symbole. Wiesbaden: Marix 2009.
- Dieter A. Binder, Heinz P. Wassermann: Die steirische Volkspartei oder die Wiederkehr der Landstände. Graz: Leykam 2008.

The following monographs were published in the Faculty series "Central European Studies", edited by Georg Kastner, Dieter A. Binder and Arnold Suppan:

- Marc Stefan Peters: Konstruiert. Kompromittiert. Musealisiert. Altösterreich und Preußen. Ein historisch-kulturanthropologischer Vergleich. Herne: Schäfer 2009.
- Henriett Kovács: Die Friedensbewegung in Österreich-Ungarn an der Wende zum 20. Jahrhundert. Herne: Schäffer 2009.

Dieter A. Binder
Dean

Elisheva Moatti

Center for Austrian Studies The Hebrew University of Jerusalem

The Center for Austrian Studies at the Hebrew University was established in May 2001 as a joint initiative of the Austrian Ministry of Foreign Affairs, the Austrian Ministry of Education, Science and Culture and the Friends of the Hebrew University in Austria.

Its goal is to promote Austrian studies and Austrian culture in Israel at the academic level, to establish and maintain contacts between Israeli and Austrian scholars and students by organizing symposia, lectures, conferences and workshops on Austrian issues. "Austrian studies" is understood in the broad sense of the word, rather than being narrowly defined as a concentration on the geographic area covered by the present Republic of Austria. The focus envisioned consists in interdisciplinary, broad Central European area studies with an Austrian core.

In May 2005, the Center for Austrian Studies was affiliated, together with the Helmut Kohl Institute for European Studies, the Marjorie Mayrock Center for Russian, Eurasian and East European Research, the Paul Desmarais Center for the Study of French Culture, and the Center for the Study of Italian Culture, into the European Forum at the Hebrew University, a framework that serves as epicenter for all the centers, chairs, funds and foundations active within the university dealing with research and teaching on issues related to Europe and the European Union. In October 2007, a new Center was added to the European Forum, the DAAD Center for German Studies. The European Forum is a trans- and multidisciplinary institution operating under three Faculties: Social Sciences, Humanities and Law.

The Center for Austrian and Central European Studies emphasizes the role of the Republic of Austria in the EU enlargement and integration processes and the role of the City of Vienna as a cultural center in European history. Attention is given to the Jewish population of the Habsburg Empire and its multifaceted impact on European culture, especially thanks to the Aaron Menczer Fund and the municipality of Vienna. The Center sponsors graduate courses about Austria, organizes international conferences and series of lectures, promotes research projects and publications of books, "Conference and Lecture Series" and "Working Papers". This broad area of interest and research gives the Center for Austrian Studies a greater visibility in research as well as in teaching, in Israel and abroad.

The activities of the center extend to teaching and research on the one hand, and to public relations in the broad sense and exchange programs with Austrian universities on the other hand. A special emphasize is put on personal encounters. This is achieved by international conferences, organized by the Center for Austrian Studies, which provide an exceptional framework, especially for graduate students and young scientists, to make personal contacts with their colleagues from the respective other country. In addition, these conferences allow the Israeli public to participate, thereby broadening and deepening the knowledge about Austria in Israel.

At the beginning of the academic year 2008/09, the research group **Consuming Memory and Constructing Identities in Modern Europe** was established at the Center for Austrian Studies, headed by Prof. Bianca Kühnel and Dr. Irit Dekel from the Hebrew University of Jerusalem. The group cooperated with Dr. Heidemarie Uhl from the Austrian Academy of Sciences. Besides the lector of the Center for Austrian Studies, Dr. Markus Helmut Lenhart, graduate and post graduate students, associated with the Center, participated in research.

During the meetings the participants introduced their own research and offered their methodological and theoretical perspectives. The group has elaborated widely on issues such as encounters with memory artifacts in everyday activities, on intentional vs. unintentional memory and on relations between memory and movement. The group has become a fertile ground for the participants' individual research, some of which resulting in presentations at international conferences.

The academic year 2009/10 started with a research workshop in Vienna, in cooperation with the Austrian Academy of Sciences and the Institute of Cultural Sciences and History of Theatre, titled "New Perspectives in Memory Studies: Rethinking Movement, Representation and Materiality". The two day workshop brought together young scholars from Jerusalem and Vienna who discussed issues of continuity, change and translation in memory studies as well as materiality and mobility as reflected in art, museums, tourism, advertisement and architecture. The papers presented at the workshop were the basis for this year's work.

During this year, the group worked on establishing a common theoretical and conceptual ground for a volume they are editing, to be published in the Conference & Lecture Series of the European Forum. The students refined their papers and submitted advanced drafts of their works, as well as commented on each others' papers. The development of their thinking and writing, and the flexibility and openness they applied to those processes were exceptional, and will be beneficial to their future work.

As an interdisciplinary group of students, they distanced themselves from some of the themes discussed in memory studies while keeping the analytical framework rich and informing. The topics for the students' research projects range from pilgrimage in replicas of Jerusalem (Neta Bodner) to boredom and identity in the EU (Avraham Rot); memory on tour in second and third generation German Israelis (Gal Engelhard); green politics and present EU identities in Europe (Michal Goren and Mark Volovici); serial photography and memory of the present (Yonatan Amir). Three of the foreign presenters in the Vienna Workshop will contribute to the edited volume (Joanna White, Ljiljana Radonic, Bernhard Forchtner). The academic exchange started in Vienna also yielded a papers session in the upcoming conference of the German Studies Association with Engelhard and White, organized by Dr. Irit Dekel in cooperation with Prof. Y. Michal Bodemann from the University of Toronto.

As in previous years, the Center for Austrian Studies provided various individual research grants so as to encourage young scholars and students to actively participate in research projects. After a call for papers was issued, the scholarship committee of the center assessed the research proposals. The research-grant recipients are required to submit the results of their year-long work in a paper to be published in the Working Paper Series of the European Forum.

Research grants were awarded to:

- Yemima Cohen, MA student at the European Forum, Construction of the Historical Memory of Judaism in Prague and Vienna
- Yossi Klein, PhD student at the Department of Geography, Paul Engelmann (1891–1956) – A Forgotten Jewish Austrian Architect in Tel Aviv
- Dr. Louise Hecht, Post-doctoral student at the European Forum, From Vienna to Jerusalem: The Journalist, Poet, and Politician Ludwig August Frankl von Hochwart (1810–1894)
- Sharon Gordon, PhD student at the Department of History, Carl Menger and Viennese Modernism

The intensive courses too, given by guest lecturers from Austria, further the personal encounters and offer an excellent opportunity for scientists from Israel and Austria to initiate common research projects.

Prof. Michael Landesmann, The Vienna Institute for International Economic Studies, 3–8 January 2010.
Cohesion and Competitiveness of the Enlarged European Union

The process of East–West European Integration as it proceeded since 1989 created an integrated economic space with a much wider range of income levels, institutional and behavioural characteristics and policy requirements than was the case in Europe before 1989. This course covers particularly economic developments in the Enlarged European Union but will also refer to 'Wider Europe'. Emphasis is on issues of 'cohesion' and 'competitiveness', the two areas which have dominated the policy debate within the European Union. We shall discuss differentiated growth processes at regional and national levels, patterns of international economic integration through trade, FDI and cross-border production networks, labour market developments and the economic analysis of the impact of migration flows; furthermore, the issues of further Enlargement and neighbourhood policy and the difficulties of policy development and policy coordination in the integrated European Union in the face of increased heterogeneity and in the wake of the global financial and economic crisis.

Prof. Wolfgang Schmale, University of Vienna, Department of History, 25–29 April 2010.
Cultural Transfers in European History

National history or the history of a nation-state is focused on master narratives and the building of the nation's unity. In general, this scheme has also largely been used with respect to European history. In this regard "European history" or "Europe's history" is nothing other than the history of growing European Unity. Contemporary European Integration History follows also this approach.

On the other hand, since the 1980s a new multidisciplinary approach on cultural transfers has infringed first the national master narratives, secondly and more recently, the narrative of European history. Not unity, but diversity can be considered as the "proprium" of Europe. Instead of unity, the growing of coherence in the diversity becomes a research topic.

The seminar treats with seven fields of interest:

- European unity – deconstruction of a master narrative
- "Cultural transfers" as a new approach to European history
- Nation building and the threat to cultural and ethnical diversity
- Types of cultural transfers in European history
- Historical mediators: Jews, Armeniens, Germans
- Religious minorities, exile groups and cultural transfers
- Europe – "liquid modernity" (Zygmunt Bauman)

Prof. Lioba Theis, University of Vienna, Department of the History of Art, 23 May – 5 June 2010.
Early Byzantine Architecture

- "Late Antique or Early Byzantine?" – The formation of the "New" on the basis of the "Old" (i.e. common architecture of Antiquity)
- "Is there a profane and a sacred architecture?" – Form and Meaning
- "Does form follow function?" – Form and Style
- "Experiential knowledge versus design?" – Measuring and Planning
- "Churches of stone, but wooden huts?" – On building material and its meaning
- "Ceiling – Vaulting – Dome – are there constructions comparable to the celestial canopy?" On building construction
- "Is there a Byzantine Style?" – Reflection on – and reflections of – Byzantine Architecture

Dr. Markus Helmut Lenhart, lector at the Center for Austrian Studies, offered this year four MA courses:
Modern Art, Design and Architecture in Central Europe (1890–1918)

The course dealt with the culture of the Austrian-Hungarian Empire, concentrating on the period from 1890 to the end of the First World War. The course pursued two objectives. One was to compare the different artistic disciplines during this period and show their interconnections. The other was to present the various cultural centers within the Austrian-Hungarian Empire and to position them vis-à-vis the overwhelming importance of Vienna in the (art) historical literature.

Modern Art, Design and Architecture in Central Europe (1918–1938)

After the disintegration of the Austrian-Hungarian Empire into several new (or renewed) states, not only did a political entity cease to exist but a closely interconnected culture fragmented into various national arts. This course examined the art, design and architecture of the successor states in terms of the differences, resemblances and new identities that emerged during the interwar period up to the outbreak of the Second World War.

Jewish Culture in the Austro-Hungarian Empire 1867–1918

Beginning with the Toleranzpatent of Emperor Joseph II, a growing number of Jews were able to participate more actively in the culture of the Austrian-Hungarian Empire. It was during the reign of Emperor Franz Joseph (1848–1916), however, that Austria's Jewish population contributed most abundantly to Austrian-Hungarian culture despite their small percentage of the population. With Vienna currently the most revered Jewish cultural center, this course presented, as well, the numerous other centers of Jewish culture in the empire till its disintegration.

The Representation of the Shtetl in Modern Art

Besides literature, art in particular plays a major role in the commemoration of East European culture. Nobody shaped our picture of the shtetl more than Marc Chagall with his numerous paintings of bearded Jews, often ignoring gravity by flying over picturesque little villages. What, however, does a critical look at relevant paintings, graphics and photographs reveal? What are the contributions of Central European artists? The course drew a connecting line from the paintings of the late-nineteenth-century Austrian artist Isidor Kaufmann to the photographs of Roman Vishniac during the 1940s in the midst of the Shoah. Along with the question of how the shtetl was represented, the participants in this course analyzed how art shaped modern, post-Shoah perceptions of the shtetl.

In cooperation with the Department of Sociology and Anthropology and the Israeli Anthropological Association, the Center for Austrian Studies invited **Prof. Matti Bunzl**, Department of Anthropology, University of Illinois, for a guest lecture on "*From Modern to Postmodern Exclusions: Anti-Semitism and Islamophobia in Europe Today – An interpretation of the historical and structural role of anti-Semitism and Islamophobia in Europe today*".

The Austrian Library, incorporated into the Bloomfield Library for the Humanities and Social Sciences, contained in 2009 3687 books. Since it is a reference library, it is not easy to estimate how often and how many of these books are used. However, 520 of these books have been borrowed in 2009.

The Center for Austrian Studies is organizing its own reference library for students and scholars. In the future it intends to set up working space for them. With these steps, the Center tries to strengthen its ties to students and scholars working on projects related to Austria and to make the Center a vivid point of intellectual exchange.

As a first step, Victoria Kumar, recipient of the Doctoral Research Fellowship for 2009/10 awarded by the Federal Ministry for Science and Research, and Nikolaus Wildner, recipient of an MA Fellowship for 2009/10 awarded by the Federal Ministry for Science and Research catalogued the books in our library.

The Center for Austrian Studies grants thirty students from the Hebrew University scholarships for a two-month intensive language course at the University of Vienna. These scholarships include flight cost as well as dormitory and tuition fees. The scholarships are funded by the Austrian Foreign Ministry, the Austrian Ministry of Science and Research, the Austrian Friends of the Hebrew University, the Center for Austrian Studies, the Helmut Zilk Fonds für internationale Beziehungen Wiens and the University of Vienna.

In addition, the center grants nineteen students from the Hebrew University scholarships for two– or three–week intensive language courses at different Austrian universities: Graz, Klagenfurt, Salzburg, Innsbruck and Linz. Theses scholarships funded by the hosting universities, the Austrian Friends of the Hebrew University and the Center for Austrian Studies are covering the dormitory and tuition fees.

The language scholarships are granted to students from different faculties and departments of the Hebrew University who need an extensive knowledge of German for their academic work. Many of these students also deal directly with Austria or the Austrian legacy in Central Europe.

The Center for Austrian Studies, in cooperation with the Austrian Library at the Hebrew University, has set up the Austrian Film Forum which provides a possibility to view a selection of Austrian movies at the university. The idea at the core of this project was to establish an open and accessible forum for the general public at the Hebrew University and beyond, so as to create a possibility to get acquainted with various aspects of Austrian history, society and culture, in addition to the few courses at the university which deal specifically with those issues.

The target audience for the Austrian Film Forum is mainly students from various departments at the Hebrew University, who have had some kind of connection with Austria. This includes students of the Center for Austrian Studies, the European Forum with its different sections, who might have dealt or wish to deal in the future with certain aspects of Austria as part of their studies and research, as well as students, who completed language courses in Austria or applied for them. In that sense we intended to establish a forum which also serves in an informal framework as a reference point for students who wish to get a basic idea about Austria, for example, as preparation to a study trip to Austria and students who seek to enhance and deepen their connection to Austrian culture after coming back from a language course in Austria or for any other reason.

The schedule of the Forum for this year included eleven movies which provided a good overview on the development of Austrian film.

Articles

Hrvoje Šugar
(University of Vienna)

The Frontiersmen (Graničari) in the Austrian Military Border in Sixteenth and Seventeenth Centuries

Introduction

This paper deals with the colonisation of the Austrian Military Border in Croatia and Slavonia during the sixteenth and seventeenth centuries. This colonisation was very pragmatic and the settled population served as a defence mechanism, primarily for the Inner Austrian lands and secondly for the lands of the Hungarian Crown against invasions of Ottoman troops. Therefore, from very early on this group had a completely different status than other groups within medieval and modern-era European feudal society. Their role was chiefly a military one. It was that of colonizers who would cheaply and efficiently defend their territory from foreign incursions, and later on the settled territory would come to constitute a specific corpus within the Habsburg Empire (principally within the lands of the Hungarian Crown). This area was known as the Military Border (*Militärgrenze*). From the seventeenth century onwards it served as a pool of soldiers for the Habsburg crown, intended to wage war throughout Europe and not only in defence against the Ottoman Empire.

This paper focuses on a few major problems:

- the main colonisation routes and colonization areas
- the ethnic and religious background of the settled population
- their social and legal status in the territory of the HabsburgMonarchy as well as a comparison with their status in earlier medieval and Ottoman society

When talking about the population settlement, I will try to answer two key questions. Firstly, what were the reasons for the settlers' arrival to the territory of the Habsburg Monarchy along with the issue of reconstructing the area from which they arrived and, secondly, the aspect of colonisation regarding the territory they were granted by the Habsburgs as well as the reasons why certain territories were awarded.

The ethnic issue is a more complex one. Although its importance has not been brought into attention during the sixteenth century, there is still no uniform answer to the question on the ethnic affiliation of the settled population. Similarly, the religious affiliation – although often stressed – is placed only in the background of economic and social issues.

Besides the question of social and economic status of the colonists, one of the most important questions is that of their religious confession. After all the Serbian and Uniate Church greatly influenced the development of their identity, paving the way for their eventual assimilation into the community of the Serbian and, to a lesser extent, Croatian people

This paper explains the emergence of the Vlach communities throughout the Balkans (as predecessors of the colonised communities in the territory of the Habsburg Empire) and the colonisation during the 1530s.

Naturally, the idea of creating a special, sedentary layer of society which would permanently be prepared to engage in warfare, but at the same time would be able to support itself (the concept of "cheapness") was difficult to put into practice. Therefore, the history of the formation of the Military Border often was a history of continuous rebellion and social unrest. Still, the Military Border did start to function as a giant pool of troops in the end, and the settled population had a special status as Frontiersmen (*Graničari or Grenzer*).

Medieval Models and the "Vlachs"

However, in studying the history of the Military Border and the colonisation in the sixteenth and seventeenth centuries, one can notice that the protagonists in this colonisation were groups of population referred to as the "Vlachs". While "Vlach" in the Middle Ages often referred to an ethnic group of the Romance language group on the Balkan Peninsula, in the Military Border, this term soon began to have a social rather than ethnic meaning referring to the status of free warriors. The Orthodox religious affiliation of the Serb Vlachs has often been equated with the social status of Frontiersmen Vlachs. But these Vlachs, due to their specific semi-nomadic shepherd-warrior lifestyle, had become famous as good soldiers in earlier historic periods and been hired by a number of Balkan states.

Vlachs in Late Medieval Croatia, Dalmatia and Dubrovnik

Sources from the 14th century often mention Vlachs in these territories, and their description coincides with the Greek and Bulgarian sources from earlier periods. According to these sources, Vlachs are nomadic or semi-nomadic herdsmen. Unfortunately, the sources remain silent about their origin and language. But one rather certain conclusion can be drawn. Vlachs do not appear in the hinterland of Dalmatian towns on a more frequent basis until the first half of the 14th century. This was caused due to the spread of the family Šubić rule to the territory of the lands of Hum and to the north towards Bosnia. Therefore, it is possible to assume that these contacts were sooner the result of the spread of this Croatian noble's rule than of a significant migration from the eastern and south-eastern Balkans. It is noteworthy, that sources from as early as this period depict the Vlachs similarly to many other sources from the sixteenth and seventeenth centuries, i.e. as pillaging, violence-prone herdsmen – mostly with a negative perception.

On the other hand, these Vlachs were well incorporated into the feudal system of the Croatian part of the Austro-Hungarian Empire, i.e. the sources do not treat them as a foreign, unfamiliar body.[1] In a document dated to the year 1345, in which Louis Anjou reconciles with the duke of Cetina, Vlachs and Croats are mentioned as the latter's subjects, even though nothing more is said about their origins.[2] A sign of equation would not be in place here, since the Latin source leaves no doubt that these are two different groups of population in question. Still, it is debatable whether this is a social or an ethnic distinction.

Vlachs in Medieval Serbia and Bosnia

By the middle of the 14th century the Serbian Emperor Dušan spread his rule over the territories of northern and central Albania, Macedonia, northern Greece and western Bulgaria. This is the very territory where ethnic Vlachs are mentioned for the first time by the Greeks. Soon after these conquests, Dušan regulated the relations with the Vlachs in his Code. This is roughly the same period when Vlachs are frequently being mentioned on the territory of Croatia, Dalmatia and Bosnia. However, it would be difficult to conclude that this mention is related to their westward migration. A different matter is in question here. The 14th century is the very period of defining and expanding the borders of the three medieval states – Bosnia, Serbia and the Kingdom of Hungary and Croatia. While in earlier periods there were large areas of no man's land in between these small states, the 14th century brought along the full affirmation of the feudal system. In the western Balkans – under the influence of the Anjou family – it gave rise to the system of knighthoods and banderiums (armed contingents), which in turn led to warfare improvements, the expansion of individual states, as well as to conflicts between them. Exactly in these times the Vlachs became of interest to the rulers under whose authority they have now come fort he first time.

---

1 „Ego quidem Galla […] vlaca confiteor, quo mediam domum lignaminis positam in territorio Damiani Volcasii dedi in pignore Marie filie […]" Monumenta historica Ragusina, vol. 4, Zagreb 1993, 106.

2 „[…] et eorum incolis seu populis Croatis et Olachis". Codex diplomaticus regni Croatiae, Dalmatiae et Slavoniae, vol. 11, 250.

Vlachs under the Ottoman Rule

The Ottomans strengthened their rule in the Balkans as early as in the 14th century. In the beginning they conquered only smaller forts and towns on the European side of the Byzantine Empire, but after the Battle of Maritsa in 1371 and their first significant victory over the Serbs, they in fact crushed the resistance of the strongest Balkan state of the time.[3] Over the following hundred years, they were able to relatively easily spread their rule over the entire Balkan peninsula and threatened the Hungarian-Croatian kingdom.

Although many older historiographies interpreted the Ottoman incursion as an unexpected, barbaric eastern element that completely interrupted all the links to the preceding civilization system and world order, in practice this was not entirely true. Despite the fact that from the very beginning the Ottomans feigned as spreaders of Islam, the so-called Gazias, their relations to the Christians were very tolerant, sometimes even friendly.[4] This tolerance, unusual in comparison to European Christian states at this time, resulted from two factors: the first is in the sheriat law itself, which tolerates all religions that are based on a "holy book" as the foundation of its teaching. The second is a pragmatic one: since the very foundation of the Ottoman state, it had been incorporating many non-turkish ethnic elements and later on even non-islamic ones.

The Ottoman incursion into Middle Europe led to significant demographic changes, which also affected the Vlachs. The Ottomans colonized the desolated medieval Serbia – from Kosovo to Smederevo – with a large Vlach population. Thus, the economic structure changed alongside with demographic changes. Namely, the Vlachs were mostly involved in cattle-breeding, and did not turn to agriculture until few generations later. Unfortunately, the Ottoman sources do not say much about the ethnic origin of the Vlachs, but a few preserved *kanun-namas* and a number of *defters* can give us some guidelines. The Ottomans legally regulated the position of Vlachs in the Pashaluk of Zvornik and Smederevo, where they enjoyed certain privileges similar to those in medieval Serbia: payment of tax per household instead of per capita, judicial and administrative autonomy, but also the obligation of providing a horse-mounted soldier for the Ottoman army. The position of Vlachs in the Ottoman border territories was very favourable. In the Pashaluk of Smederevo the privileges were not lost until 1536, when the area was no longer part of the border line. However, "Vlach" became an explicitly social denominator already during the Ottoman era. When Požega was conquered and the border region

---

[3] Josef Matuz, Das osmanische Reich, Darmstadt 1996, 37f.

[4] For example, the founder of the Ottoman state, Osman, maintained very friendly relations with his Byzantine neighbours. Matuz, Reich, 30f.

(*krajište*) was formed in the 1540s, the Ottomans granted the status of Vlachs to all the inhabitants (*raja*), although it was Hungarian and Croat (or Serb) population.

History of the Military Border until 1699

The history of the Military Border in Croatia and Slavonia can be generally divided into several periods. It is an outline division, not relevant to all the aspects of the Military Border history, but when it comes to its colonisation and organization, there are several solid benchmarks:[5]

From the formation to 1590

This is the period of the Habsburgs' entrance into the territory of Croatia and Hungary. Although it can be divided into several shorter periods, among other things characterized by the civil war in Hungary, conflicts with the Ottomans, but also the Habsburg's relations with the Western countries, primarily its French rival, it was an important period for the Croatian and Slavonian Military Border because it resulted in the formation and consolidation of the Border itself. The colonisation of Vlachs as the primary defenders of the Military Border was a part of its strategy, but it is still not as massive as in the period to come.

From 1590 to 1606

This period started with smaller introductory wars, followed by the 13-year Long War (1593 – 1606) between the Habsburg and the Ottoman Empire. It was the very period when the Military Border, with all its deficiencies, showed its full efficiency. The largest colonisation wave on its territories also took place during this period.

From 1606 to 1683

This rather long period of time is interesting for its break with the Habsburg policies of the earlier periods, when the attitude of the Croatian and Hungarian nobility towards the Military Border was still taken into consideration. Now the Military Border definitely became a separate territory, excluded from the authority of the Croatian and Hungarian parliaments. This period brought efforts in legally organizing the life of Vlachs in the Military Boarder, but it was also characterized by frequent uprisings caused either by

---

[5] A Similar division was suggested by Fedor Moačanin, *Vojna Krajina do kantonskog uređenja 1787.* in: Dragutin Pavličević (Ed.), *Vojna krajina, povijesni pregled–historiografija–rasprave*, Zagreb 1984, 23f.

broken promises of the Imperial authorities or by their attempts to introduce a more rigid control.

From 1683 to 1699

This period is a turning point in the Military Border history, especially, after The Great Serb Migration under Arsenije III Črnojević in 1690, when the status of the Frontiersmen changed. The Military Border was greatly expanded, and the newly settled Serb population and Serbian church authorities were granted privileges and rights that often were in conflict with the rights and habits of the Frontiersmen. This period is a prologue for the total disintegration of their social status. They lost a significant amount of their earlier rights. Their way of living changed, and the Military Border and its Frontiersmen turned into a sessile population under direct Imperial control, without any of its previous autonomy.

The Formation of the Military Border

The first thing to be highlighted when talking about the Military Border is that up until the end of the seventeenth century it was not a clearly defined territory, it rather encompassed territories bordering the Ottoman Empire, and was under control of the Emperor or the Inner Austrian Estates, i.e. it was directly associated with the military garrisons under the command of Imperial officers.[6]

Until 1522 almost the entire territory of the medieval Croatian kingdom was conquered or pillaged by the Ottomans who, in the course of their raids, pushed forward far into the western Austrian lands. Because the Hungarian–Croatian ruler Louis II. (1516–1526) was considered to be too weak, the Croatian parliament called on the Austrian archduke Ferdinand to assistance.[7]

The Ottoman incursions into Austrian lands in 1521 and 1522, along with the particularly difficult defence situation of the Hungarian-Croatian kingdom after the fall of Belgrade in 1521, were proof enough for the Austrian Estates that Croatia and Hungary were completely incapable of taking care of the defence system, so Ferdinand suggested the establishment of a garrison be-

---

6 As early as 1578, one document mentions military garrisons in Zagreb, Ljubljana, Trieste and Goriza as parts of the Military Frontier. So the concept of the Military Frontier was still not connected to territory, but rather to military organization and persons under the military command. Fedor Moačanin, *Vojna Krajina do kantonskog uređenja 1787,* 29f.

7 Jakob Amstadt, Die k.k. Militärgrenze 1522–1881, Würzburg 1969, p. 4. and Monumenta Habsburgica I, 2.

tween Una and Kupa, and the building of fortifications in Rijeka and Metlika.[8]

As early as July 1522 the Austrian troops took hold of several towns (Zemay (?), Knin, Skradin, Klis, Ostrovica).[9] By now, Ferdinand and the parliament of the Holy Roman Empire were already trying to form a defence mechanism within Croatia in order to prevent the Ottoman incursions into the Austrian lands. At the very beginning they tried to rely on the Croatian Estates, but later on they realized that the only possible defence would be to subject the border troops directly to one central command. In November and December 1522, the Nuremberg *Reichstag* approved 4000 men for the defence of Hungary, and additional forces for the garrisons of Senj, Krupa, Bihać, Jajce and Klis[10] in Croatia.

The fall of Belgrade in 1521 was a turning point in the defence of the Hungarian-Croatian kingdom. Within the next 30 years, the Ottoman Empire spread its hold deep into Central Europe, took most of Hungary, Croatia and Slavonia, and its troops immediately threatened Vienna. However, during this period the Habsburgs completely took charge of the defence of Central Europe and created an efficient defence system in the Military Border.

Main Problems of the Military Border defence

The Military Border system in the sixteenth and seventeenth centuries had to cater for the needs of new warfare technologies introduced by the long-lasting wars against the Ottoman Empire. Namely, the earlier system of medieval fortifications, feudal defence systems, could not handle the massive number of soldiers and technology of the Ottomans. One of the basic drawbacks of the Croatian and Slavonian defence system were the outdated me-

---

8 Gunther E. Rothenberg, Die österreichische Militärgrenze in Kroatien 1522 bis 1881, Wien-München 1970, 25f. Louis II. supposedly let over the towns of Senj, Klis, Krupa, Jaska and some other fortifications to Croatia as early as 1521, and colonized them with the Uskoks from Bosnia and Montenegro. However, it is not certain whether the mentioned towns were settled by these Uskoks by that time or only later on. „Il abandonna à l'empereur Ferdinand, son beau-père Senj (Zengg), Klissa, Krupa, *Lika* [sic!], Jaska et plusieurs autres places de la frontière croate, pour les défendre contre les Turcs. Ferdinand concentra dans ces villes *émigrés de la Bosnie et du Montenegro* (op.aut.), qu'on désignait sous le nom d'Uskoci (fugitifs). Ce fut l'origine des Confins militaires de l'Autriche." Emile Picot, Les Serbes de Hongrie, Prague 1873, 47 (see footnote 1). Unfortunately, Picot does not give any sources whatsoever for these facts, but it can be assumed that works of Csaplovics, Bartenstein and other Austrian historians and clerks from the eighteenth and nineteenth centuries were at his disposal.

9 Amstadt, Militärgrenze, 4.

10 Rothenberg, Militärgrenze, 26–28.

dieval forts whose position and function did not meet the newly formed requirements.[11]

Therefore, the existing forts were either left over to the enemy and ruination or, more rarely, transformed into new Renaissance–type fortifications.[12] Apart from the larger forts, blockhouses or watchtowers played an important role in the defence system.[13] These are smaller, mostly wooden constructions with a garrison of six to twelve soldiers distributed along the front line, mostly serving as an advance–post and a notification system.

This huge type of system exceeded the financial capacities and interests of an average noble, so a central, imperial authority was necessary for its functioning and organisation.[14] Therefore, the process of transferring the authority in the Military Border over to the central authority in Vienna was both justified and the only possible solution for a successful functioning of the system. Naturally, the construction of this system lasted for several decades and did not show its full functionality until the end of the sixteenth century, when the Ottoman advance had finally been stopped.

Similarly, one of the basic problems for the defence of the Kingdom of Croatia and Slavonia consisted in different conceptions and desires of several involved sides. To the Habsburgs, the Croatian–Slavonian Military Border was part of a larger and more complex

---

[11] The greatest drawbacks of medieval forts were their position, the small size and a high wall. Medieval forts were mostly built on inaccessible locations providing protection only for the nobles. The new forts were intended as a part of a larger defence mechanism which covered a much larger area. At the same time, most of the medieval forts were too small to fit a larger number of soldiers and equipment. If such a fortification was used for defence purposes, the height of its walls posed a large problem. In the Middle Ages, the wall height was the main defence against both cavalry and infantry, which were mostly equipped with cold weapons while in defence from artillery such walls have practically no function. Milan Kruhek, *Krajiške utvrde i obrana hrvatskog kraljevstva tijekom 16. st.*, Zagreb 1995, 14f.

[12] New, Renaissance–type fortifications encompass an entire system which in its essence reminds of an organism. Several different sections need to function in harmony. A Renaissance fortification is lower, its towers have transformed into low bastions surrounded by earth, and not stone (for better protection against artillery fire), the defence has been strengthened by ditches, it is spatially larger and each section of the fortification has to be accessible to soldiers. Such fortifications are parts of a larger strategic defence belt; thus, the idea is not to have an isolated location for constructing such a fort, but just the opposite – it must serve to prevent enemy incursions as well as a base for entering the enemy territory. More about this in: Kruhek, *Krajiške utvrde i obrana hrvatskog kraljevstva tijekom 16. st.*, 24–36.

[13] Kruhek, *Krajiške utvrde i obrana hrvatskog kraljevstva tijekom 16. st.*, 36.

[14] Žejko Holjevac – Nenad Moačanin, *Hrvatsko–slavonska Vojna krajina u ranome novom vijeku*, Zagreb 2007, 14–16.

military system, reaching from the Adriatic Sea all the way to the Carpathian Mountains. It is important to stress that the territory of Croatia and Slavonia was under the attack of local Ottoman forces throughout the sixteenth and seventeenth century, primarily from Bosnia and Slavonia. The main Ottoman advances were directed towards Vienna, via Hungary, therefore this territory demanded a far better defence system and far more investment.

For that reason the Emperor was constantly trying to shift the expense of financing the Croatian–Slavonian Military Border to the Inner Austrian Estates, since they were mainly under the attack of Ottoman troops when these would move across Croatia.

It took some time for Croatian nobles to realize that the medieval system of defence for their feudal possessions had no function against the Ottomans. Therefore they reluctantly agreed to the defence system being controlled by the central Imperial authorities. Of course, the most powerful nobles like the Kaptol of Zagreb, the family Zrinski and the Frankopans, never gave up on their feudal rights.

The Inner Austrian Estates accepted the financing system of the Military Border in principle, but even in this respect their particular interests had to be met. Thus, the interests of the Inner Austrian Estates, the Croatian Estates and of the Habsburgs were often diametrically opposed. Let us take only one example; the Inner Austrian Estates insisted on their independency from the central authorities and on maintaining the feudal system. But when it came to the Military Border, the same Estates supported the ruler because their involvement in the Military Border provided them with additional profits – despite the fact that this was indirectly undermining the existing feudal system. Naturally, this also put them in conflict with the Croatian nobles although, nominally, they had to acknowledge their rights.

In the Military Border itself, all interested parties had to satisfy the interests of the Frontiersmen. With the arrival of new population from the territory of the Ottoman Empire, the methods of warfare changed, as well as the mentality and the organisation of the feudal system in the area.

The Emperor had a difficult job in satisfying all the sides, especially considering the Habsburg inclination towards creating a modern and centralised state capable of standing alongside France and other western countries. However, during the sixteenth and the first half of the seventeenth century, the ruler simply could not afford to neglect any of the involved sides but rather had to carefully balance between all of them.

First Colonisations of Vlachs in Žumberak

The first colonisations of people from the Ottoman territories were conducted by the Habsburgs on the territory of Inner Austrian lands, mostly on the feudal possession of Žumberak in Carniola. This area was not within the Hungarian–Croatian kingdom; nevertheless it was included into the Karlovac General Command[15] after 1578.

After Ferdinand had ascended the throne of the Hungarian–Croatian kingdom, he had no larger estates at his disposal where he could freely settle military colonists, and a civil war between the supporters of Zapolja and Ferdinand was raging in Croatia as well as in Hungary. Therefore, the first colonisations were conducted in Carniola, where he did have certain possessions.[16] In Žumberak the land possessions were greatly devastated by the Ottoman raids and the yields were low, yet it was close enough to the battlegrounds on the Croatian–Ottoman border to play an active role as a Military Border.[17]

However, the most important role in this process was played by Ivan Kobasić, a nobleman who was, next to the Croatian *ban* Ivan Karlović, one of the most faithful supporters of Ferdinand. Ivan Kobasić was granted the town of Žumberak by Nikola Semenić in 1526. This estate was owned by the Court Treasury, but the Treasury did not take it back the same year; Ferdinand committed not to take the possession from the Kobasić family as long as they lived. The reason was that the Kobasić family had most of their estates around Bihać, which was devastated at that time due to Ottoman raids and brought low yields. By that point there was probably a plan for the settlement of population to the territory of Žumberak from the less safe, bordering areas. At any rate, there are no direct sources talking about this first group of the Uskoks, but there is a document dated 1564 in which Ferdinand confirms the privileges awarded in 1526.[18]

Many estates in Croatia were plundered and there was the possibility of colonizing these areas. But the Croatian nobility was not always enthusiastic to accept Vlachs and to free them of their feudal duties, as the Vlachs would usually expect. Naturally, there will be later exceptions and some Croatian feudal lords will later colonize the Vlachs (the so-called "private Vlachs"). Only after the King has

---

[15] Vojin S. Dabić, Karlovački generalat (1683–1746), Beograd 1996, 29–31.

[16] Colonisation of population from Croatia, Bosnia, and perhaps Serbia as well, on the territories of Carinthia, Styria and Carniola, but other Austrian lands as well, also took place in the fifteenth century and sources precisely specify its origin. However, this does not involve military colonists the likes of those settled in the 20s and the 30s of the sixteenth century, so they are not within the scope of this research. Cf Јоцип Мал, Ускочке сеобе и словенске покрајине, Љубљана 1924, 16; and Hermann Ignaz Bidermann, Neuere slavische Siedlungen auf süddeutschem Boden, Stuttgart 1888, 361–394.

[17] Dabić, Karlovački generalat, 29–31.

[18] Мал, Ускочке сеобе, 15f.

acquired some possessions in Croatia, during the sixteenth century, will he start colonizing this area as well.[19]

Still, it is worth mentioning that Vlachs were also settled on the territory of Styria, especially during the mid-sixteenth century, but their settlements were relatively quickly included into the existing feudal system and as such did not become a part of the Military Border.[20]

The colonisation of Vlachs in Žumberak started as early as 1526, but their numbers were much lower than as those settled after 1530,[21] when a wave of migration to the Habsburg Empire started. It is known that the Vlachs inhabited a broad territory of the Balkans, and performed their military role on the side of the Ottomans. Their migrations to the Habsburg Empire were almost always caused by deterioration of their financial status or privileges they enjoyed in the Ottoman Empire, and never by emotional or religious reasons. The cause for the Vlachs' arrival to Žumberak was probably the introduction of new taxes for the Vlachs in the Ottoman Empire.[22]

When the Habsburg diplomat Benedikt Kuripešić travelled to Constantinople in September 1530, he passed through Bosnia and made notes on interesting observations concerning the status of the population under Ottoman rule. This was the year when the taxes for Serb/Vlach i.e. Christian population were raised, and their dissatisfaction grew to the point at which many of them considered going over to the Habsburg side.[23] Since Kuripešić travelled near

---

19 Dabić, Karlovački generalat, 73f.

20 See: Hermann Ignaz Bidermann, Die Serben-Ansiedlungen in Steiermark und im Warasdiner Grenz-Generalate, Graz 1883.

21 Karl Kaser, Freier Bauer und Soldat, Graz 1986, 48f; see also footnote 2 on page 48, 526f.

22 The information concerning where the Vlachs and Serbs which cross over to the Habsburgs come from are not always known, but since the Ottomans would always introduce their regular privileges in the border regions last, a revoke them last in the earlier occupied territories distant from the battlegrounds, we may assume that the majority of Vlachs arriving to Žumberak in the 30s of the sixteenth century came from the territories of medieval Serbia or Bosnia. Holjevac-Moačanin, *Hrvatsko-slavonska Vojna krajina,* 129–131.

23 „Sy seint auch von irem erpauten gründten kheinen anndern zynnß, dann jahrlich ainen gulden hungerisch, das ist fünffzig asper, von ainem hauß zugeben schuldig gewest. Aber yezt in disem iar, seit er nun Crabaten am maisten erobert und des Hungerlanndts ainen grossen tail unnder sich gebracht, hat er angefangen, beid vorgemelte stendt der Kristen höher zu beschwern und mit neuen aufsatzungen, wie hernachvolgt, zu belestigen: [...] Darumben die bemelten Cristen baider stendt vasst übl zufrieden; und ist zu gedenkhen, daß sy leichtlich von dannen an Cristenliche orter zu bewegen wärn." Benedikt Curipeschitz, Itinerarium oder Wegrays Küniglich Mayestät potschafft gen Constantinopel zudem Türkischen Keiser Soleyman. Anno 1530, (Reprint) Klagenfurt 1997, 57f.

the areas from where Vlachs came to Žumberak, we may even assume that he was in contact with the very people who would later become colonizers of this region. Even if this is not the case, the deterioration of Christians' status in Bosnia and Serbia in the 1530s was so widespread that large sections of the population were affected by the new tax system. The cause for this was a very logical one. Namely, after the fall of Belgrade in 1521 and Jajce in 1528, the Ottomans transferred the "*krajište*" (border region) deep into the north of Hungary and westwards. Bosnia and Serbia lay no longer on the borderlines of the Ottoman Empire. This expansion annulled the need for extending the privileges of the Vlach and Christian population.

Through the travel logs of Benedikt Kuripešić – which are far more detailed in some aspects than those of his contemporaries – we can follow the movement of the Vlach population from the Balkans towards the West. During his stay in Bosnia he wrote that the new inhabitants of Bosnia arrived precisely from Serbia:

> *"Die annderen sein Surffen, die nenen sie Wallachen und wir nenens Zisttzn oder Marthalosen. Die khamen von dem ort Smedravo, und Khriechisch Weissenburg und haben Sanndt Pauls glauben"*.[24]

In June 1531 another group of *„der her vbergefalnen Türgken"* arrived. There were about 1.000 of them, out of which as many as 700 capable of military service.[25] They brought with them as many as 15.000 heads of large cattle and were looking for a place to settle. Ivan Katzianer advised them to settle in the area of Kostel and Poljana along the river Kupa, not far from Žumberak, i.e. south of Črnomelj and Kočevje.[26]

Since a truce was in force at that time, and the Ottomans started with very rigorous controls of the population in order to prevent them from leaving for the Habsburg Empire, Katzianer also tried to prevent further colonisation. Furthermore, a few months earlier Ivan Kobasić, who was far more in favour of the colonisation process than

---

[24] Curipeschitz, Itinerarium, 56f.

[25] Both Josip Mal and Karl Kaser talk about these Uskoks as the Uskoks from the Cetina river area, although the stated source (Acta historiam confinii militaris Croatici illustrantia, vol. 3, *Spomenici hrvatske krajine*, Zagreb 1889, 387) does not speak of them specifically as the Uskoks from Cetina. The only possibility would be that the mention of the Cetina area Vlachs in a letter dated 7 June 1531, sent by the Captain of Bihać Petar Rebrović, refers to these Vlachs, mentioned two weeks later.

[26] Radoslav Lopašić, Acta historiam confinii militaris Croatici illustrantia, vol. 3, *Spomenici hrvatske krajine*, Zagreb 1889, 387. Karl Kaser mistakenly writes about 1500 heads of cattle. Kaser, Freier Bauer, 49.

the other nobles, had died. Shortly after him the Croatian ban Ivan Karlović died as well. It is important to remember that the Inner Austrian Estates also exerted pressure in order to prevent the Uskok raids on the Ottoman territories, fearing Ottoman retribution.[27]

Military service was the chief activity of the settled Vlachs. They served either as light cavalry or infantrymen. However, since the movements of large Ottoman armies towards Inner Austria were rarely routed through Croatia and Slavonia, and military actions were focused on the vicinity of Jajce and Bihać, the role of the Uskoks–Vlachs in spying on the Ottomans was particularly important.[28]

As early as March 1531, the Inner Austrian Estates met in Unterdrauburg (Dravograd). Carniola was represented, among others, by Bishop Christoph Lamberg and *Feldhauptmann* Hans Katzianer. One of the decisions adopted was that 300 mercenary infantrymen (Martolos) were to protect Croatia from the Ottomans, and as many as 400 cavalrymen were to defend Styria. It is explicitly stated that these were Christian refugees (*Christenflüchtlinge*), so we may assume that most of them were recruited by the Uskoks which had arrived the previous winter.[29]

Other Colonisation Routes

Žumberak was a part of the Inner Austrian region of Carniola, but during the 40s and the 50s of the sixteenth century – and especially during the 1593–1606 War – the Habsburgs were trying to settle as many soldiers as possible on the territory of the Slavonian Military Border between Sava and Drava (the Varaždin General Command), and in the south into the Croatian Military Border (the Karlovac General Command). The colonisation process was more intense on the territory of the Varaždin General Command, because in the Karlovac General Command there was still a strong influence of some noble families (like the family Zrinski and the Frankopans) which did not want to colonise their territories with a population that would not be under their direct control but rather under that

---

27 Мал, Ускочке сеобе, 20–23.

28 Naturally, this espionage was not merely a communication of information from the Ottoman territories, but more of a commando military action. For instance, in January 1531 one group of "*prebezy*" caught an Ottoman soldier near Udbina, after which Karlović immediately sent them on surveillance deep into the Ottoman territory: „*Misimus iterum nostros prebegos ad explorandum*". Emil Lazsowski, Monumenta Habsburgica regni Croatiae, Dalmatiae et Slavoniae – *Habsburški spomenici Kraljevine Hrvatske, Dalmacije i Slavonije*, Vol. 2. Zagreb 1916, 6.

29 August Dimitz, Geschichte Krains von der ältesten Zeit bis auf das Jahr 1813, Vol. II, 135–136.

of the Court. Still, the number of settlers on the territory of the Slavonian Military Border was so high that even the autochthonous population sought to be awarded the "Vlach rights", in which they often succeeded if they were to assume the same obligations as the "Vlachs". Due to the homogeneity of this population, as well as their numbers, after 20 years (which was the average period for the duration of privileges) the Habsburgs failed to subdue them to regional jurisdiction so Ferdinand II. enacted the "Vlach Statutes" for all the Vlachs of the Varaždin General Command, thereby regulating their military status and privileges. Except for religious freedoms, these privileges in fact greatly limited the autonomous life of the Vlach communities and placed them under stronger control of their rulers and officers. With each new granting of privileges, the number of the Vlachs that were given the status of "Frontiersmen" was expanding, but their autonomy was shrinking. The process of colonisation of the "old" Vlachs was mostly finished by the Great Turkish War 1683–1699, when a shift in the relations on the Balkans took place. At the beginning of the seventeenth century the Serbian Orthodox Church was already granted the right of spiritual caretaking of the Vlach population in the Habsburg Empire. But the crossing of Patriarch Arsenije III Črnojević over to the Hungarian territory and under the jurisdiction of the Habsburg Empire resulted in the "Vlach issue", increasingly becoming a question of relationship between the central powers and the Serbian Orthodox Church, and not of the Vlach Frontiersmen themselves. This, unavoidably, worsened their status evermore, and made their military duty a permanent obligation.

The Venetian Military Border under the Rule of Venice

It was already mentioned that the Ottomans had special "*krajišta*" bordering the West, where the Vlach population defended their borders. However, a third power also had its own Military Border of a kind in the small area between the Drava and the Adriatic Sea. According to seventeenth century sources, we can see that the rights of these Vlachs were much the same as those required by the Habsburg-ruled Vlachs. Additionally, they also invoked their medieval rights which they enjoyed in Dalmatian communes. The basic right that the Vlachs under the Venetian rule possessed was that of holding gatherings (*legas*) where they would discuss their demands and made their decisions – but, naturally, under Venetian control.[30] A good part of these Vlachs was also relocated from the Ottoman territories, but the invoking of privileges from the pre-Ottoman era makes it obvious that Vlachs had a special status in

---

[30] Branko Sučević – Boško Desnica, *Istorija kotarskih uskoka 1646–1749, Beograd 1950–1951,* in: *Historijski zbornik V*, Zagreb 1952, 138–145.

Dalmatia ever since the Middle Ages, and which was primarily based on their nomadic and semi-military lifestyle.

The Venetian rule abundantly rewarded the Uskoks who were loyal to them, thereby stimulating the layering of the Vlach communities. It also tied notable and brave soldiers to particular towns thereby separating them from their Vlach footing, encouraged marriage into respectable civil families and awarded citizen rights or nobility titles.[31] All these Venetian activities were aimed at completely subduing the Vlachs to their control, in which they succeeded by the end of the seventeenth century. Similarly to the Habsburgs, Venice later used these Vlachs in its wars on Italian territory and not only against the Ottomans.[32]

Conclusion

The Habsburg colonisation of the Military Border was based on at least two prior experiences: one of individual settlements throughout Europe in the Middle Ages, and the other of the semi-military colonisation of population on the territory of the Hungarian Crown Lands and other Balkan countries. In the same historic period we have a compact area between the Drava and the Adriatic Sea which formed a triple-border region of three conflicting states: the Habsburg Empire, the Ottoman Empire and the Venetian Republic. Interestingly, all three states formed similar military institutions - Borders (*Krajinas*), which were based on the same "Vlach" population. Still, the Habsburg Military Border was the most longevious, best organized and best utilized one. Although the colonisation process started in the Habsburg territories - and they did not hesitate to colonise population deep into the north of Styria and even all the way to Lower Austria - the majority of the population was settled onto the territory of the Croatian Kingdom i.e. that of the Hungarian Crown. In time, this Vlach population became completely Slavenized - although we may assume that the majority had already reached the Habsburg Empire Slavenized - and a good part of this population has later itself identified with the Serbs, owing both to the affiliation to the Orthodox Church and the influence of the Serbian Orthodox Church.

---

31 The Venetians paid special attention to religious difference of the Vlachs. Namely, they appointed special serdars (heads of the lower officers, *harambašas*) for the Orthodox Vlachs. Although many of the groomsmen and godfathers in respectable Orthodox Vlachs' weddings and christenings were Catholic Venetians, Venice was quite vigorous at refusing the Catholic priests' attempts to Christianize the Orthodox population. Sučević, 142–143.

32 Sučević, 145.

This very colonisation became the territorial basis for the formation of two General Commands which became the backbone of the Military Border. The Military Border itself remains the subject matter of future scientific research as a special social and military system.

Yochai Ben-Ghedalia
(The Hebrew University of Jerusalem)

Empowerment: Great Powers, Jewish Philanthropy and European Identity[1]

The Crimean War (1853-6), which saw both England and France join forces with the Ottoman Empire against Russia, and Austria move its forces toward the Danubian principalities in an attempt to force the Tsar to withdraw his forces, constituted a watershed in the European Powers' interest in the Ottoman Empire. Despite its distance from the main battlegrounds, Jerusalem, nonetheless, played an important role in the war. Struggles between the French-oriented Catholics and the Russian-oriented Greek Orthodox over domination of Christian holy sites were among the triggers – or excuses – for the breakout of war in the first place.[2] Jerusalem was also directly affected by the conflict: The Europeans' involvement in favor of the Sultan ultimately led to a series of legislative reforms in the Ottoman Empire that enabled the Powers to strengthen their grasp on the Holy City.[3] It is worth mentioning here that the rising importance of Jerusalem had also a significant Jewish sub-context, as the Powers' interest in the city was followed by parallel concerns expressed by affluent Jewish communities in the West.

Beginning in the eighteenth century, new centers of Jewish life arose in Western and Central Europe, areas that had mostly been devoid of a Jewish presence since the late Middle Ages. Populated and led by wealthy Jews who concentrated in banking and commerce, these new communities adopted a modern lifestyle and saw themselves as an integral part of the surrounding society. Each struggled, in its own unique way, for emancipation, and sought to demonstrate its patriotism toward its respective monarch or state authority.[4] The Crimean war was a good opportunity for these communities to express their loyalty towards their empires, and to demonstrate their patronage over their co-religionists in the East, in addition to other, more altruistic, motivations. The Jews of Lon-

---

1 I want to thank my colleague and friend, Dr. Noah Gerber, for his valuable remarks on this paper.

2 For an account of the Crimean War from a diplomatic perspective see David M. Goldfrank, The Origins of the Crimean War, London 1994; David Wetzel, The Crimean War. A Diplomatic History, Boulder 1985.

3 Abdul Latif Tibawi, A Modern History of Syria. Including Lebanon and Palestine, London 1969, 94–120.

4 Jacob Katz (Ed.), Toward Modernity. The European Jewish Model, New Brunswick/Oxford 1987.

don, Paris, Vienna and other Western metropolises were reflecting the Powers' involvement in the Orient by means of intensive philanthropic activity, functioning as 'Jewish Great Powers'.[5]

***

Jewish activity on behalf of the Jews of *Zion* in those years may be divided into four categories. The first is the traditional one, which sought to enable the pious Jews of Jerusalem to live a life of *Torah* study and sanctity. Like the Franciscan Friars, these pious Jews were representing their brothers around the globe, who contributed funds to the Holy Land. Nor did the modernization of Jewish societies in the nineteenth century lesson support of this kind; on the contrary, it only underpinned its rationality, stationing it on modern methods of banking and money-transfer.

The second category is the humanitarian one. In the wake of the war, and the inability of funds from Eastern Europe to get through to the Holy Land, hunger was rampant in Palestine. This was the official catalyst for a fundraising drive, headed by Sir Moses Montefiore (1784–1885) and Britain's chief rabbi, Nathan Marcus (Mordecai) Adler (1803–90). Their campaign was unexpectedly successful, appealing as it did to both Jews and non-Jews in England, in the Continent, and in the New World. Armed with substantial cash reserves, Montefiore arrived in Jerusalem in July 1855, with the goal of distributing part of this money for purely relief purposes, directly to the needy themselves.[6]

Montefiore did not limit himself to the humanitarian mode of philanthropy alone, however, and, as a matter of fact, he was active in all four categories. Humanitarian responses to the economic and natural disasters that ravaged the Holy Land were preceded by earlier efforts that belong to the third category of philanthropic activity: civil-rights. Campaigns for improving the Ottoman Empire Jews' civil status were part of the all-European enterprise in the East. In 1840, during the diplomatic and military crisis accompanying the end of Egyptian occupation of the Levant, a united mission of prominent Jews from France and England came to Alexandria, on behalf of the Jews of Damascus. A local blood-libel against the Jews of this distant city awakened unprecedented campaigns among the Jews of the Occident. The double-headed mission, led by Mon-

[5] For more on this subject see Yochai Ben-Ghedalia, The Habsburgs and the Jewish Philanthropy in Jerusalem during the Crimean War (1853–6). Working Papers. Aharon Menczer Fund. European Forum at the Hebrew University, Jerusalem 2009, 11–14.

[6] Abraham Schischa, The Saga of 1855. A Study in Depth, in: Sonia Lipman – Vivian D. Lipman (Eds.), The Century of Moses Montefiore, Oxford 1985, 269–346.

tefiore and Adolphe Crémieux (1796–1880), did not limit its efforts to the acquittal of the Syrian Jews, but also fought for the civil status of their Oriental brethren.[7]

The same may be said of Jewish philanthropy during the Crimean War. Emulating the Powers' efforts, the Jewish 'powers' demanded that civil rights be granted to Jewish residents of the Ottoman Empire. The diplomatic campaign preceded the humanitarian initiatives, and started even before the official eruption of the war. As early as December 1853,[8] a few months before England and France joined Ottoman Empire and declared war on Russia, the Jewish leaderships in the West commenced its diplomatic lobbying. They lobbied government officials at home and abroad, dispatching delegations to the Sublime Porte with the demand, that the civil status of the Ottoman Jews be regarded as equal to that of the Christian minorities of the Empire in any future legislation.[9] The Jewish press in Western Europe both covered this diplomatic activity and actively supported it,[10] thus creating, and enhancing awareness of the Jewish great powers in play.

This awareness laid the foundations for the fourth category, almost unknown previously in Jerusalem: modern philanthropy. This sort of philanthropic activity embraced aims, strategies and attitudes that differed dramatically from those of the traditional patterns of charitable giving. Whereas the latter concentrated on supporting individuals, modern philanthropy founded public institutions, ranging from hospitals, pharmacies, well-baby clinics and welfare institutions to schools, vocational education and industry. The attitude of these donors towards their beneficiaries was also different: Whereas Diaspora Jews had regarded their brethren in the Holy City as an avant-garde of holiness and piety, the Europeanized philanthropists looked down on their oriental counterparts as uncouth, even embarrassing relatives. Therefore, as opposed to the traditional and Orthodox approaches to giving, modern philanthropy did not seek to preserve the values and lifestyle of the Jewish community of Jerusalem, but rather to modernize and to regenerate it.

Both the civil-rights and the reconstruction campaigns were also intended to serve a greater Jewish Occidental project: the Europeanization of the Jews of the East. From their new position of

---

7 See Jonathan Frankel, The Damascus Affair. "Ritual Murder", Politics, and the Jews in 1840, Cambridge 1997.

8 Nathan Michael Gelber, Dr. Albert Cohen and his visit to Jerusalem, in: Jerusalem 2, 1949, 176 [in Hebrew].

9 Isidore Loeb, Biographie d'Albert Cohn, Paris 1878, 47–54.

10 The most prominent figure in this context was the editor of the leading Jewish newspaper – Allgemeine Zeitung des Judenthums, Ludwig Philipsohn (1811–89).

wealth and influence, the European Jewish powers sought to guide their "backward" brethren through the very same process they themselves had undergone just a few years earlier. The two interrelated methods of accomplishing this goal were either bringing the Jews of Jerusalem closer to Europe by means of reconstructional, regenerating, philanthropy,[11] or bringing Europe closer to the Jews by means of civil-rights.[12] However, the real beneficiaries of these philanthropic campaigns were not the Jews of the Orient, but rather the European Jews themselves, the emerging Great Powers of the Jewish microcosm. The *empowerment* of Jewish centers in the West was an additional step in these communities' own struggle to become an integral part of European society.

This struggle was not only externally directed, however; it also had strong intra-Jewish ramifications. Lacking territory, a form of central-governance, or any means of expressing a "national", intra-diasporal collectivity, philanthropy came to serve a central role in European Jewry's politics, symbolically positioning the leading philanthropists – whether individuals or organizations – as *bona fide* Jewish powers.

***

The Jewish philanthropists were an integral part of their respective states' involvement in the East. Thus, while in the East, Montefiore, former Sheriff of the City of London, met the Sultan, and disembarked at Jaffa in "full uniform." In the course of his philanthropic missions, he served both the interests of the Jewish congregations of the Isle and those of the British government, as has been emphasized lately by Abigail Green.[13] The same may be said of Ludwig August Frankl (1810–94), whose strong Austrian affiliations I have discussed elsewhere.[14]

However, the nationalist aspect of Jewish philanthropy was not always so apparent, as in the case of Albert Cohn. Following the French declaration of war on Russia, the Central Consistory of French Jews sought means of improving the civil, cultural, and physical situation of the Jews in the Ottoman Empire. They there-

---

[11] Better known in the discourse over European Jewry by the terms enlightenment and acculturation.

[12] Or: emancipation.

[13] Abigail Green, Rethinking Sir Moses Montefiore. Religion, Nationhood, and International Philanthropy in the Nineteenth Century, in: American Historical Review 110, Bloomington 2005, 631–658.

[14] Yochai Ben-Ghedalia, "To Worship the Rising Sun of Austria". Ludwig August Frankl's Mission to Jerusalem (1856), in: Arnold Suppan – Richard Lein (Eds.), From the Habsburgs to Central Europe, Europa Orientalis 6, Vienna 2008, 101–111.

fore decided to send Dr. Albert Cohn (1814–77), the almoner of the local branch of the Rothschild family and the director of the Jewish Relief Committee of Paris – the *comité de bienfaissance* – as a one-man mission to the East.[15] Cohn's mission was not limited merely to exploring and reporting back on the situation he found there. Rather, he was to start a network of philanthropic institutions in Jerusalem, similar to the one he nurtured throughout his years in Paris. Cohn left Paris for the Orient on 11 June, 1854. He stayed in Jerusalem only three short weeks, in which time he nevertheless managed to lay the groundwork for a comprehensive, and quite successful, network of health, education, and relief institutions.

Nonetheless, the national identity of the Jerusalem institutions Cohn established is far from clear. Cohn, a man of the Jewish–French center,[16] sent to Jerusalem by the Consistory thanks to his experience in France and Algeria, was supposedly French through and through. The network of institutions he founded in the holy city was a duplicate of those he had established in Paris, many of them even carrying the names of their original Parisian equivalents. Those institutions were also perceived as French achievements, as was pointed out by contemporaries.[17]

After leaving Paris, however, Cohn did not turn southward to Marseille, the main French port in the Mediterranean and its gateway to North Africa and the Orient. Instead he headed eastward, to Vienna. There he met with *Kaiser* Francis Joseph (1830–1916), as well as Alexander Freiherr von Bach (1813–93), the minister of the interior, and Graf Karl Ferdinand von Buol-Schauenstein (1797–1865), the foreign minister, who provided him with official letters of recommendation to all the Austrian consular delegations in the Ottoman Empire. Equipped with these recommendations, Cohn left Trieste – Austria's nautical entry to the Mediterranean – for Jerusalem. The institutions he founded there were done so with the *Kaiser's* support, and were closely accompanied by the Austrian consul in Jerusalem – and not, as might be expected, by the French consul. The Austrian involvement in Cohn's philanthropic mission was even more apparent upon his arrival in Constantinople, where

---

15 On Cohn see his autobiographical letters, published in l'Univers Israélite, 20–21, 1864–6; his Franco centered biography by Isidore Loeb, Biographie; as well as the Austro-Hungarian-oriented biography by Ignaz Reich, Beth El. Ehrentempel verdienter ungar. Israeliten, vol. 1, Pesth ^{2}1868, 80–105. On his 1854 journey see also Gelber, Cohen, 175–195.

16 According to the terminology used by Michael Graetz, The Jews in Nineteenth-Century France. From the French Revolution to the Alliance Israélite Universelle, [trans. Jane Marie Todd], Stanford 1996.

17 For a description of the perception of world-politics of Jewish Philanthropy by contemporary Jewish public opinion and press, see Ludwig August Frankl, Nach Jerusalem, 2 vols., Leipzig 1858, vol. 1: 10.

he launched diplomatic efforts to improve the Ottoman Jews' civil status, with the help of the Austrian diplomatic corps in the Ottoman capital. Moreover, his first stop upon returning to Europe was Vienna, where he merited another audience by the *Kaiser* and a meeting with his senior ministers. These meetings led later on to official Austrian consular protection for Cohn's institutions in the East.

***

The national dissonance that permeates Cohn's activity in Jerusalem can be understood from various angles, such as the various powers' complexes of diplomatic interests, the intricacy of identities manifest in the House of Rothschild, as well as Cohn's own complex identity.

In the diplomatic arena, France was simply not interested in extending its complex network of patronage to Jewish causes. The French consul in Jerusalem enjoyed a stable infrastructure of both Christian institutions as well as local lay Catholic subjects, seeing no reason to broaden it.[18] This stands in stark contrast to Austria – the minor Catholic power – to whom Jewish interests were the means to deepening its anchor in the Holy City.[19] In this sense, Cohn's mission is a good example of the potential gap between the assumed national character of an entity and the formal consular protection actually granted it.

A look at Cohn's patrons – the Parisian Rothschild House – sheds a new light on the complexity of these institutions' identity. Contrary to Montefiore or Frankl, whose national identity was clear-cut, the national affiliation of the Rothschilds was much more complex.[20] The Rothschilds were often accused in the ultramontane and anti-Semitic press as cosmopolitan, and to some extent, rightly so. The House, whose members were spread over numerous countries, managed a matrix of family interests, including Jewish ones, which more than once overshadowed the political tendencies of the states in which the various members of the Family resided. The Parisian branch provides an excellent example of this complexity in action: The head of the House, James (1792–1868), was born in Frankfurt am Main and was awarded the title of Austrian general consul in the

---

18 Tudor Parfitt, The Jews in Palestine, 1800–1882, Woodbridge 1987, 127–158; Simon Schwarzfuchs, The French Consulate in Jerusalem in the Nineteenth Century and the French Protected Jews, in: Shalem 8, 2008, 478–573 [in Hebrew].

19 Mordechai Eliav – Barbara Haider (Eds.), Österreich und das Heilige Land. Ausgewählte Konsulatsdokumente aus Jerusalem, 1849–1917, Vienna 2000, 29–63.

20 On the Rothschilds see Niall Ferguson, The House of Rothschild, 2 vols., New York 1998–1999.

French capital, where he resided for most of his life. His sons Alphonse (1827–1905) and Gustave (1829–1911) – and later on the youngest son, Edmond (1845–1934), were 'real' French, being fully involved in the Jewish consistorial network. The Parisian House's French identity was even further emphasised following the 1848 events.[21] If that is not enough, members from various branches of the family throughout Europe were appointed patrons of the Rothschild Jerusalem institutions,[22] complicating the question of their national identity even further.

In spite of all this complex web of macro-associations, it seems that Albert Cohn's personal status and identity had the greatest influence on the national affiliation of the institutions he established. Born in Bratislava (Pressburg), he moved to Vienna as a young boy to receive a secular education. On account of his religion, he was barred from studying everything but medicine in the university, and so, he pursued Semitic studies privately. He became a disciple of Baron Joseph von Hammer-Purgstall (1774–1856), the Viennese leading Orientalist of those days, who, in 1836, advised his Jewish pupil to leave for Paris, where he would be able to formalise his Oriental education. There, Cohn studied under prominent French Orientalists of the time, and served as personal tutor to the local Rothschild children. He quickly became the family's almoner, and director of the Jewish Relief Committee of Paris.

Having spent his formative years in the Habsburg capital, Cohn remained completely "Austrian" years after his arrival in Paris. His affinity, however, had also a juridical aspect. Indeed, as prosaic as it may sound, since Cohn bore Austrian citizenship, he had to merit the recommendation of the Habsburg administration in order to embark on his mission to the Ottoman Empire in the first place. Only in 1862,[23] after twenty-five years of residence in Paris, and over twenty years of public activity, unmistakably affiliating him with French Jewry, did Cohen shed his Austrian citizenship in favour of a French one.

***

The national identity of Cohn's philanthropic institutions likewise points to the complex of affiliations, in the Jewish – and general – nineteenth century experiences. As opposed to the far more rigidly defined post-World War I European identities, the national affiliation of various personages and entities was more elusive in the pre-nation-state era.

---

21 Graetz, The Jews, 79–109.

22 Loeb, Biographie, 71–76.

23 Ibid., 169f.

Still, it seems that Cohn's example demands a more solid definition. What was Cohn's identity: Austrian? Hungarian? French? or – Jewish? And how does he differ from his patron, James de-Rothschild, or from Count Joseph von Pizzamano (1809–60), the Austrian consul in Jerusalem, of a Venetian noble family with Bohemian roots?[24]

This jumble of identities surely requires a broader answer. With his face turned toward the Orient, Albert Cohn – both Albert Cohn the philanthropist and Albert Cohn the Orientalist, a member of the French société asiatique – was undoubtedly – European.

In this, the Jewish confrontation with the East was no different than the one exhibited by the powers during the Crimean War, on both the battlefield as well as the negotiation table. Facing the Jewish East, the forces of Jewish philanthropy displayed a unified European frontier, while each philanthropic power represented, at the same time, its own particular national interest – or interests.

---

[24] Frankl, Nach Jerusalem 2, 17.

Markus Helmut Lenhart
(The Hebrew University of Jerusalem)

Austria as a Cradle of Jewish Art History

The following text deals with the rather interesting fact that at the beginning of art-historical research regarding Jewish art, an Austrian scholar – to be precise, an Austro-Hungarian scholar – stands out: David Kaufmann. Of course, he was not alone in his research and it has to be pointed out that contemporary steps in this field of research were taken by several scholars (but also non-scholars) at the same time, for example in France and in Russia.[1] Nevertheless, taking his impact on later times into consideration, I strongly support the position of David Kaufmann as a sort of "midwife" for the birth of Jewish Art as an accepted field of research in art history. My aim is, by concentrating on one particular text by Kaufmann, to present his key arguments and to show how he tried to position Jewish art within the broader field of art historical research.

To prove the existence of Jewish art and to secure its standing was insofar important, as the classification and definition of the term "Jewish art" represented a special problem within the art-historical research of the nineteenth and the early twentieth century. Most art historians held that there was no such thing as Jewish art. This argument was primarily supported by the emphasis on the ban on depictions appearing in different parts of the *Tora* and other Jewish religious writings.

However, in one sense a certain form representing Jewish art – it was not called by this term at the time – could not be negated completely and had to be accepted, at least as a section of biblical archaeology. Within this, proving of biblical history played an outstanding role. One of its concerns was to find evidence of the exis-

---

1 I want to thank Ziva Amishai-Maisels from the Hebrew University, Jerusalem for reminding me of this fact. One of these projects was initiated in Russia by Vladimir Stasov in cooperation with David Günzburg resulting in an outstanding publication, translated into several languages. The best known one was the French version: Vladimir Stasov – David Guenzburg, L'Ornement Hébreu. Ornementation des anciens manuscrits hébreux de la Bibliothèque Imperiale Publique de St. Pétersbourg, Berlin 1905. The continuing importance of (and fascination with) this publication is revealed by the fact that a facsimile of the book, including additional material, was published in 1990: Bezalel Narkiss, with Illuminations from Hebrew Bibles of Leningrad. Decorations in Hebrew medieval manuscripts from the Imperial Public Library in St. Petersburg, now the Saltikov-Shchedrin Collection at the State Public Library in Leningrad. Original published by David Gunzburg and Vladimir Stassoff. Facsimile of the 27 original large colour plates accompanied by a new introduction with 25 additional plates, Jerusalem 1990.

tence of the temple of Salomon. Interestingly enough, the capability of the biblical Jews to achieve something extraordinary in the field of arts was pointed out by referring to the erection of the temple. But in the same breath, the dictum of the "art-less" Jew was also exemplarily confirmed because the Jewish people had, according to the biblical sources, even in their "golden age" been dependent on foreign artists - in this case Phoenician artists - to build their temple.[2] Nevertheless, the examination of biblical stories, although more often used as proof of the non-existence of Jewish art, was something of a starting point.

Besides being biblical archaeology, it was a movement within Judaism, which aimed at investigating Jewish history and culture independently, especially from the Jewish point of view, and which was responsible for the later scholarly research into Jewish art. The *Wissenschaft des Judentums*, as they called themselves, was founded in the early nineteenth century. Even though they were often excluded from the academic world, the more important representatives managed to influence the perception of Jewish history - at least within Judaism - decisively. In the beginning, its principle interests lay in the examination of general history, literary studies and linguistics, a direction that it kept until the end of the nineteenth century. Although some of its members shared common prejudices towards scientific investigation of Jewish art, it is inconceivable without it. David Kaufmann's scholarly education was strongly influenced by the *Wissenschaft des Judentums*, and as a publisher of one of its major journals, *Monatsschrift für Geschichte und Wissenschaft des Judentums*, he was closely connected to it. He was one of the first Jewish researchers to examine and also collect Jewish art. The scholars who followed in his wake, such as Rachel Wischnitzer-Bernstein, Karl Schwarz, Ernst Cohn-Wiener and Franz Landsberger, can only be understood in relation to the "tradition" founded by him.

In addition to this we should not forget the artists themselves. In the nineteenth century several Jewish artists started to deal with Jewish themes, making them more visible for a wider audience. Moritz Daniel Oppenheim, Maurycy Gottlieb and Isidor Kaufmann are only the better known figures from a whole range of Jewish artists dealing with Jewish themes. But what has to be added is the fact that none of them were presenting something along the lines of a "manifesto" in favour of Jewish art. Their importance lies solely in the fact that they may have given some art historians cause to think.

---

2 Margaret Olin, Nationalism, the Jews, and Art History, in: Judaism. A Journal of Jewish Life & Thought 45/4, New York 1996, 466f.

David Kaufmann and the *Haggada of Sarajevo*

At the beginning of the positive scientific investigation of Jewish art that went beyond biblical archaeology stands the appendix of David Kaufmann, written as a supplement to a facsimile of the *Haggada of Sarajevo* in 1898.[3] This text forms an important link between the historical, linguistic and literary studies of the Wissenschaft des Judentums and the beginning of art-historical investigation of objects of Jewish culture.

David Kaufmann was born in Kojetein (today Kojetín), a town in the province of Moravia, on 7 June 1852, and died in Karlsbad (Karlovy Vary) on 6 July 1899. From 1867 to 1877 he visited the rabbinical seminar in Breslau (today Wrocław, located in Poland) and additionally also enrolled at the University. He completed his doctorate in religious philosophy in 1874. After this, he taught Jewish history, religious philosophy and Homiletics at the rabbinical seminar in Budapest. He held this post until his death. In addition, he was active as journalist and editor of the previously mentioned *Monatsschrift für Geschichte und Wissenschaft des Judentums*, one of the most important Jewish magazines in the Austro-Hungarian Empire.[4]

As a scholar he is primarily to be seen as a historian and linguist (and surely not as an art historian), both due to his academic training and the clear main emphasis of his research. As editor of the *Monatsschrift für Geschichte und Wissenschaft,* which appeared regularly between 1851 and 1939, he was, in this position, a successor of the historian Heinrich Graetz, one of the most outstanding representatives of Jewish historiography. Kaufmann himself performed his function as editor from 1892 until his death in 1899.[5]

His earliest article dealing with Jewish art – which is available – deals with his impression of two sections of the Parisian World Exhibition of 1878: on the one hand, the works of the Jewish

---

[3] David Heinrich Müller – Julius von Schlosser (Eds.), Die Haggadah von Sarajevo. Eine spanisch-jüdische Bilderhandschrift des Mittelalters. Nebst einem Anhange von Prof. Dr. David Kaufmann in Budapest. Mit einem Frontispiz in Chromotypie, 38 Lichtdrucktafeln, 18 Textabbildungen und einem Atlas von 35 Tafeln, Wien 1898. Kaufmanns supplement is bearing the title Zur Geschichte der jüdischen Handschriften-Illustrationen, 173–228.

[4] Moshe Zobel, David Kaufmann, in: Cecil Roth – Geoffrey Wigoder (Eds.), Encyclopaedia Judaica, 16 vols., Jerusalem 1971–1972, columns 842f.

[5] The journal itself is thanks to a project of the DFG completely digitalized and is today freely accessible in the internet: Hans Otto Horch – Rachel Heuberger – Annette Haller (Eds.), Compact Memory – Deutsch-jüdische Literaturgeschichte im Web. Institut für Germanistische und Allgemeine Literaturwissenschaft. Lehr- und Forschungsgebiet Deutsch-jüdische Literaturgeschichte, RWTH Aachen, http://www.compactmemory.de/.

French painter Henri Leopold Lévy and on the other, the collection of Judaica of Mr. Strauß. The works of Lévy, which were primarily sketches for the decoration of a Roman Catholic Church, allowing the question to arise within him as to which works of art – or themes, to be more precise – would be fitting for a Jew. Much more interesting and important for the topic of this presentation were the questions in connection with the represented Judaica. The exhibited objects stimulated Kaufmann to ideas regarding research yet to be undertaken in the field of synagogue architecture and the equipment of synagogues.[6] Interestingly enough, each of the examples suggested by him was of Italian origin – a suggestion that will be of further importance in his appendix to the *Haggada of Sarajevo*.

Of equal importance are two other aspects of this article. Firstly, he had already talked about Jewish national artists without revealing any references to relations to a sort of proto–Zionism. Secondly, almost in the same breath he opposed any ideas concerning the idea of an iconophobic Judaism, based on the already mentioned argument of the ban on depictions appearing in the *Tora*. This opposition seems to be directed against inner–Jewish confirmations and non–Jewish ones alike.[7]

David Kaufman earns special attention, not so much for the text mentioned above – although in itself it is quite an interesting one – but for his appendix to a facsimile of the *Haggada of Sarajevo*, published in 1898. His contribution bears the title *Zur Geschichte der jüdischen Handschriftenillustrationen*.[8] This article was the first modern and positive examination of a medieval handwritten manuscript in Hebrew, which was part of the Jewish community and not one of the few manuscripts for the use of the Catholic Church. Its importance, however, does not exhaust itself in a simple sort of stock–taking. Kaufmann introduced several aspects and ideas represented in the following and for a long time continued to have an effect – not to be underestimated – for the classification and definition of the term "Jewish art".[9]

---

6 David Kaufmann, Etwas von jüdischer Kunst, in: David Kaufmann, Gesammelte Schriften, ed. by. Marcus Brann, 3 vols., Frankfurt am Main 1908–1915, vol. 3, 150–153.

7 Kaufmann, Etwas von jüdischer Kunst, 151f.

8 See footnote no. 3.

9 Eva Frojmovic, Buber in Basel, Schlosser in Sarajevo, Wischnitzer in Weimar. The Politics of Writing about Medieval Jewish Art, in: Eva Frojmovic (Ed.), Imagining the Self, Imagining the Other. Visual Representation and Jewish–Christian Dynamics in the Middle Ages and Early Modern Period, Cultures, beliefs and traditions. Medieval and Early Modern People 15, Leiden/Boston/Köln 2002, 4.

The *Haggada of Sarajevo* is one of the oldest Sephardic Haggadot in the world, originating in Barcelona around 1350. The *Haggada* is presently owned by the National Museum of Bosnia and Herzegovina in Sarajevo, where it is on permanent display. The editors of the facsimile were David Heinrich Müller and Julius von Schlosser, the latter an important art historian in the Austro-Hungarian Empire. Although he co-edited the facsimile of the *Haggada,* he was not positively inclined towards the idea of Jewish art; in his article, accompanying the facsimile, also he made some ineffectual suggestions that even Jews might be capable of artistic works. The whole tone of his writing was nevertheless against Jewish art in the sense of how it is used today. David Kaufmann, on the other hand, began his article by drawing up a short summary of the current research situation in the field of illustrations of handwritten books in general, mentioning palaeography and history of art in particular.[10]

His further efforts went to proving that Jews were active as artists, and that there was continuity in Jewish art. As a linguistic expert in illustrated, handwritten manuscripts, and in part due to the fact that his article had accompanied the facsimile of such a manuscript, he based his hypothesis particularly on this medium, but not on this alone. The scrolls which were reserved for the service at the synagogue are, even today, still subject to the strictest of rules including the ban on illustrations, whereas the books offered for private use continue to provide opportunity for illustration. Kaufmann introduced these different kinds of books using numerous examples, commenting on and describing them more or less extensively, including certain types of picture-Bibles, Esther-scrolls, prayer books and Haggadot. In addition, he also mentioned Ketubbot and other manuscripts still more seldomly analyzed today; for example all manner of books regarding religious laws and Bible commentaries or medicinal treatises. In this way, he revealed a wide knowledge concerning works from Germany and Italy, and the fact that he knew something about the inventory of various English collectors.[11]

In his opinion, the writers would have started adding small images on the edges in addition to their actual work, which consisted of writing the letters themselves. The reason may have lain in the clarification of the meaning of the text, although aesthetic aspects are also possible. Another source that he suspected of being still more closely connected to the written word was the art of micrography. Letters are written minutely, so that the details lose coher-

---

10 Kaufmann, Zur Geschichte der jüdischen Handschriften-Illustrationen, 173f.

11 Kaufmann, Zur Geschichte der jüdischen Handschriften-Illustrationen, 175–212.

ence from a certain distance, and the letters become blurred into smaller or broader lines, and even noticeably darker areas. This is made use of to the effect that one "paints" whole pictures with this technique. The artist also ensures that the chosen text and the image are matching thematically. The result stands between painting and calligraphy. For Kaufmann, marginal notes and micrography formed the nuclei of illustrations in Hebrew books. He saw two motives as the impulses behind this: The first one had simply been fantasy in itself, which one may presuppose as existent among all humans – in this way, a strong reproach against all anti-Semites was stated, who thought Jews to be devoid of normal human feelings. The other reason may have been in expectation of renown and glory, which could have encouraged the writers to become active as artists too, an all-too human habit.[12]

By vehemently arguing in favour of the existence of Jewish illustrators he entered new ground and opposed the opinion – predominant until then – that there were no Jewish illustrators but instead only Christian ones. Until this moment scholars had reacted by negating Jewish illustrators and declaring that the executing artists for the existing, undeniably Hebrew books – merely seen as remittance works – were Christians, at least in respect to the illustrations. Kaufmann's argumentation in favour of Jewish artists was based on different facts. As a rule, the publishers had never hidden any Christian-Jewish cooperation that took place in the form of a Christian illustrator and a Jewish writer. Kaufmann held the view that when there is a silence about any particular collaboration, and thus about the illustrator, one can logically assume it to be a purely Jewish work. Another argument was based on the already mentioned assumption that the illustrators recruited themselves from among the rows of writers. This made it quite possible for illustrator and writer to be one and the same person. Since the writers were unquestionably Jews, the executing artists then would be logically Jews as well. This would be valid also in case the illustrator was not mentioned, as in most cases, in the colophon. Kaufmann also recalled the case of a manuscript – a Machsor from Pesaro from the fifteenth century – where proof would arise from the fact that the pictures would suggest an intimate knowledge of Jewish customs in such a precise way that the artist was undoubtedly a Jew. Furthermore, Kaufmann mentions Mose dal Castellazzo, a known Jewish painter from Venice of the fifteenth century. Castellazzo also served as a starting point for a whole row of names of known Jewish artists, which Kaufmann included in this part of his article, elegantly building a continuous

---

12 Kaufmann, Zur Geschichte der jüdischen Handschriften-Illustrationen, 174 and 215.

chain from the fifteenth century up to the end of the nineteenth century.[13]

Here we enter the second theme of his article. He developed the thought of a "chain of tradition" - without directly calling it as such. In a next step he traced - in a virtual timeline - medieval book production back into antiquity and in the same breath linked it to modern book production. In the case of the modern book production he once again mentioned Mose dal Castellazzo, whose illustrations were cut into wood for printing. Thus, Kaufmann was able to find one connection from the handwritten and illustrated book to the letterpress. By offering a "chain of tradition" up until his own times, he constructed a time-line of Jewish book production from antiquity until the nineteenth century, even projecting it to the future. Of course, he could not prove an unbroken line of books illustrated by hand through all these centuries, taking into consideration all the various changes that had taken place in book production. Nevertheless, he did not let go of his idea of a "chain of tradition" and used in addition to various types of books, every illustrated piece containing text, such as the Ketubbot.[14]

Overlooking the text in its entirety, it reveals a very interesting and also important fact in the context of the weighting of single epochs and countries. Kaufmann obviously preferred manuscripts from the Italian area. This does not mean that he disregarded the performances of the Jews of medieval Spain and Germany, far from that. But within the different epochs, he held the considerable performances of the Jewish-Italian Renaissance in high regard, a judgment which he repeats in different sections of his work. In contrast to his positive evaluation of the books of the Renaissance, he regarded the Baroque period to be of lesser importance and quality.[15]

What makes this judgment so interesting is its parallelization with the surrounding art-historical research concerning Christian art. In contemporary art-historical writings an outstanding meaning was also attributed to the culture of the Italian Renaissance. One can suspect that Kaufmann wanted to achieve an "upgrading" of Jewish art, which until then had been utterly negated, or at best marginalized. By presenting an artistic continuity through the centuries, and in pointing out that by chance, time and place of its artistic peak where the ones most favoured by European art histori-

[13] Kaufmann, Zur Geschichte der jüdischen Handschriften-Illustrationen, 213–228.

[14] Kaufmann, Zur Geschichte der jüdischen Handschriften-Illustrationen, 198, 219f and 225.

[15] This fact was already noted by other scholars dealing with Kaufmanns text. Frojmovic, Buber in Basel, Schlosser in Sarajevo, Wischnitzer in Weimar, 16f.

ans, he seemed to have tried to prove that Jewish art is in no way inferior to Christian art. One also gets the impression that at the same time, by proving how narrowly connected Jewish culture was with the surrounding one, he tried to establish the impression that Jews formed an integral part of European cultural history. This idea was not self-evident in his time.

However, by connecting Jewish art with that of the surrounding societies, Kaufmann reached a kind of crisis concerning his concept of Jewish art. By analyzing the text it becomes clear that Kaufmann moved back and forth between two positions. On the one hand, he followed national boundaries and outlined the Jewish contribution to the respective fields of art, for example Italian art. On the other hand he tried to establish the idea of a supranational art, seeing Judaism as a religious community connected across all nation states. To be able to counter this dilemma, he decided to subdivide his article not according to countries but according to "literary" genres. However, he did not escape from the basic problem, which also touched on the question of a Jewish national art[16] – a topic he had already mentioned in his first article dealing with Mr. Strauß's collection of Judaica, presented at the Parisian World Exhibition of 1878. This problem may be attributed not only to the fact that Jews formed – in Kaufmanns time – no nation at all, but it may also be a faint echo of the nationalistic problems within the Austro-Hungarian Empire.

One may not agree with all theories he presented in his work, but he undisputedly holds the honour to have been the first Jewish scholar to have drawn attention to the rich artistic inheritance of the Jewish community.

However, his contribution to the investigation of Jewish art history was not restricted to the supplement of the *Haggada of Sarajevo*, although this was indeed his most notable and also most noted contribution. In the year of his death he presented an extensive examination with the title *Die Bilderzyklen im deutschen Typus der alten Haggada-Illustration*, dealing exclusively with Haggadot from Germany.[17] His "mission" to spread the idea of caring for and researching artistic items of Jewish origin included the founding of the *Gesellschaft für Sammlung und Konservierung von Kunst- und historischen Denkmälern des Judentums in Wien* – a society which was con-

16 This was especially noted by Olins analyzes of Kaufmanns text. Margaret Olin, The Nation without Art. Examining Modern Discourses on Jewish Art, Lincoln/London 2001, 88.

17 David Kaufmann, Die Bilderzyklen im deutschen Typus der alten Haggada-Illustration, in: David Kaufmann, Gesammelte Schriften, ed. by. Marcus Brann, 3 vols., Frankfurt am Main 1908–1915, vol. 3, 229–261.

nected to the founding of the first Jewish museum in Vienna.[18] With this institution another man with the surname Kaufmann, unrelated to David, played an important role by "designing" as part of the exhibition a Sabbath room – this was Isidor Kaufmann, a then prominent Jewish artist, known for his paintings of East-European Jewish life.

David Kaufmann was a fervent collector, not only as a member of the *Gesellschaft für Sammlung und Konservierung von Kunst- und historischen Denkmälern des Judentums in Wien* but also as a private person, whose library contained many valuable manuscripts – one of them, the *Kaufmann Haggada*, bears his name even today –, incunabula and even genizah fragments. His collection is now owned by the Hungarian Academy of Sciences.[19]

Concerning Kaufmann's publications: according to the Encyclopaedia Judaica he produced an astonishing amount of work – 30 books, and over 500 articles and book reviews. After his death, a selection of his articles was published in three volumes by Marcus Brann. A small part of this output even appeared in a Hebrew translation. The lion's share of his work constitutes historical studies – primarily biographical outlines – and linguistic treatises.[20] Only a very small part of his work was dedicated to art-historical subjects in the broadest sense. That may also be the cause for the fact that the judgment of his immediate contemporaries turned out to be slightly different by stressing not his contribution to Jewish art, but concentrating on his achievements as a scholar of historical and linguistic topics.

The situation changed some years later, in the interwar period, when art-historians in Germany such as Rachel Wischnitzer-Bernstein, Karl Schwarz, Ernst Cohn-Wiener and Franz Landsberger began to do research on Jewish art, citing Kaufmann's articles and (partly) adopting his arguments.[21]

---

18 Zobel, David Kaufmann, column 842f.

19 Hungarian Academy of Sciences, Budapest, Ms.A. 422. Mentioned in: Andreas Nachama et.al. (Eds.), Jüdische Lebenswelten. Martin-Gropius-Bau, Berlin, 12. Jänner – 26. April 1992, 2 vols., Frankfurt am Main 1991, vol. 2 (catalogue), 460.

20 A more detailed bibliography and account of his scholarly research than the dry dropping of numbers in the *Encyclopaedia Judaica* can be found in: Marcus Brann – Ferdinand Rosenthal (Eds.), Gedenkbuch zur Erinnerung an David Kaufmann, Breslau 1900.

21 Besides several articles their most important publications, which were partly republished in later years or even translated to different languages, are: Rachel Wischnitzer-Bernstein, Gestalten und Symbole der jüdischen Kunst, Berlin 1935. Karl Schwarz, Die Juden in der Kunst, Berlin 1928. Karl Schwarz, Die Juden in der Kunst, Berlin 1928. Ernst Cohn-Wiener, Die Jüdische Kunst. Ihre Geschichte von den Anfängen bis zur Gegenwart, Berlin 1929. Franz Landsberger, Einführung in die Jüdische Kunst, Berlin 1935.

These were as follows:

- After Kaufmann, the existence of Jewish illustrators of handwritten manuscripts was no longer questioned, which was the pre-condition for arguing in favour of Jews being artistically active and, of course, the existence of a Jewish art tradition at all.
- Though Kaufmann's sometimes shaky "chain of tradition" was not accepted in all its particulars, the acceptance of a continuing Jewish art became visible at last in the interwar period, when the first monographs on the history of Jewish art through the times appeared.

Today, Kaufmann's contribution to the investigation of Jewish art is generally appreciated and his validity as a pioneer in this field of studies is stressed. His importance is insofar visible, as his texts can still be found in the lists of cited literature in modern scholarly works.[22]

[22] For further details regarding the theme of this article: Markus Helmut Lenhart, Du sollst Dir ein Bild machen. Jüdische Kunst in Theorie und Praxis von David Kaufmann bis zur Kultur-Lige, Schriften des Centrums für Jüdische Studien 15, Innsbruck/Wien 2009.

Andreas Rathberger
(University of Vienna)

Austria–Hungary, the Cretan Crisis and the Ambassadors' Conference of Constantinople in 1896

Introduction

In the past, publications analyzing the Cretan Crisis of 1896–1898 mainly did so in the context of researching the emergence of the Great Power alliance blocs of World War One, focusing on the dealings of foreign ministers and cabinets, while a recently published diploma thesis deals with the military and naval aspects of the international intervention.[1] Other recent publications in the field of international history emphasize the role played by professional diplomats for the development of both informal and codified standards in nineteenth century international politics, analyzing its structures below the level of governments and cabinets.[2] My PhD thesis[3] accordingly analyzes the methods and functionality of the *Ambassadors' Conference of Constantinople* as the most

---

[1] E.g.: J. A. S. Grenville, Gołuchowski, Salisbury and the Mediterranean Agreements 1895–1897, in: Slavonic and East European Review 36/87, London 1958, 340–369; Peter Stein, Die Neuorientierung der österreichisch-ungarischen Außenpolitik 1895–1897, Göttinger Bausteine zur Geschichtswissenschaft 44, Göttingen 1972; Berthold Sutter, Die Großmächte und die Erhaltung des europäischen Friedens zu Beginn der Kreta-Krise 1897, in: Südost-Forschungen 21, München 1962, 214–369; Eva Wolf, Die Beziehungen Österreich-Ungarns zu Deutschland unter Gołuchowski (1895–1906), PhD thesis, Vienna 1967; More recent publications likewise focus on cabinet politics: Mehmed Ekinci, The Origins of the 1897 Ottoman-Greek War, MA thesis, Ankara 2006; Ariadni Moutafidou, Die Politik Österreich-Ungarns gegenüber dem osmanisch-griechischen Krieg von 1897, Hamburg 2003; Stephan Verosta, Kollektivaktionen der Mächte des Europäischen Konzerts 1866–1914, Vienna 1988; The most recent publication on the Cretan Crisis is an MA thesis analyzing the military and naval aspects of the international intervention: Irmgard Pangerl, Die Kreta-Mission der k.u.k. Kriegsmarine, MA thesis, Vienna 2008.

[2] See Matthias Schulz, „Wächter der Zivilisation?": Institutionelle Merkmale und Normative Grundlagen des Europäischen Konzerts im 19. Jahrhundert, in: Historische Mitteilungen 17, Stuttgart 2004, 35–47; Matthias Schulz, Normen und Praxis: Das Europäische Konzert der Großmächte als Sicherheitsrat, 1815–1860, Studien zur Internationalen Geschichte 21, München 2009; Marija Wakounig, Ein Grandseigneur der Diplomatie: die Mission von Franz de Paula Prinz von und zu Liechtenstein in St. Petersburg 1894–1898, Europa Orientalis 1, Vienna/Berlin 2007.

[3] The PhD thesis this paper is based on was funded by a research stipend granted by the University of Vienna (FNr. 220) from August to December 2008.

thoroughly institutionalized, yet so far least researched organ of the so-called "European Concert of Powers".[4] The Ambassadors' Conference played a particularly important role during the Cretan Crisis of 1896–1898, serving as a semi-independent institution for resolving international crises and preventing conflicts among the Great Powers. My thesis aims to explore the extent to which the Ambassadors' Conference acted independently or in concert with governments, as well as the extent to which its work influenced the political course of the Great Powers.

In order to achieve the latter goal, the work of the Ambassadors' Conference regarding the Cretan Crisis is put in context with the decision-making processes of Austro-Hungarian foreign politics and checked for its impact there: Austro-Hungarian Foreign Minister Agenor Count Gołuchowski the Younger after all, was particularly vocal in claiming that Austria-Hungary had no special interest in Crete beyond the maintenance of the *status quo* and of unanimity and cooperation among the Great Powers.[5] At the same time, however, his early years of office were characterized by the constant fear of a possible attempt by the Russian Empire to seize control of Constantinople[6] and the Dardanelles. Whenever crises threatened to destabilize the Ottoman Empire, he displayed a remarkable readiness to claim the initiative in starting and directing international interventions, attempting to bind all Great Powers to a collective course of action in order to prevent unilateral Russian intervention, using the structures of the Concert of Powers to protect what he perceived as Austro-Hungarian "vital interests".[7] This ambiguous motivation

---

4 Unlike other "ambassadors' conferences" convoked by the concert as merely temporary bodies to mediate specific conflicts, the Ambassadors' Conference in Constantinople served as a de facto permanent institution since 1856: Schulz, Wächter, 39; It is often casually mentioned in historical studies, but so far has not been the target of in-depth analysis; A comparatively extensive overview of what is known about it is given in Verosta, Kollektivaktionen, 15, 18f.

5 See the annual speeches on Foreign Politics Gołuchowski held in front of the Delegations of the Austrian and Hungarian Parliaments in 1896 and 1897: Das Exposé des Grafen Goluchowski, in: Fremdenblatt, Vienna, 9. 6. 1896, evening edition, 2–3; Die Delegationen, in: Fremdenblatt, Vienna, 10. 6. 1896, morning edition, 1–5; Das Exposé des Grafen Gołuchowski, in: Fremdenblatt, Vienna, 21. 11. 1897, morning edition, 1–6.

6 Modern Turkish: İstanbul; Ottoman Turkish: قسطنطينيه, Kostantiniyye (formal); İstanbul (informal); Modern Greek: Κωνσταντινούπολη, Kōnstantinoupolē; η Πόλη, ē Polē.

7 See e.g.: Isabel Friederike Pantenburg-Lankheit, Alternativen zum Zweibund? Probleme Österreichisch-Ungarischer Bündnispolitik 1897–1908, PhD thesis, Bonn 1993, 159, 176; Marija Wakounig, „Das Sitzen zwischen zwei Stühlen." Sozial-politische Entwicklungstendenzen in den Anfangsjahren der Ära Agenor Gołuchowski, in: Studia Historica Slovenica 2/2, Maribor 2002, 387–398, here: 390–393, 395; Wakounig, Grandseigneur, 21f, 147.

makes Austro-Hungarian foreign politics during the Cretan Crisis an interesting case study of the extent to which governments were willing to look beyond their own power politics and tactics and cede decisions to the ambassadors in Constantinople in the genuine spirit of international cooperation and peace. In order to gain a broad understanding of international perception of the Ambassadors' Conference, research is not limited to documents from the Austro-Hungarian Foreign Ministry and diplomatic service, but includes the records of the British and German Foreign Offices as well.[8] In accordance with the current status of my research, this paper focuses on 1896, the first year of the Cretan Crisis.

The Cretan Crisis

The roots of the Cretan Crisis of 1896–1898 go back to the Greek War of Independence of the 1820s, after which Crete with its mainly Greek-speaking, but mixed Christian and Muslim population remained part of the Ottoman Empire. The following decades saw a series of uprisings and revolts on the island, as calls for independence or greater autonomy of the island mixed with Greek nationalism and demands to reduce Muslim privileges and increase representation of Christians in local administration. After a number of concessions had been included in the *Réglément Organique* and the *Halepa Convention* or *Halepa Pact* of 1878, the rule of the Ottoman Governor of Crete was balanced by a local *General Assembly* and an *Administrative Council*, both of which had fixed quotas of Christian and Muslim representatives.[9]

Even though these reforms were confirmed and theoretically put under international guarantees by the Berlin Treaty of 1878, in 1889 the Sultan once more tried to tighten his control of the notoriously unruly island by suspending the Halepa Pact. Local power was put exclusively in the hands of a civil governor (*Vali*) and a military commander, both of which were appointed directly and indefinitely by the Sultan, while the hierarchy between both positions was left deliberately ill-defined, encouraging rivalry and mutual supervision.[10]

By the mid 1890s calls for reform were expressed throughout the Ottoman Empire, leading to increased unrest in Macedonia and

---

8 The following abbreviations will be used to describe archives and libraries in citations: HHStA Wien = Haus-, Hof- und Staatsarchiv, Vienna; TNA: PRO London = The National Archives: Public Records Office, Kew, Greater London; I have not yet conducted my research at the German Politisches Archiv des Auswärtigen Amts in Berlin, the results of which will be included in the final version of my PhD thesis.

9 Ekinci, Origins, 16f; Moutafidou, Politik, 27.; Verosta, Kollektivaktionen, 34–37.

10 Moutafidou, Politik, 27; Verosta, Kollektivaktionen, 37f.

among Armenians and Kurds, triggering government retaliation in the shape of the infamous 1895 Armenian Massacres. On Crete a newly formed Committee for Reform[11] demanded the immediate convocation of the General Assembly. The suggested changes in the legal and political representation of the religious communities not only triggered a conflict with the Ottoman authorities, but also caused severe tensions between Christians and Muslims living on the island.[12]

As the authorities refused to make concessions, Christian guerrilla forces started an armed resistance movement against government forces in the countryside of Western Crete in the spring of 1896. Skirmishes between rebels and government military forces escalated into something worse, as Christian and Muslim irregular fighters each started terrorizing the villages of the opposing religious group, plundering, killing and burning homes. As violence erupted in the island capital of Canea[13] on 24 May 1896, the local consuls representing the Great Powers sent alarming reports to their governments, causing warships to be despatched to Crete for the protection of foreign nationals. At the same time, the attempt of the ambassadors in Constantinople to negotiate the retreat and save conduct of the Ottoman garrison of a military fort besieged by rebels marked the beginning of international intervention in the Cretan Crisis.[14]

The months between May and September 1896 saw various attempts by the Great Power governments, their ambassadors in Constantinople and the consuls in Crete to negotiate a peaceful resolution of the conflict.[15] The Great Power governments were particularly worried about the threat of unrest spreading to Macedonia, possibly escalating into a full-blown war between the Ottoman Empire and Greece, where nationalists were putting intense pressure on government and King to intervene on behalf of the Cretan Christians. It was a widespread fear that further desta-

---

[11] In contemporary sources it is often referred to as Epitropi, from the modern Greek word for "committee": επιτροπή, Epitropē.

[12] Ekinci, Origins, 17; Moutafidou, Politik, 27f; Verosta, Kollektivaktionen, 38; on the general issue of reforms in the Ottoman Empire and the developments concerning Armenians and Kurds see: Donald Bloxham, The Great Game of Genocide, Oxford/New York 2005, 29–57; Rainer Fritz, Die Armenische Frage im europäischen Kontext, diploma thesis, Vienna 2006, 31–64; Werner Zürrer, Die Nahostpolitik Frankreichs und Russlands 1891–1898, Wiesbaden 1970, 89–107.

[13] Modern Greek: Χανιά, Chania; Ottoman Turkish: خانيه, Hanya; Venetian Italian: Canea.

[14] Moutafidou, Politik, 27f; Verosta, Kollektivaktionen, 38–43.

[15] Moutafidou, Politik, 27–29; Verosta, Kollektivaktionen, 38–54.

bilization might cause the long-expected collapse of the Ottoman Empire, in which case competing ambitions of individual Great Powers might trigger a World War.[16]

G. Montbard, The Trouble in Crete: Turkish Troops returning to Canea after firing Native Villages, in: The Illustrated London News, London, 4. 7. 1896, 12.

Despite the common interest in preventing this, the Great Power governments in this case found it difficult to agree on collective diplomatic intervention, which was the traditional approach adopted by the so-called *European Concert of Powers* to resolve challenges to the established political *status quo*. Suspicions and mutual distrust were strong among the governments in 1896, as various rumours of British, French or Italian plots to occupy Crete circulated and were complemented by reports of the German Empire employing an active spy on the island.[17]

---

16 This fear was frequently referred to as the main reason for the necessity of maintaining unity and cooperation within the European Concert, e.g.: Liechtenstein an Gołuchowski, St. Petersburg 1896 July 17, HHStA Wien, PA XII/ 278 50A–B; It was also discussed in newspapers, along with the possible social and political upheaval, which might be caused by a World War: Kritische Zeiten, in: Pester Lloyd, Budapest, 13. 11. 1895, 3.

17 See e.g.: Calice to Gołuchowski, Buyukdere 1896 June 18, HHStA Wien, PA XII/277 27 D; Calice to Gołuchowski, Buyukdere 1896 July 9, HHStA Wien, PA XII/278 30 B; Calice to Gołuchowski, Buyukdere 1896 July 9, HHStA Wien, PA XII/278 30 C; Liechtenstein to Gołuchowski, St. Petersburg 1896 July 17, HHStA Wien, PA XII/278 50A–B; Vélics to Gołuchowski, Berlin 1896 July 18, HHStA Wien, PA XII/278 23B; Széchény to Gołuchowski, Athens 1896 July 24, HHStA Wien, PA XII/278 36A–B;

British Prime Minister Lord Robert Cecil Marquess of Salisbury was unwilling to assume an active let alone interventionist stance, remembering how his last attempt at intervention during the Armenian Crisis of 1895 had lead to embarrassment and isolation.[18] Russian Foreign Minister Aleksei Borisovich Prince Lobanov-Rostovskii displayed a genuine interest in preventing a serious crisis in the Near East at this time by cooperating with Austria-Hungary; Gołuchowski, however, preferred to alleviate his fears of Russian expansionism by relying on British and German support of his attempts at initiating "collective actions" designed to minimize the political options of the Russian Empire, only to be disappointed by both of his preferred allies.[19] The ruling Ottoman Sultan Abdul Hamid on the other hand, displayed a particular unwillingness to grant reforms or indeed any concessions, as he generally viewed internationally supported demands for local autonomy and reform as the first step towards further disintegration of his Empire and saw minorities raising such demands as traitors, a view that had already led to the Armenian massacres of 1894–1895.[20] Wishing to prevent or delay any reforms in his provinces, his skill in playing on discord among the Great Powers to sabotage international intervention was widely acknowledged and frequently blamed for the stalling of negotiations during the Cretan Crisis.[21]

In the end it was not the Great Power governments but the Ambassadors' Conference of Constantinople that succeeded in brokering a compromise reform program for Crete acceptable to all, which in early September 1896 at least temporarily defused the conflict.[22]

---

[18] On Salisbury and his response to the Armenian Crisis in 1895 see: Stein, Neuordnung, 34–36; Wakounig, Grandseigneur, 148f; Zürrer, Nahostpolitik, 108–117.

[19] Stein, Neuorientierung, 132–137; Wakounig, Sitzen, 391; Wakounig, Grandseigneur, 163f.

[20] On the background and consequences of this attitude see: Bloxham, Game, 37–57; Fritz, Armenische Frage, 53–57; Zürrer, Nahostpolitik, 90–94; some contemporaries even acknowledged the cruel "logic" behind these tactics of Abdul Hamid: Ardern G. Hulme-Beaman, Twenty Years in the Near East, London 1898, 305.

[21] Calice to Gołuchowski, Buyukdere 1895 July 18, HHStA Wien, PA XII/161 30G; Calice to Gołuchowski, Constantinople 1895 November 14, HHStA Wien, PA I/462 47D; Deym to Gołuchowski, London 1896 July 28, HHStA Wien, PA XII/278 28; Calice to Gołuchowski, Buyukdere 1896 July 30, HHStA Wien, PA XII/278 33A-F; Gołuchowski to Calice, Vienna 1896 August 15, HHStA Wien, PA XII/279 private;.Hulme-Beaman, Twenty Years, 303f; Eduard Ritter von Steinitz (Ed.), Wladimir Giesl, Zwei Jahrzehnte im Nahen Orient, Berlin 1927, 34f.

[22] Moutafidou, Politik, 29; Verosta, Kollektivaktionen, 56–59.

The Ambassadors' Conference of Constantinople and the Cretan Crisis

What precisely was the Ambassadors' Conference of Constantinople? It was not an official institution constituted by an international treaty.[23] Indeed the ambassadors representing the Great Powers in Constantinople had no official collective mandate to act beyond the instructions set for individual ambassadors by their respective governments. Nevertheless, in practice the ambassadors in Constantinople were granted much greater freedom to act than the ambassadorial corps at other capitals and in times of crisis often acted collectively as an unofficial international body. In the Cretan Crisis of 1896–1898, the "*Six Representatives*", as they were often called, played a particularly active role as an instrument of international conflict resolution.[24] While the Concert of Powers in other cases convoked "ambassadors' conferences" as merely temporary bodies to mediate specific conflicts, the Ambassadors' Conference of Constantinople served as a de facto permanent institution since 1856.[25]

The extraordinary role of the ambassadors in Constantinople arose from privileges granted to foreign powers by the Sultan in the eighteenth century and from a general understanding among the Great Powers in the second half of the nineteenth century, that to coordinate their political and economical interests in the Ottoman Empire would be beneficial to all.[26] Fearing that rivalry among them might trigger a great war in the case of the Empire's eventual collapse, they attempted to postpone the latter. This attitude was expressed most clearly in the Treaty of Berlin in 1878, which obliged the Ottoman Empire to introduce certain reforms, partially put under guarantee of the Great Powers.[27] Representing the Concert of Powers accordingly, the ambassadors started to act more and more like a board of supervisors of the Ottoman Empire, drawing

---

[23] Neither the 1856 Treaty of Paris, nor the 1878 Treaty of Berlin, nor the older bilateral "Capitulations" between the Ottoman Empire and individual Great Powers include any reference to the ambassadors in Constantinople having a special mandate for collective action or collective representation of "Europe"; for a reprint of the treaties see: Karl Strupp (Ed.), Urkunden zur Geschichte des Völkerrechts, vol. 1, Gotha 1911, 48–67, 187–222, 282.

[24] In this function, the Ambassadors' Conference was eventually institutionalized as the official Board of Arbitration for disputes regarding the Greek–Ottoman peace treaty of 1897: Verosta, Kollektivaktionen, 185–197.

[25] Schulz, Wächter, 39.

[26] See e.g. Steinitz, Giesl, Jahrzehnte, 54, 56.

[27] See § 23 and 61 of the Berlin Treaty regarding reforms for Crete, the European Provinces and the Armenian Provinces of the Ottoman Empire: Strupp, Urkunden, 211, 220; Verosta, Kollektivaktionen, 35f.

up reform plans and offering "advice" whenever there was unrest in the provinces.[28]

When they were acting collectively in this sense, the ambassadors of the Great Powers in Constantinople were regarded not just as representatives of their respective governments, but as representatives of the so-called "collective will of Europe", before which all lesser powers were expected to bow.[29] The fact that they merely represented the rulers and governments of six self-proclaimed Great Powers, who had never received a universally acknowledged legal mandate to represent the entire continent and force their "suggestions" on other countries, was conveniently ignored.[30]

The importance assigned to the ambassadors in Constantinople was expressed and enhanced by the choice of diplomats assigned to this post, who were usually highly experienced and widely respected, occasionally having considerable personal influence on their respective governments:

The Austro-Hungarian ambassador at the time of the Cretan Crisis for example was Heinrich Baron Calice, the longest-serving ambassador in Constantinople of his day. Having been accredited to this post since 1880, he would remain there until 1906, adding up to an

---

[28] As Wladimir Giesl Freiherr von Gieslingen, military attaché to the Austro-Hungarian embassy in Constantinople during the Cretan Crisis explains in his memoirs, the extensive prerogatives they enjoyed caused the ambassadors to feel and to be regarded as the "caretakers of Turkey": Steinitz, Giesl, Jahrzehnte, 54.

[29] This tendency to claim representation of the "will of Europe" and the expectations that collective decisions of the Concert of Powers should therefore be regarded as binding was frequently expressed by diplomats, politicians and newspapers alike.: Fremdenblatt, Vienna, 3. 7. 1896, 181/50, morning edition, 1; Telegram from Calice to Gołuchowski, Buyukdere 1896 July 22, HHStA Wien, PA XII/278 102; Telegram from Liechtenstein to Gołuchowski, St. Petersburg 1896 August 3, HHStA Wien, PA XII/279 57; Gołuchowski to Calice, Vienna 1896 August 15, HHStA Wien, PA XII/279 private; when the ambassadors negotiated with the Ottoman government on behalf of Christian minorities within the Empire, the latter were expected to literally "surrender unconditionally" to the proposals of the ambassadors: Telegram from Pinter to Gołuchowski, Canea 1896 September 4, HHStA Wien, PA XII/280.

[30] The right of the Great Powers to speak for all of "Europe" and enforce their decisions against the will of weaker powers was widely, but not universally acknowledged by experts of international law in the 1890s: Schulz, Normen, 563f; The particularly patronizing attitude the representatives of the Great Powers adopted towards the inhabitants of the "Orient" is exemplified by their advice against abolishing censorship on Crete, stating that "the Cretans are not yet ripe for freedom of the press". Herbert to Salisbury, Therapia 1896 August 10, TNA: PRO London, FO 78/4712 633.

impressive twenty-six years of service in the same post.[31] By 1896 he had already served in Constantinople for sixteen years, establishing close personal ties with a number of Ottoman government officials and influential dignitaries from the court of the Sultan.[32]

The Crisis in Constantinople: The Ambassadors of the Great Powers, in: The Graphic, London, 19. 9. 1896, 372. (from left to right: Paul Cambon [France], Alberto Pansa [Italy], Heinrich Baron Calice [Austria-Hungary], Aleksandr Ivanovich Nelidov [Russia], Hugo Prince Radolin [Germany, since 1895 actually replaced by Anton Baron Saurma-Jeltsch], Sir Philip Currie [Great Britain])

Due to his age and expertise, he not only served as the widely respected *doyen* or honorary chairman of the diplomatic corps in Constantinople, but could also afford to offer his advice to his superior, Foreign Minister Gołuchowski, who usually did not ap-

31 Steinitz, Giesl, Jahrzehnte, 60f; Berthold Sutter, Machtteilung als Bürgschaft des Friedens. Eine Denkschrift des Botschafters Heinrich von Calice 1896 zur Abgrenzung der Interessensphären zw. RUS und ÖU am Balkan, in: Mitteilungen des Österreichischen Staatsarchivs 37 (1984), 290–324, here: 291–293.

32 See: Calice to Gołuchowski, Buyukdere 1895 October 10, HHStA Wien, PA XII/162 42C; He was also treated particularly respectfully by the Sultan, who honoured him with personal receptions after formal dinners and invited him to private piano concerts by his favourite son: Steinitz, Giesl, Jahrzehnte, 32f.

prove of his ambassadors expressing their own opinions or ideas, especially if they deviated from his own.[33]

The advice of French ambassador Paul Cambon, who was not only a respected diplomat but had previously held high-ranking administrative positions in several French provinces, was likewise frequently asked for and followed by French Foreign Minister Gabriel Hanotaux.[34]

The Russian ambassador in Constantinople in 1896, Aleksandr Ivanovich Nelidov, hardly lacked the confidence to make his voice heard in St. Petersburg: During the "interregnum" in the Russian foreign ministry after the death of Lobanov-Rostovskii on 30 August 1896 he virtually tried to take control of Russian foreign politics, demanding personal audiences with the Tsar and bypassing the acting head of the ministry Nikolai Pavlovich Shishkin in pursuit of his personal pet project of a Russian occupation of the Dardanelles.[35]

The German Emperor in 1897 even appointed the former State Secretary from the Ministry of Foreign Affairs Adolf Freiherr Marschall von Bieberstein as the German ambassador in Constantinople, which was apparently seen as an acceptable post for somebody who had up to then served as the de facto „Foreign Minister" of Germany.[36]

Yet more prestige and political weight than the ambassadors wielded individually could be brought to bear if they worked together as a group, representing the *Concert of Powers* as a whole.

The most basic form of cooperation was the mutual exchange of information, which was also practiced by ambassadors elsewhere. In the case of the ambassadors in Constantinople, sharing not just excerpts from their instructions but also telegrams they received from the consuls based in various provinces of the Ottoman Empire, they gained a broad understanding of developments throughout the Empire and of the way these developments were viewed by

---

[33] See e.g.: Helmut Rumpler, Die Rechtlich-Organisatorischen und Sozialen Rahmenbedingungen für die Aussenpolitik der Habsburgermonarchie 1848–1918, in: Adam Wandruszka – Peter Urbanitsch (Eds.), Die Habsburgermonarchie 1848–1918, Vol. 6/1: Die Habsburgermonarchie im System Internationaler Beziehungen, Vienna 1989, 1–121, here: 79f; Wakounig, Sitzen, 393–395.

[34] Zürrer, Nahostpolitik, 189–191, 194.

[35] Zürrer, Nahostpolitik, 183–189.

[36] The extensively self-confident behaviour of the former German State Secretary led to personal rivalry between Calice and Marschall, as the former expected more respect for his age and experience than the latter was willing to give to his Austro-Hungarian colleague: Steinitz, Giesl, Jahrzehnte, 58f.

the various Great Power governments they represented.[37] This not only provided the expertise necessary for working out possible remedies to internal problems of the Ottoman Empire, but also made it easier to anticipate the positions represented by colleagues when trying to reach a compromise. Based on this information exchange, sometimes only two or three ambassadors would work together to demand a commonly desired action or reform from the Ottoman government, when universal accord was not seen as necessary or else was silently assumed in the issue at hand.[38]

The special role played by the ambassadors in Constantinople became more pronounced when it came to dealing with an immediate crisis demanding collective but particularly fast action: in such cases, the ambassadors could employ the necessity of a quick response to coordinate their actions without previously asking their governments for instructions, briefly consulting each other at a spontaneous meeting or *reunion*, followed by presenting common demands to the Sultan, either individually or in the form of a *collective note*. Examples of this type of semi-independent collective action in cases of emergency can be found in the immediate efforts to have the Armenian massacres in Constantinople suppressed in 1895[39], the attempts to negotiate safe conduct for the besieged Ottoman garrison of Fort Vamos on Crete in May 1896[40], and the efforts to resolve the hostage situation in late August 1896[41], when

---

[37] E.g.: Telegram from Calice to Gołuchowski, Buyukdere 1895 October 19, HHStA Wien, PA XII/162 93; Telegrams from Calice to Gołuchowski, Pera 1895 November 12, HHStA Wien, PA XII/162 108, 109; Telegram from Calice to Gołuchowski, Constantinople 1895 December 8, HHStA Wien, PA XII/162 131; Herbert to Salisbury, Constantinople 1896 July 2, TNA: PRO London, FO 78/4710 514; Herbert to Salisbury, Therapia 1896 July 21, TNA: PRO London, FO 78/4711 580; Calice to Gołuchowski, Buyukdere 1896 July 23, HHStA Wien, PA XII/278 32A–E; Herbert to Salisbury, Therapia 1896 August 13, TNA: PRO London, FO 78/4713 653.

[38] E.g. the close cooperation and intense information exchange between Calice and British representative Herbert in July 1896, as they were pushing for the Cretan military commander Abdullah Pasha to be sacked by the Ottoman government: Herbert to Salisbury, Therapia 1896 July 21, TNA: PRO London, FO 78/4711 580.

[39] Calice to Gołuchowski, Buyukdere 1895 October 3, HHStA Wien, PA XII/162 41 A–D; Telegram from Calice to Gołuchowski, Buyukdere 1895 October 8, HHStA Wien, PA XII/162 81;

[40] Calice to Gołuchowski, Constantinople 1896 June 4, HHStA Wien, PA XII/277 25A–E; Herbert to Salisbury, Pera 1896 June 4, TNA: PRO London, FO 78/4709 438.

[41] Telegram from Calice to Gołuchowski, Buyukdere 1896 August 28, HHStA Wien, PA XII/280 128; Herbert to Salisbury, Therapia 1896 August 31, TNA: PRO London, FO 78/4713 688.

Armenian revolutionary activists stormed the *Ottoman Bank* headquarters in Constantinople.

The most visible manifestation of the Ambassadors' Conference, however, was the long series of *reunions* and negotiations that took place when the ambassadors at Constantinople were charged with resolving more complex issues behind a crisis in the Ottoman Empire or called upon to work out plans of reform. In these instances, the *reunions* would be more frequent, formal and time-consuming than the ad-hoc meetings in emergency situations. The ambassadors would typically base their negotiations on general instructions received from their respective governments, using the leeway provided by the phrasing of the instructions to find common ground, eventually working out a compromise program.[42] Once a plan of action or a catalogue of reforms acceptable to all was established, the ambassadors would collectively try to convince their respective governments to approve. Once they felt their actions were sufficiently covered by instructions from their governments, the ambassadors would present their concepts to the Sultan as collective "suggestions".[43] This official transmission was usually followed and in some cases preceded by laborious, unofficial negotiations with the Ottoman Foreign Minister and various influential dignitaries from within the Palace and the "inner circle" of Sultan Abdul Hamid.[44] Eventual acceptance of such collective "suggestions" by the Sultan was not seen as optional and generally expected, relying on the authority of the Concert of Powers and the efforts made by this point to antici-

[42] The ambassadors in Constantinople had already resorted to such an independent course of action before the Cretan Crisis of 1896: During the Armenian Crisis of 1895 they contributed to the prevention of potentially dangerous naval interventions by individual Great Powers, initiating and negotiating a plan for a very limited, collective increase of Great Power naval presence inside the Dardanelles, which was entirely compatible with existing treaties: Telegrams from Calice to Gołuchowski, Pera 1895 November 12, HHStA Wien, PA XII/162 108, 109, 110; Telegram from Calice to Gołuchowski, Pera 1895 November 17, HHStA Wien, PA XII/162 113; Telegram from Calice to Gołuchowski, Constantinople 1895 November 18, HHStA Wien, PA XII/162 116.

[43] For continuation of the above-mentioned example from 1895 see: Telegram from Calice to Gołuchowski, Constantinople 1895 November 21, HHStA Wien, PA XII/162 48 C; Telegrams from Calice to Gołuchowski, Pera 1895 November 25, HHStA Wien, PA XII/162 118, 119.

[44] For these negotiations in the case of the 1895 proposition see: Telegram from Calice to Gołuchowski, Pera 1895 November 19, HHStA Wien, PA XII/162 117; Telegram from Calice to Gołuchowski, Pera 1895 November 28, HHStA Wien, PA XII/162 120; on the ability of close confidants of the Sultan to overrule government decisions and the often difficult procedure of getting their approval see: Hulme-Beaman, Twenty Years, 291–298; Steinitz, Giesl, Jahrzehnte, 34f.

pate possible objections. If the Sultan or any other conflict parties however did refuse to comply with "suggestions" made by the Great Powers, everything depended on the questionable readiness of the Ambassadors' Conference and the Great Power governments to agree on so-called "*coercive measures*", forcing compliance by a collective show of military force.[45]

It was the Ambassadors' Conference acting in accordance with these mechanisms of conflict resolution, which ended the first dangerous phase of the Cretan Crisis in 1896, showing the superior speed and quality of conference diplomacy performed by a circle of experienced experts, where a number of individual government initiatives had foundered on mutual suspicions and insufficient coordination.[46] At first the ambassadors had restricted themselves to passively reacting and intervening in specific issues, such as demanding a stop of Ottoman military punitive expeditions threatening to escalate the conflict on Crete, negotiating the reinstitution and convocation of the General Assembly and asserting the replacement of the Ottoman military commander on Crete with an officer of lower rank than the *Vali* to enforce the authority of the civil governor.[47] As these specific interventions failed to encourage meaningful negotiations between Cretan Christians, Muslims and Ottoman authorities, while ill-coordinated efforts by individual Great Power governments likewise failed to achieve results, the ambassadors decided to seize a much broader initiative to work out a reform program for Crete themselves in a series of *reunions* between 18 July and 1 August 1896:

As representatives of the Christian and Muslim community on Crete had each addressed the Great Powers with petitions and memorandums explaining their respective demands for a modified version of the Halepa Pact, the ambassadors used these conflicting

---

[45] This dilemma was frequently lamented by the ambassadors, e.g.: Telegram from Calice to Gołuchowski, Constantinople 1896 June 10, HHStA Wien, PA XII/277 69; Herbert to Salisbury, Pera 1896 June 10, TNA: PRO London, FO 78/4709 458; it was a particularly important aspect during the Armenian Crisis of 1895, when the resulting threat of separate naval intervention by one or two Great Powers was seen as very real danger to peace.

[46] See the attempts made by Gołuchowski to initiate collective government action: Stein, Neuorientierung, 132–137; Wakounig, Sitzen, 391; Wakounig, Grandseigneur, 163f.

[47] Calice to Gołuchowski, Buyukdere 1896 July 2, 9, HHStA Wien, PA XII/278 29C, 30; Herbert to Salisbury, Constantinople 1896 July 4, TNA: PRO London, FO 78/4710 518AB; Telegram from Herbert to Salisbury, Therapia 1896 July 15–16, TNA: PRO London, FO 78/4724 283; Calice to Gołuchowski, Buyukdere 1896 July 16, HHStA Wien, PA XII/278 31B; Herbert to Salisbury, Therapia 1896 July 21, TNA: PRO London, FO 78/4711 580.

demands to work out a compromise.[48] They started to systematically categorize Christian demands as being either potentially "acceptable", "less acceptable" or "not acceptable" to the Muslims and the Ottoman government.

Henry Marriott Paget, The Eastern Question – A Meeting of Ambassadors in Constantinople at the House of Baron Calice, in: The Graphic, London, 7. 11. 1896, 589.

Taking the decision on this distinction away from the Ottoman authorities, the ambassadors would drop or modify everything that fell into the latter two categories and present the accordingly revised reform program to their respective governments and to the Sultan for ratification.[49] This initiative was taken without prior authorization from any government and took place while the cabinets of the Great Powers were mainly engaged in a debate of whether weapon shipments from Greece to Crete

[48] Christian and Muslim deputies of the Cretan General Assembly alike had transmitted their respective programs of reform to the ambassadors via the local consuls between the 15 and 17 July: Biliotti to Salisbury, Canea 1896 July 15, 17, TNA: PRO London, FO 78/4636 50, 51; Telegram from Calice to Gołuchowski, Constantinople 1896 July 17, HHStA Wien, PA XII/278.

[49] Calice to Gołuchowski, Buyukdere 1896 July 23, HHStA Wien, PA XII/278 32A–E; Telegram from Calice to Gołuchowski, Buyukdere 1896 August 1, HHStA Wien, PA XII/279 106; Herbert to Salisbury, Therapia 1896 August 10, TNA: PRO London, FO 78/4712 633.

should be stopped by an international naval blockade.[50] While some of the ambassadors were obviously uncomfortable with such independent action, they nevertheless proceeded. Facing their governments, the ambassadors explained how their inactivity would have damaged the reputation of the Concert of Powers, stressing the character of their work as being a catalogue of mere "suggestions".[51] After weeks of *reunions* carried out independently from the intense arguments between governments, the ambassadors finished their compromise program of reforms for Crete, which was then ratified by the governments as the only readily available, universally acceptable response to the crisis.[52] The compromise was accepted by the Sultan on 27 August and on 4 September 1896 the consuls on Crete reported that the Christian deputies to the Cretan General Assembly had likewise "surrendered unconditionally" to the program.[53] The situation on Crete at least temporarily stabilized, and the Ambassadors' Conference had proven that it could act as a catalyst and not just as a passive tool of international conflict resolution.

However, this system of conflict resolution had its flaws, which would contribute to the eventual failure of preventing the Cretan Crisis from escalating into the Greco-Ottoman War of 1897. Lacking a formal collective mandate, the ability of the Am-

---

50 The ambassadors themselves were well aware of the independence of their action: Calice to Gołuchowski, Buyukdere 1896 August 6, HHStA Wien, PA XII/279 34A–H.

51 Calice to Gołuchowski, Buyukdere 1896 August 6, HHStA Wien, PA XII/279 34A–H; The ambassadors also took care to keep the governments informed of their progress by transmitting drafts of their work: Telegram from Herbert to Salisbury, Therapia 1896 August 10–11, TNA: PRO London, FO 78/4724 318; Calice to Gołuchowski, Buyukdere 1896 August 11, HHStA Wien, PA XII/279 35.

52 Telegram from Gołuchowski to Calice, Vienna 1896 August 15, HHStA Wien, PA XII/279 53; Telegram from Herbert to Salisbury, Therapia 1896 August 16, TNA: PRO London, FO 78/4724 332; Calice to Gołuchowski, Buyukdere 1896 August 20, HHStA Wien, PA XII/279 37B; Telegram from Calice to Gołuchowski, Buyukdere 1896 August 21, HHStA Wien, PA XII/279 116; Telegram from Gołuchowski to Calice, Vienna 1896 August 21, HHStA Wien, PA XII/279 57; Herbert to Salisbury, Therapia 1896 August 24, TNA: PRO London, FO 78/4713 673; Telegram from Herbert to Salisbury, Therapia 1896 August 25–26, TNA: PRO London, FO 78/4724 354.

53 See the final reports from ambassador Calice and representative Herbert, including the final draft of the compromise program: Calice to Gołuchowski, Buyukdere 1896 August 27, HHStA Wien, PA XII/279 38A–C; Herbert to Salisbury, Constantinople 1896 August 29, TNA: PRO London, FO 78/4713 684A; On the "unconditional surrender" of the Christian deputies see: Telegram from Pinter to Gołuchowski, Canea 1896 September 4, HHStA Wien, PA XII/280.

bassadors' Conference to function was completely dependent on the goodwill and leeway granted to the ambassadors by their respective governments. Indeed, the Ambassadors' Conference often had its responsibilities contested by other entities of international politics.[54] Individual governments, the consuls on Crete and the ambassadors at Constantinople often worked parallel to or even seemingly against each other, the situation getting even more complicated in 1897, when a newly formed *Council of Admirals*, which represented the international naval forces at Crete, demanded its share of authority.[55] The fights for responsibility and a place in this ill-defined, yet hierarchical system, cost much time and energy and at times overshadowed and severely hampered international politics surrounding the Cretan Crisis.[56]

Prejudices and suspicions so prevalent among the governments at that time also existed among the ambassadors, as did personal rivalries. Austro-Hungarian ambassador Calice continuously suspected his French and Russian colleagues of secretly conspiring with the Greek government for the benefit of Greek nationalist interests.[57] The French and Russian ambassadors in turn frequently expressed their own suspicions regarding British ambitions of being the dominant power in the Eastern Mediterranean.[58] The British representative claimed that the entire Cretan Crisis was a Franco-Russian conspiracy intended to bring about a new, all-European "Orient Conference", where the Austro-Hungarian occupation of Bosnia and the more recent British occupation of Egypt would be challenged as illegal.[59] When the German ambassador approached Calice with his own rumours about a British conspiracy on Crete, he was in turn challenged with the question whether he had received

---

54 See e.g.: Dumba to Gołuchowski, Paris 1896 August 3, HHStA Wien, PA XII/ 279 private; Calice to Gołuchowski, Buyukdere 1896 August 6, HHStA Wien, PA XII/279 34A-H; Dumba to Gołuchowski, Paris 1896 August 7, HHStA Wien, PA XII/279 43A-C.

55 On the Council of Admirals see: Pangerl, Kreta-Mission, 58-62; Verosta, Kollektivaktionen, 130-149.

56 See e.g.: Dumba to Gołuchowski, Paris 1896 August 3, HHStA Wien, PA XII/ 279 private; Calice to Gołuchowski, Buyukdere 1896 August 6, HHStA Wien, PA XII/279 34A-H; Dumba to Gołuchowski, Paris 1896 August 7, HHStA Wien, PA XII/279 43A-C.

57 E.g.: Telegram from Calice to Gołuchowski, Constantinople 1896 June 8, HHStA Wien, PA XII/277 67; Calice to Gołuchowski, Buyukdere 1896 June 11, HHStA Wien, PA XII/277 26A-C.

58 E.g.: Calice to Gołuchowski, Buyukdere 1896 June 11, 18, HHStA Wien, PA XII/277 26A-C, 27D; Calice to Gołuchowski, Buyukdere 1896 July 9, HHStA Wien, PA XII/278 30B.

59 Calice to Gołuchowski, Buyukdere 1896 June18, HHStA Wien, PA XII/277 27D.

this information from a German spy supposedly active on Crete everybody had been talking about.[60] From 1897 onwards, the atmosphere of cooperation between the ambassadors would be further damaged by an apparent personal struggle for prestige between Calice and the new German ambassador Marschall, the latter challenging the former's position as *doyen* of the diplomatic corps on the basis of his own background as a leading figure in the German Foreign Ministry.[61]

As mentioned before, the ability of the Ambassadors' Conference to enact its influence on international affairs depended strongly on the presence and personal influence of individual ambassadors. Nevertheless, the British, Russian and French ambassadors each took leave from their post during various critical periods of the Cretan Crisis, leaving affairs in the hands of mere temporary "representatives". These "representatives" often lacked the confidence necessary for independent or at least semi-independent action, severely reducing the effectiveness of the Ambassadors' Conference.[62]

Ambassador Calice himself explained in an official report from 11 June 1896 that the "friendly traffic" and the "exchange of information" between the ambassadors was invaluable for preventing certain misunderstandings and reducing suspicions among the Great Power governments. He further acknowledged the useful ability of the ambassadors to independently initiate collective action in emergency situations. He however also acknowledged the difficulty of reaching common ground and starting a common initiative in the absence of an immediate emergency, remarkably openly criticizing the governments for keeping the ambassadors on too tight a leash and rewarding independent action with rebukes, which caused his colleagues to display great reluctance to act without having been told to do so by their governments.[63] Gołuchowski would not take this hint to heart, as shown by his lack of cooperation with the Ambassadors' Conference in August 1896.

Cabinet Politics versus Conference Diplomacy: The Austrian Foreign Ministry and the Ambassadors' Conference

Due to his prestige and his long years of experience as Austro-Hungarian ambassador in Constantinople, Heinrich Baron Calice had the

---

60 Calice to Gołuchowski, Buyukdere 1896 July 9, HHStA Wien, PA XII/278 30C.

61 Steinitz, Giesl, Jahrzehnte, 58f.

62 Calice to Gołuchowski, Buyukdere 1896 June 11, HHStA Wien, PA XII/277 26A–C.

63 Calice to Gołuchowski, Buyukdere 1896 June 11, HHStA Wien, PA XII/277 26A–C.

confidence to act in concert with his colleagues without constantly asking his government for permission. When the Ambassadors' Conference initiated its compromise program to settle the Cretan Crisis through reform without having been explicitly authorized to do so by the governments, Calice confidently informed Gołuchowski that it had been necessary to follow this semi-independent course of action so that the reputation of the European Concert would not be damaged by the inability of the Great Power governments to reach an agreement.[64] While the general ideal in the Austro-Hungarian diplomatic service was to have ambassadors restricted to acting as reliable eyes, ears and mouthpieces of the Foreign Minister, Calice refused to limit himself to that role.[65]

He even went so far as to withhold or distort information to influence and manipulate his superior when he deemed it necessary to prevent the Foreign Minister from making mistakes, or to protect the work of the ambassadors from unwanted interference. One such case is revealed by comparing the respective reports of Calice and British representative Michael Herbert, submitted on a particular *reunion* of the ambassadors on 9 June 1896. According to Herbert, French ambassador Paul Cambon had explained that despite its value and expertise the Ambassadors' Conference could not make a difference in the crises that riddled the Ottoman Empire, unless their respective governments would be willing to back up its collective decisions with naval or military force. He had therefore suggested that the ambassadors should persuade their governments to engage in some joint "action", demonstrating military might and forcing the Ottoman Empire to abstain from violence and massacres on Crete. Cambon had explained that the precise nature of this "action" would be of little importance, as long as all Great Powers would participate unanimously. According to Herbert *all* the ambassadors had embraced this idea and promised to suggest it to their respective governments.[66] Herbert himself stayed true to this promise in his report to Lord Salisbury.[67]

Calice however, who according to Herbert had likewise promised to support the idea expressed by Cambon, did no such thing. In his report to Gołuchowski on the *reunion*, the subject was not

---

64 Calice to Gołuchowski, Buyukdere 1896 August 6, HHStA Wien, PA XII/279 34A–H.

65 On the attitude expected from Austro-Hungarian ambassadors see: Rumpler, Rahmenbedingungen, 79f; Wakounig, Sitzen, 393–395.

66 Telegrams from Herbert to Salisbury, Pera 1896 June 10, TNA: PRO London, FO 78/4723 200, 204; Herbert to Salisbury, Pera 1896 June 10, TNA: PRO London, FO 78/4709 458.

67 Herbert to Salisbury, Pera 1896 June 10, TNA: PRO London, FO 78/4709 458.

even mentioned. According to Calice, Cambon had merely stated the futility of diplomatic actions without backup by force in order to argue *against* further ambassadorial interventions in the Cretan crisis. Calice concluded by explaining that the consensus among the ambassadors had been to assume a more passive stance for the time being and wait to see how the situation on Crete would develop before getting involved more deeply, presenting a result that could not have been more contradictory to the report made by the British representative.[68]

It seems unlikely that Herbert, who was a mere substitute for the absent British ambassador Sir Philipp Currie and usually eager to have every step he made acknowledged and confirmed by his superiors, would have consciously distorted facts and invented a collective pledge of the ambassadors to support an idea that had never been put forward. Looking at the version presented by Calice however, the "consensus" to abstain from putting more pressure on the Ottoman Empire fits suspiciously well with his own reported particular reluctance to embrace the idea of Ottoman concessions going beyond a mere reinstitution of the Halepa pact.[69] The idea as reported by Herbert in turn seems remarkably similar to some of the ideas put forward by Gołuchowski and may well have triggered unpleasant memories of the "Stationary Question" of 1895: At the height of the Armenian Crisis, Gołuchowski had been all too ready to champion a collective naval show of force in the Dardanelles, even though it would have violated international treaties, leading to the embarrassment of a suddenly diplomatically isolated Austria-Hungary.[70] In June 1896 Calice may therefore have thought it prudent to stay quiet about the suggested "collective action", knowing how the idea might tempt his Minister to rashly assume an all too exposed position.

When his government attacked and undermined the position and functionality of the Ambassadors' Conference, Calice was just as willing to use the weight of his expertise to subtly but effectively oppose the plans of his own Minister. In August 1896 he did not openly criticize Gołuchowski for his plan of an international naval blockade of Crete, which was intended to stop weapons and volunteers reach-

---

68 Telegram from Calice to Gołuchowski, Constantinople 1896 June 10, HHStA Wien, PA XII/277 69; Calice to Gołuchowski, Buyukdere 1896 June 11, HHStA Wien, PA XII/277 26A–C.

69 Herbert assigned particular importance to Calice being the last of the ambassadors to abandon this view in early August: Herbert to Salisbury, Therapia 1896 August 10, TNA: PRO London, FO 78/4712 633A.

70 On Gołuchowskis initiatives during the Armenian Crisis of 1895 and the „Stationary Question" see: Stein, Neuorientierung, 38–45; Wakounig, Grandseigneur, 149–154; Wakounig, Sitzen, 390; Zürrer, Nahostpolitik, 117–122.

ing the island from mainland Greece.[71] The plan however threatened the simultaneous efforts of the Ambassadors' Conference to establish a compromise reform program, as it included the suggestion to take responsibility for the Cretan reform away from the ambassadors and bestow it upon a newly established *Consular Commission* on Crete.[72] Calice, in his reports to Gołuchowski, vigorously defended the role of the Ambassadors' conference, stressing their superior expertise and experience compared to the consuls, whereas the maintenance of a government monopoly of initiative would significantly slow down the process of reaching a compromise. At the same time, he was very eager to present the entire blockade idea as futile, explaining that the Sultan would never cooperate.[73] Calice expressed similar points of view to his colleagues in Constantinople, displaying a remarkable readiness to present the initiative of his superior as hopeless.[74] When the ambassadors in Constantinople, having received instructions from their respective governments, rejected the idea of a formally established Consular Commission supervising and controlling the reform process on Crete, Calice told Gołuchowski the suggestion had been vetoed by Russian ambassador Nelidov.[75] However, at the same time Herbert reported to Salisbury that "*most of*" the ambassadors had opposed the plan.[76] None of the sources clearly indicate let alone prove that Calice was among the ambassadors opposing the suggestion made by his superior. If he *did* play a part in the refusal however, this conspicuous playing on Gołuchowski's well-known suspi-

---

[71] See the original proposal in a circular telegram Gołuchowski sent on 24 July: Telegram from Gołuchowski to Liechtenstein, Wolkenstein, Deym, Vélics, Mezey, Vienna 1896 July 24, HHStA Wien, PA XII/278 41, 30, 19, 39, 34; for the first response from Calice see: Calice an Gołuchowski, Buyukdere 1896 Juli 30, HHStA Wien, PA XII/278 33A–F.

[72] Gołuchowski amended his original proposal accordingly on 31 July, after having sought and received approval from Lobanov-Rostovskii: Telegram from Gołuchowski to Liechtenstein, Vienna 1896 July 28, HHStA Wien, PA XII/278 43; Liechtenstein to Gołuchowski, St. Petersburg 1896 July 30, HHStA Wien, PA XII/278 54; Telegram from Gołuchowski to Vélics, Mezey, Wolkenstein, Clary, Vienna 1896 July 31, HHStA Wien, PA XII/278 40, 35, 31, 21.

[73] Calice an Gołuchowski, Buyukdere 1896 Juli 30, HHStA Wien, PA XII/278 33A–F; Telegram from Calice to Gołuchowski, Buyukdere 1896 August 1, HHStA Wien, PA XII/279 106; Calice to Gołuchowski, Buyukdere 1896 August 6, HHStA Wien, PA XII/279 34A–H.

[74] Herbert to Salisbury, Therapia 1896 August 10, TNA: PRO London, FO 78/4712 633A.

[75] Calice to Gołuchowski, Buyukdere 1896 August 20, HHStA Wien, PA XII/279 37B.

[76] Telegram from Herbert to Salisbury, Therapia 1896 August 19–20, TNA: PRO London, FO 78/4724 337.

cions regarding Russia to evade blame for the failure makes a lot of sense.

The suggestion of a naval blockade made by Gołuchowski in July 1896 deserves to be examined in closer detail, as it reveals a tendency of the Foreign Minister, who claimed to value unanimity of the "European Concert" so highly, to embark on initiatives that ran parallel to or even competed with the efforts of the Ambassadors' Conference, effectively endangering international cooperation.

Ever since Gołuchowski had first proposed the blockade on 24 July, the British Prime Minister had outright refused to participate in anything the British public could perceive as support for Sultan Abdul Hamid, who since the Armenian massacres of 1895 was widely despised as the "bloody Sultan".[77]

Ludwig Grillich, Agenor Count Gołuchowski the Younger, Vienna (undated).

In a particularly painful surprise to Gołuchowski, the German Empire, thought to be the closest ally of Austria–Hungary, likewise refused to participate due to "naval technical issues" and merely of-

[77] Telegrams from Deym to Gołuchowski, London 1896 July 26, 28, HHStA Wien, PA XII/278 45, 46; Deym to Gołuchowski, London 1896 July 28, HHStA Wien, PA XII/278 28.

fered “moral support” of the blockade, suggesting that participation of every single Great Power would not be necessary.[78]

It was the hope of gaining British support for the blockade by guaranteeing close supervision of the reform process and the conduct of Ottoman military forces that made Gołuchowski amend his proposal on 31 July 1896 with the suggestion of establishing a formal “Consular Commission” on Crete charged with these tasks.[79] At first, neither the Austro-Hungarian consul on Crete, Julius Pinter, nor ambassador Calice were even informed of this proposal, which threatened to undermine the position of the Ambassadors’ Conference just as it was working on the very reform plan that was to stabilize the situation on Crete in September 1896.[80]

Besides this bad timing of the suggestion, the consuls representing the Great Powers on Crete generally lacked the diplomatic training and experience of the ambassadors in Constantinople, not to mention prestige and influence, and were hardly qualified to work together as a commission. Any rivalries that might have existed among the ambassadors pale in comparison to the intense personal dislike some of the consuls felt for their colleagues, suspecting each other of things such as conspiring with rebel leaders or committing murder with poisoned lemonade. Some of them were in constant conflict with the local population and some of the Consuls were known for the extraordinary bias with which they viewed the conflict between the local Christian and Muslim

---

[78] Telegrams from Vélics to Gołuchowski, Berlin 1896 July 25, 26, HHStA Wien, PA XII/278 116, 117; Vélics to Gołuchowski, Berlin 1896 July 31, HHStA Wien, PA XII/278 24A–B.

[79] Telegram from Gołuchowski to Liechtenstein, Vienna 1896 July 28, HHStA Wien, PA XII/278 43; Indeed, on 29 June an earlier but similar British proposal of forming the consuls and naval commanders present on Crete into a commission to mediate negotiations with the Christian deputies and rebels had already been withdrawn due to the disapproval of the ambassadors in Constantinopel: Telegram from Herbert to Salisbury, Therapia 1896 June 29, TNA: PRO London, FO 78/4723 244; While the British government had asked the ambassadors for their opinion and acted accordingly, Gołuchowski tried to push his proposal through, disregarding the ambassadors.

[80] While the ambassadors knew about the original blockade proposal, they were apparently originally kept in the dark about the additional proposal of transferring some of their responsibilities to a Consular Commission; As they even lacked information on the reactions of their governments to the original proposal, they anxiously demanded to know on 3 August: Telegram from Herbert to Unknown, Therapia 1896 August 3, TNA: PRO London, FO 78/4724 private.

communities.[81] Gołuchowski soon found himself unsupported and isolated in what developed into a debate of the structures of international conflict resolution and the responsibilities of ambassadors and consuls: French Foreign Minister Hanotaux quoted the discord and lack of professionalism displayed by the consuls to argue against the creation of a Consular Commission, demanding instead that the status and responsibilities of the Ambassadors' Conference should be enhanced.[82] The German government did not go that far, but likewise expressed its support of leaving the Cretan reform in the hands of the Ambassadors' Conference.[83]

The proposal of a Consular Commission nevertheless complicated and hindered the efforts of the Ambassador's Conference. While the Great Power governments showed no sign of reaching the common ground necessary for a joint initiative and before the ambassadors could finish their reform program, the Sultan sent his own "special envoy" to Crete in order to establish direct negotiations between government authorities and the Christian deputies of the Cretan General Assembly. The deputies refused to negotiate directly and instead demanded mediation from the consuls, which would have put the latter in a position similar to that of the "Consular Commission" suggested by Gołuchowski. This would have enabled the Sultan to sideline the reform program the ambassadors had been working on and deal with the less experienced consuls instead. Realizing this, the ambassadors refused to authorize the consuls to mediate on any basis except that of their own reform pro-

[81] The Austro-Hungarian consul Julius Pinter in 1895 readily believed and extensively reported on rumours that the French consul Paul Blanc had poisoned the British director of a telegraph company so that he could marry the widow: Pinter to Gołuchowski, Canea 1895 July 18, HHStA Wien, PA XXXVIII/Konsulate 1895 C–J 25; The allegations were being kept alive by local enemies of Blanc in 1896, damaging his reputation on the island and being reported by newspapers as far away as New York: Grave Crisis in Crete, The New York Times, New York 7. 8. 1896, 9; British consul Sir Alfred Biliotti faced the constant mistrust of his colleagues, being suspected of pursuing secret schemes and supporting the Cretan rebels. He correspondingly complained about them constantly sabotaging his work and questioned whether the consuls could ever function as a group: Biliotti to Salisbury, Canea 1896 July 8, 11, TNA: PRO London, FO 78/4636 48, 49; Pinter in turn described all his colleagues either as untrustworthy schemers or old, decrepit and weak-willed: Pinter to Gołuchowski, Canea 1896 November 27, HHStA Wien, PA XII/280 321.

[82] Dumba to Gołuchowski, Paris 1896 August 3, HHStA Wien, PA XII/279 private; Telegram from Dumba to Gołuchowski, Paris 1896 August 20, HHStA Wien, PA XII/279 57.

[83] Telegram from Vélics to Gołuchowski, Berlin 1896 August 10, HHStA Wien, PA XII/279 124.

gram, which had not been finished yet.[84] Gołuchowski had unwittingly offered the Sultan an opportunity to weaken, if not shake off completely, Great Power mediation of the Cretan Crisis.[85] Seemingly paradoxically killing off an opportunity for meaningful negotiations by preventing consular mediation, the ambassadors remained in control and bought the time they needed to complete their own compromise program. The conclusion made by Calice on 19 August 1896, somewhat contentedly stating that "nothing more can be expected from talks in Canea" and that only the ambassadors would be able to offer a solution for the Cretan Crisis, indicates the struggle for influence and responsibility underlying the entire affair.[86]

Lack of cooperation among governments, ambassadors and consuls could cause all kinds of confusion and severely hamper conflict resolution. In the end it was an important factor contributing to the failure of the international reform attempt on Crete, after the ambassadors had succeeded in completing their compromise program. Misunderstandings between consuls and ambassadors could be used by nationalist agitators to spread misinterpreted versions of the proposed reform program to sabotage its acceptance by the Cretan population, while Ottoman authorities likewise appear to have used further opportunities to delay the reform process.[87] Petty rivalries among the consuls combined with rivalling special interests and speculation by banks and boards of investors. This delayed negotiations over a loan desperately needed for reform and relief to both Christian and Muslim refugees, which consequently dragged

---

[84] Telegrams from Calice to Gołuchowski, Buyukdere 1896 August 13, HHStA Wien, PA XII/279 112, 113; Telegram from Herbert to Salisbury, Therapia 1896 August 13–14, TNA: PRO London, FO 78/4724 325.

[85] The ambassadors denounced the mission of Zihni Pasha as "one of the ordinary Turkish devices" to weaken the international mediation efforts: Telegram from Herbert to Salisbury, Therapia 1896 August 14–15, TNA: PRO London, FO 78/4724 328; Whether it was intended as such or not, Zihni Pasha even copied the argument brought forward by Gołuchowski, stating that a Consular Commission could serve as a substitute for an international guarantee of the reforms and proper conduct of the Ottoman authorities on Crete: Telegram from Herbert to Salisbury, Therapia 1896 August 19–20, TNA: PRO London, FO 78/4724 335.

[86] Telegram from Calice to Gołuchowski, Buyukdere 1896 August 19, HHStA Wien, PA XII/279 114.

[87] See e.g.: Telegrams from Biliotti to Salisbury, Canea 1896 September 8, TNA: PRO London, FO 78/4637 126, 128; Telegram from Kosjek to Gołuchowski, Athens 1896 September 9, HHStA Wien, PA XII/280 60; Telegram from Gołuchowski to Pinter, Vienna 1896 September 9, HHStA Wien, PA XII/280; Telegrams from Pinter to Gołuchowski, Canea 1896 September 10, HHStA Wien, PA XII/280 AB; Telegram from Calice to Gołuchowski, Buyukdere 1896 September 11, HHStA Wien, PA XII/280 137.

on from September 1896 to January 1897.[88] Even though the work of the international commissions charged with reforming the judicial system and local police forces had been similarly delayed by struggles over individual candidates for the commissions, when they finished their work in January 1897 they still lacked the financial means to enact the reforms.[89] Reports from Crete explicitly stated that without a loan there could be no police reform, that without a reformed, effective police force the planned regional elections could not take place, and that without elections there would be no peace on Crete.[90] Nevertheless the Great Power governments seemed unwilling or unable to directly assist the reform commissions, while the ambassadors in Constantinople had moved on to work on a general reform plan for the entire Ottoman Empire and individual ambassadors took extended leave from their posts.[91] By the time the Ambassadors' Conference saw the danger and once more actively engaged in assisting the Cretan reform in late January 1897, it was apparently too late: the renewed outbreak of armed rebellion and violence in February 1897 meant that a great chance to resolve the Cretan Crisis by diplomatic means and reform had been wasted.[92]

The Ambassadors' Conference of Constantinople was not an officially established international institution, lacking a collective mandate or any official acknowledgement of the extent and limits of its responsibilities beyond the instructions given to individual ambassadors. In the absence of properly institutionalized structures for international conflict resolution, its ability to function de-

---

88 Pinter to Gołuchowski, Canea 1896 September 17, 25, HHStA Wien, PA XII/280 260, 267; Pinter to Gołuchowski, Canea 1896 October 2, 9, 17, 24, 31, HHStA Wien, PA XII/280 277, 288, 296, 298, 301; Pinter to Gołuchowski, Canea 1896 November 26, 27, HHStA Wien, PA XII/280 320, 321; Pinter to Gołuchowski, Canea 1896 December 11, 23, HHStA Wien, PA XII/280 329, 336; Pinter to Gołuchowski, Canea 1897 January 12, HHStA Wien, PA XII/281 3; Telegram from Pinter to Gołuchowski, Canea 1897 January 26, HHStA Wien, PA XII/281.

89 Pinter to Gołuchowski, Canea 1897 January 1, HHStA Wien, PA XII/281 1; Calice to Gołuchowski, Constantinople 1897 January 7, HHStA Wien, PA XII/281 1.

90 Pinter to Gołuchowski, Canea 1897 January 16, HHStA Wien, PA XII/281 4.

91 Between 12 and 26 November 1896 neither Calice nor Pinter appear to have been at their posts, reports from both Constantinople and Canea being written by temporary representatives: Macchio to Gołuchowski, Constantinople 1896 November 12, 19, HHStA Wien, PA XII/280 49C, 50D; Telegram from Pflügl to Gołuchowski, Canea 1896 November 12, HHStA Wien, PA XII/280; Pflügl to Gołuchowski, Canea 1896 November 14, 21, HHStA Wien, PA XII/280 313, 316.

92 On the renewed outbreak of armed rebellion on Crete in 1897 and the consequences see e.g.: Moutafidou, Politik, 29–95; Verosta, Kollektivaktionen, 60–99.

pended mainly on the personal qualities, experience, influence and willingness of the ambassadors to think beyond the interests of individual Great Powers and work together in the interest of maintaining the peace. The Cretan Crisis reveals that the attempts to resolve the crisis peacefully were not only hampered by mutual distrust among the Great Powers and by the lack of cooperation displayed by Greek nationalists and Ottoman authorities. The governments, consuls and ambassadors of the Great Power all too often wasted time and energy working against each other rather than working together. However, despite its flaws, the Ambassadors' Conference displayed a certain ability to reach compromises based on a mutual understanding of the common interest in peace and initiate international cooperation. The ambassadors could in some cases exact limited influence on their governments and push through compromise programs they had reached out of their own accord, serving as a catalyst rather than just as a tool for solving international conflicts. Even though the success would not last, in 1896 the Ambassadors' Conference temporarily succeeded in preventing an escalation of the Cretan Crisis, providing a compromise plan for reform acceptable to all and creating the basis for an international attempt to resolve the causes behind the crisis. As such, the Ambassadors' Conference of Constantinople was an important factor in international politics in the 1890s and deserves to be the target of further research.

Sources and Literature

Unprinted Sources

Haus-, Hof und Staatsarchiv, Vienna, Austria (HHStA)
Politisches Archiv des Ministeriums des Äußeren (PA)
PA XII (Türkei/ Osmanisches Reich)

Presseleitung (PL)
PL 68–70 (1895–98)

Österreichische Nationalbibliothek, Vienna, Austria (OeNB)
Sammlung Mikroformen
Austro-Hungarian newspapers from 1896–1898 on microfilm

The National Archives: Public Records Office, Kew, Greater London, UK (TNA: PRO)
Foreign Office Records (FO), General Correspondence
FO78 (Turkey/ Ottoman Empire)

Images

All images used in this paper are in the public domain. The undated photography of Agenor Count Gołuchowski the Younger was taken from Wikimedia Commons (File:WP Agenor Goluchowski der Jüngere.jpg,
http://commons.wikimedia.org/wiki/File:WP_Agenor_Goluchowski_der_Jüngere.jpg, 3.1.2010).

All other images come from the author's own collection of nineteenth century prints.

Printed Sources

- Ardern G. Hulme-Beaman, Twenty Years in the Near East, London 1898.
- Eduard Ritter von Steinitz (Ed.), Wladimir Giesl, Zwei Jahrzehnte im Nahen Orient, Berlin 1927.
- Karl Strupp (Ed.), Urkunden zur Geschichte des Völkerrechts, vol. 1, Gotha 1911.

Literature

- Donald Bloxham, The Great Game of Genocide, Oxford/ New York 2005

- Mehmed Ekinci, The Origins of the 1897 Ottoman-Greek War, MA thesis, Ankara 2006.
- Rainer Fritz, Die Armenische Frage im europäischen Kontext, MA thesis, Vienna 2006.
- J. A. S. Grenville, Gołuchowski, Salisbury and the Mediterranean Agreements 1895–1897, in: Slavonic and East European Review 36/87, London 1958, 340–369.
- Ariadni Moutafidou, Die Politik Österreich-Ungarns gegenüber dem osmanisch-griechischen Krieg von 1897, Hamburg 2003.
- Irmgard Pangerl, Die Kreta-Mission der k.u.k. Kriegsmarine, MA thesis, Vienna 2008.
- Isabel Friederike Pantenburg-Lankheit, Alternativen zum Zweibund? Probleme Österreichisch-Ungarischer Bündnispolitik 1897–1908, PhD thesis, Bonn 1993.
- Helmut Rumpler, Die Rechtlich-Organisatorischen und Sozialen Rahmenbedingungen für die Aussenpolitik der Habsburgermonarchie 1848–1918, in: Adam Wandruszka – Peter Urbanitsch (Eds.), Die Habsburgermonarchie 1848–1918, Vol. 6/1: Die Habsburgermonarchie im System Internationaler Beziehungen, Vienna 1989, 1–121.
- Matthias Schulz, „Wächter der Zivilisation?“: Institutionelle Merkmale und Normative Grundlagen des Europäischen Konzerts im 19. Jahrhundert, in: Historische Mitteilungen 17, Stuttgart 2004, 35–47.
- Matthias Schulz, Normen und Praxis: Das Europäische Konzert der Großmächte als Sicherheitsrat, 1815–1860, Studien zur Internationalen Geschichte 21, München 2009.
- Peter Stein, Die Neuorientierung der österreichisch-ungarischen Außenpolitik 1895–1897, Göttinger Bausteine zur Geschichtswissenschaft 44, Göttingen 1972.
- Berthold Sutter, Die Großmächte und die Erhaltung des europäischen Friedens zu Beginn der Kreta-Krise 1897, in: Südost-Forschungen 21, München 1962, 214–369.
- Stephan Verosta, Kollektivaktionen der Mächte des Europäischen Konzerts 1866–1914, Vienna 1988.
- Marija Wakounig, „Das Sitzen zwischen zwei Stühlen.“ Sozial-politische Entwicklungstendenzen in den Anfangsjahren der Ära Agenor Gołuchowski, in: Studia Historica Slovenica 2/2, Maribor 2002, 387–398.

- Marija Wakounig, Ein Grandseigneur der Diplomatie: die Mission von Franz de Paula Prinz von und zu Liechtenstein in St. Petersburg 1894–1898, Europa Orientalis 1, Vienna/Berlin 2007.
- Eva Wolf, Die Beziehungen Österreich-Ungarns zu Deutschland unter Gołuchowski (1895–1906), PhD thesis, Vienna 1967.
- Werner Zürrer, Die Nahostpolitik Frankreichs und Russlands 1891–1898, Wiesbaden 1970.

Sara O.M. Yanovsky
(The Hebrew University of Jerusalem)

Jewish Religious Education in Vienna 1918–1938 Consensus and Friction between the Austrian State and the Viennese Jewish Community

Introduction

With nearly 200,000 Jews, Vienna had one of the largest urban Jewries in pre-holocaust Europe, managed by a powerful communal organization, the Israelitische Kultusgemeinde (IKG).[1] Since 1952 the IKG formulated policies and strategies, weighed alternatives and set priorities in order to organize communal Jewish life in the city.

With nearly 20,000 Jewish pupils in primary and secondary education yearly during the interwar period, the realm of Jewish education was one of the key functions undertaken by the IKG. In Austria, religious education was by law a public, communal function, regulated by the Imperial Law of May 25, 1868,[2] which reserved the paramount control and supervision to the state, but at the same time made the Church and other religious associations, in case of the Jewish community the IKG, directly responsible for organizing religious education for children under their authority. This not only compelled the IKG to organize religious instruction for Jewish children in the public sphere, but also made close cooperation with state authorities inevitable. Jewish communal leaders entered into a direct exchange with state authorities in the shaping of religious instruction for Jewish children, but on a wider scale in shaping the sphere in which Jewish children were educated in a largely non-Jewish society.

The Viennese Jewish community clearly had unprecedented resources, but was also burdened by an unprecedented range of prob-

* This research project and the publishing of its findings were made possible by the generous support of the Center for Austrian Studies at the European Forum of the Hebrew University. It is part of a PhD thesis titled "Facing the Challenge of Jewish Education in the Metropolis - A Comparative Study of the Jewish Communal Organizations of Budapest and Vienna, from 1867 to World War II", conducted under the supervision of Michael K. Silber. The author continues her research at Scholion - Interdisciplinary Research Center in Jewish Studies at the Hebrew University and is supported by the Leo Baeck Fellowship Program of the Studienstiftung des deutschen Volkes.

1 On the Jews of Vienna see Marsha Rozenblit; Die Juden Wiens, 1867–1914: Assimilation und Identität, Wien 1989; Robert Wistrich, Die Juden Wiens im Zeitalter Kaiser Franz Josephs, Wien 1999.

2 Reichs-Gesetz-Blatt für das Kaiserthum Oesterreich. Jahrgang 1868, http://anno.onb.ac.at/cgi-content/anno-plusapm=0&aid=rgb&datum=18680004&seite=00000097&zoom, 2010 January 24.

lems. Particular challenges of the interwar period included the consequences of World War I, such as human losses, a financial crisis, rising anti-Semitism and the definition of a Jewish identity in an atmosphere of advanced integration into Austrian society, which itself was forced to deal with the effects of World War I and the formation of an Austrian identity.[3]

This essay aims to assess how the leaders of the IKG balanced their interests in the management of Jewish education, and therefore their expectations in terms of fostering a certain type of Jewish identity, with state laws and policies. Educational strategies formulated within urban settings both enabled and constrained integration into larger society. Education provides a perspective that helps to gain a better grasp of Jewish society in the metropolis, the decision-making and the often conflicting ideologies within the Jewish community as well as between the Jewish community and Austrian state authorities. Looking at the decisions made on Jewish education by community leaders and the way they dealt with challenges on a state level, sheds new light on the role that communal governance played in responding to challenges Jews, and in particular Jewish education, faced during the interwar period.

The state was generally represented either by the Ministry of Education or in the particular case of Vienna by the Lower Austrian Education authority, the municipality of Vienna and particularly the Vienna School Board.

The main questions this essay aims to answer are: What were the visions of the Jewish community leaders concerning Jewish education? How did these fit in with those of state authorities and state-schools? How did the IKG and state authorities cooperate in order to make their visions come true? When did cooperation between state authorities and the Jewish community turn into compromise or even conflict? In what way did state laws and policies influence the strategy of the IKG in responding to one of the key challenges facing Jews in the modern era, namely the transmission of Jewish identity via Jewish education to future generations?

Decision Making in the IKG

The IKG in Vienna had an executive committee and several permanent commissions, one of the main ones (*Sektion II*) responsible for educational issues. The commission, whose members were generally members of the IKG's executive committee, met from the 1860s

[3] On interwar Vienna see Günter Bischof – Anton Pelinka – Alexander Lassner (Eds.), The Dollfuss/Schuschnigg Era in Austria: A Reassessment, Contemporary Austrian Studies 11, New Brunswick 2003; see also the upcoming volume 19 of Contemporary Austrian Studies on interwar Austria.

until 1937 several times a year in order to discuss matters concerning Jewish education and made decisions in this respect.[4] When crucial decisions had to be made on educational matters, the issues were discussed by the executive committee in addition to the school commission. The main responsibilities of the school commission included the organization of religious instruction at public, non-Jewish schools or education centers, so-called *Sammelstationen* for children, who did not have religious classes at their school. It was responsible for the curriculum including text books, time tables, as well as the employment and allocation of teachers and inspectors, in cooperation with state authorities. This cooperation was regulated by state law, which required on the one hand the agreement of the respective religious authority before any teacher for religious instruction could be employed at a school and on the other hand the authorization by state authorities before any text book was permitted to be used in class.[5] The state law also gave religious authorities permission to establish private schools and courses. The IKG, in addition to public religious classes, ran Bible schools, organized weekly or bi-monthly youth services at Viennese synagogues in cooperation with the teachers and cantors as well as lectures with slide shows for children who had dropped out of school. It also granted financial aid to a large number of societies that ran their own educational institutions including bible schools, Hebrew classes and youth organizations, a Jewish primary school and a Jewish secondary School. In 1935 the IKG opened its own Jewish primary school.

Conversion, Intermarriage and the Denomination of Children

Cases of conversion and inter-marriage during the interwar period created situations in which the denomination of children became unclear. In several cases, state authorities, the IKG and parents were involved in a decision-making process, which determined whether children were officially to be considered Christian, Jewish or undenominational and the respective religious instruction.

The law of inter-denomination regulated the denomination of children born of mixed marriages as well as of children, whose parents converted.[6] In case of mixed marriages girls were to follow the

---

4 Protocol books of the IKG's school commission meetings (Sektion II), Central Archives for the History of the Jewish People (hereafter CAHJP), Jerusalem

5 Reichs-Gesetz-Blatt für das Kaiserthum Oesterreich. Jahrgang 1868, http://anno.onb.ac.at/cgi-content/anno-plus?apm=0&aid=rgb&datum=18680004&seite=00000097&zoom=2, 2010 January 24.

6 Ibid, http://anno.onb.ac.at/cgi-content/anno-plus?apm=0&aid=rgb&datum=18680004&zoom=2&seite=00000099&x=18&y=7, 2010 January 24.

religion of their mother, boys the religion of their father unless the parents decided otherwise through a contract. Children born out of wedlock followed the religion of their mother and if none of the above–mentioned scenarios were relevant, the legal guardian decided the denomination. Generally, the denomination of a child could not be changed until he or she reached the age of fourteen and was therefore regarded as mature to choose his or her own denomination. The parents, however, were allowed to change the denomination of children through a contract, if the children had not yet reached the age of seven. In the case of conversion of one or both parents to another religion, children followed the conversion of their parents as long as they were under the age of seven. Parents as well as religious authorities were responsible for the adherence to these laws. In case of a violation of law they had the right to turn to state authorities. This law therefore set clear guidelines which had to be adhered to and directly controlled, amongst others by the IKG. However, it also left room for disputes, primarily when it came to children aged seven to fourteen or when parents did not convert to another religion, but decided to become undenominational.

The IKG, with strict adherence to this state law, used it as a tool to keep children from leaving the IKG and its sphere of influence. State regulation had given the IKG an important opportunity of influence through compulsory Jewish education for those who were members of the community. It should be stated at this point that the efficiency of religious instruction at public schools was not taken for granted and the option of abolishing religious education at public schools was debated in Austria at the beginning of the interwar period, a step, which would have enlarged the separation between the state and the Church and would have further decreased the Church's influence on public schools. Proponents of the abolition of religious instruction were concerned about the contradictions between sciences and religious teachings. From the Jewish point of view, as the IKG school inspector Heinrich Redisch pointed out in an article he published in 1919 in the monthly Jewish teachers' magazine *Freie Jüdische Lehrerstimme*, the contradiction between sciences and religion was less problematic, as it could be explained logically. The years passed since the history of the creation, for instance, could be explained with the mythological character of numbers in religious texts and did therefore not necessarily contradict science. In any case, as he wrote "Jews will not be able to influence the solution of the debated question, our religious instruction shares the destiny of the Catholic and Protestant. If Christian religious instruction will be abolished, so the Jewish of course will fall too."[7] But Christian religious instruction did not fall and, as e-

[7] Heinrich Redisch, in: Freie Jüdische Lehrerstimme, 1919 November 15.

laborated later, gained significant importance in the 1930s. Therefore also Jewish religious instruction at public schools stayed on, and although orthodox Jewish circles repeatedly criticized the inefficiency of two lessons a week, usually not at a satisfactory level, public religious instruction still gave the IKG a basis to gather Jewish children and to recruit them for further activities in Jewish circles such as the very well frequented youth services. It was therefore seen as worthwhile to make efforts to keep Jewish children IKG members in the following cases:

On 31 March 1921 Thomas Luzian August Brunner's Jewish father Heinrich Brunner and his undenominational mother Irene Brunner, notified the municipal authority (*Magistrat*) of the nineteenth district that they were planning to raise their nearly seven–year old child according to the religion of the mother, who had just left Jewish religion and the IKG the day before to become undenominational and was planning to convert to the Evangelical (Lutheran) religion. The child had been raised Jewish up to that date. After being informed about the parents' decision by the municipal authority, the IKG objected, claiming that the marriage of the parents was not a mixed one as the mothers' changed status to undenominational was not regarded a conversion and therefore the parents were not allowed to change the denomination of their child. The sources on the case do not provide information on its outcome, but the Federal Chancellery was asked by the Ministry of Education to make the final decision on the case. Four years later, after the mother had already converted to the Evangelical religion, it was still being discussed, as correspondence between the Federal Chancellery and the Ministry of Education shows.[8] The age of the child, being over seven years by that time, probably complicated the issue further. The IKG clearly made efforts to keep Thomas Luzian August a member of the Jewish community after the mother had left. It might also be worthwhile to note that the parents had decided to change the denomination of the child shortly before his seventh birthday, possibly being aware that after the age of seven they would not have been allowed to do so.

In another case in 1922, Elsa and Siegfried Brecher, both Jewish, agreed that after their divorce their two children should be raised Roman Catholic. The mother stated her plan to convert to the Roman Catholic religion too. At that point both children were younger than seven years. When the IKG received notification of the planned conversion of the children, it objected to the municipal authority of the thirteenth district stating that converting the child-

[8] Federal Chancellery to Federal Ministry of Education, 1925 February 13, Federal Chancellery Z1. 149314/9/1921, Österreichisches Staatsarchiv (hereafter ÖStA) Wien, 52 D8 Neuer Kultus, Isr. Kultus.

ren was against the law because both parents were Jewish and there was no case of a mixed marriage, which would have been covered by the law of inter-denomination. Therefore the parents were not allowed to alter their children's religion. The municipal authority decided that the children were to be considered Jewish. However, by that time, the children had already converted with their mother, after the elder son had celebrated his seventh birthday. Documents of the Ministry of Education show that after the conversion of the mother, the state authorities brought up the question whether the decision of the municipal authority could still be adhered to, as it might not be in the interest of the children to force them to grow up as Jewish children in the Catholic household of their mother.[9] Again, it is not clear how this case ended, but it repeatedly shows that with the help of state law, or loopholes in the state law, the IKG made efforts to prevent children from leaving the Jewish community. This ensured those children would receive basic Jewish education through religious instruction classes at public schools.

A third case is a good example of a dispute on the denomination of a child without direct involvement of the IKG, when in 1923 the Jewish mother Olga Haas (born Janowitz) and the Roman Catholic father Eugen Haas, wanted to register their newborn daughter Hilde as undenominational. The municipal authorities decided that according to the law the girl had to be registered at the IKG. This particular case turned out to be more complicated because the parents were, although living in Vienna, citizens of Czechoslovakia, where the law of inter-denomination had been slightly changed in 1920. When the parents appealed against the decision of the municipal authorities, the case was passed to higher instances such as the Federal Chancellery and the Ministry of Education, where it was discussed further.[10]

It is interesting to note that the disputes on children's denomination generally did not appear to be directly between the state authorities and the Jewish community, but rather between the Jewish community and the parents, while state authorities got involved for legal reasons; or, as the last case shows, directly between state authorities and parents. The state authorities apparently adhered to the law in disputes with parents and if they believed the law required it, ordered them to register their children as Jewish even without the IKG being involved directly. The law of

---

9 Federal Ministry of Education, 1922 October 25, 2934; 1923 December 3, 3096; 1924 Jan 17, 1538, ÖStA, 52 D8 Neuer Kultus, Isr. Kultus.

10 Federal Ministry of Education 1924 July 22, 1924 July 25, Z. 88.158–24.18210; 1924 September 30, Z. 18210–17/Kultus; 1924 November 4, Z12Z129;18210; 1925 January 23, 2201–IZ; Federal Ministry of Foreign affairs, 1925 January 7, Z. 124.250–24., ÖStA, 52 D8 Neuer Kultus, Isr. Kultus.

inter-denomination, which applied to all recognized religions, ensured that Jews were treated equally by law and the IKG was treated equally to other religious authorities. In 1935, the Federal Court of Justice decided that all children, whose parents belonged to a denomination at the time of their child's birth and only later became undenominational and stayed undenominational until the child had reached the age of seven, had to attend religious education according to the religion their parents had belonged to at the time of the child's birth.[11] The state had thus narrowed the loophole in the law significantly when it came to children of undenominational parents. Hence, more children had to attend religious classes, than before.

To take the issue one step further, without state legislation, the law as well as the enforcement of the law, the Jewish community would not have been able to proceed legally against parents' decisions to take their children out of the IKG. Although it restricted their authority in many cases for the sake of freedom of religion of the parents, the IKG learned to use the law and the loopholes in the law to prevent children from leaving the Jewish community.

Similarly, cooperation between the state and the Jewish community seemed to have worked quite well when it came to children's attendance of religious instruction classes, as the following letter from the Vienna School Board to the IKG concerning an intervention of the IKG president in the year 1928 shows: "Concerning the intervention of the president of the IKG on 9 February 1928 [...] I am honored to disclose in the name of the Vienna School Board, that it surely cannot be put into doubt, that parents [...] are obliged to make their children participate in the obligatory religious instruction and that inefficiently excused absence from this instruction represents an unexcused absence from school. The Vienna School Board will therefore turn its attention to the compliance with this statutory obligation."[12] In this case too, only the state had the authority to make the attendance of religious education obligatory. Without state law, the Jewish community could hardly have made religious classes anything more than voluntary.

Religious Exercises and Customs in Public Schools

Some aspects of public schooling contradicted Jewish religious laws and customs. To find compromises in issues such as prayer in school, head covering and keeping the laws of the Sabbath, the IKG and state authorities were in continuous correspondence.

---

[11] IKG, 1936 April 23, IKG Z.1660 ex 1936, A/W 1562, CAHJP.

[12] Stadtschulrat für Wien to IKG, 1928 June 21 , A/W 1518.8, CAHJP.

Religious Exercises

The so-called *Glöckel-Erlass*, passed in 1919 by Social Democrat politician Otto Glöckel, declared participation in religious exercises such as religious services to be voluntary and no longer mandatory.[13] During a revision of these voluntary religious exercises at public schools in 1922, the religious authorities, including the Catholic Church, the Protestant Church and the IKG representatives, were asked by the Vienna School Board to hand in their proposals for religious exercises for the children under their authority, which those would attend in addition to the regular religious instruction. The exercises for Jewish children were the regular youth services at several Viennese synagogues, which were announced by the Vienna School Board. Christian children also attended religious services as part of their religious exercises, but the archiepiscopal representatives also requested a confessional prayer before and after daily instruction at schools. The Vienna School Board denied this request because of the "objections by other religious associations" and explained further that a "celebration of a confessional prayer by the teacher in the presence of all the children who attend the class, including children of other confessions, is perceived by these as a disregard of their religious sentiments."[14] Further, the Vienna School Board argued that a confessional prayer before and after regular instruction contradicted the inter-confessional character of primary schools. The Vienna School Board had no objection to confessional prayers during religious instruction classes.

The year before, in 1921, the school commission of the Jewish community had asked their inspector Heinrich Redisch to intervene at the Vienna School Board after the Christian parents association of the nineteenth district in Vienna had decided to introduce prayer before and after classes. Following this, the commission decided to send a letter to the Vienna School Board, stating that in consideration for the upcoming revision of religious exercises, the executive committee of the IKG was objecting against the fact that Jewish students were forced to participate in religious exercises with other confessions.[15] The decision of the Vienna School Board in 1922 against such exercises did not solve this issue for long. In April 1933 Minister of Education Anton Rintelen in the Engelbert Dollfuß government abolished the *Glöckel-Erlass* and religious exercises once again became obligatory.[16] In November that year the

---

[13] Glöckel-Erlass, http://de.wikipedia.org/wiki/Glöckel-Erlass, 2010 February 27.

[14] Stadtschulrat für Wien, 1922 July 24, A/W 1555, CAHJP.

[15] Protocol books of the IKG's school commission meetings (Sektion II), A/W 1518.8, CAHJP .

[16] Glöckel-Erlass, http://de.wikipedia.org/wiki/Glöckel-Erlass, 2010 February 27.

archiepiscopal representatives ordered all Roman Catholic children in public and private primary schools to say the following prayer, asking the Holy Spirit for assistance in learning:

Heiliger Geist, komm zu verbreiten
über uns dein Gnadenlicht,
dass wir immer weiter schreiten
in Erlernung unserer Pflicht!
Mache uns zum Lernen Lust,
hilf, dass wir in unserer Brust
das Erlernte wohl behalten
und im Guten nicht erkalten.[17]

Additionally the children were ordered to say the prayer "Our Father Who Art in Heaven" with the Angelic Salutation and make the Sign of the Cross before and after prayer while saying "In the name of the Father and the Son and the Holy Spirit." In classes, in which Catholic pupils were the minority it was sufficient to say the prayer "*Heiliger Geist, komm zu verbreiten*" at the beginning of instruction and at the end say the following prayer, this time asking the Father to bless the knowledge learned in the lesson:

Vater, segne diese Lehren,
die du durch des Lehrers Mund
deinen Kindern machtest kund,
uns zum Heil und dir zu Ehren.
Präge sie durch deinen Geist
tief ins Herz, dass wir im Leben
stets zu handeln uns bestreben
so, wie dein Gebot uns heisst.[18]

The executive committee of the IKG was asked by the Vienna School Board to comment on the order for Catholic children.[19] The IKG argued against confessional prayers at Viennese primary schools, promoting in the interest of all pupils and for educational reasons an unconfessional prayer. In case the confessional prayer would be implemented, the IKG requested that in schools where Jewish children were the majority, the words "Holy Spirit" would be replaced by "Holy God". The IKG did not object to Jewish

---

[17] Stadtschulrat für Wien to IKG, 1933 October 18, Stadtschulrat für Wien Z1. I-6723/33; copy in the protocol books of the IKG plenary meetings A/W 71.20, CAHJP.

[18] Ibid.

[19] Ibid.

children staying in class during the Catholic school prayer.[20] The cases of Christian Prayer services clearly show that all official parties involved were more or less prepared to compromise.

The Catholic Church did not request Catholic children in classes, where they were the minority, to cite all the prayers generally required. State authorities asked the Jewish community representatives to comment on the planned implementation of Catholic prayer during class. Although the IKG representatives clearly did not support confessional prayer, they were ready to accept it, as long as Jewish children would not have to directly participate in it. Alternatively they were ready to allow Jewish children to participate in prayers if they were rephrased in an un-confessional or confessionally neutral way. The question whether the respective bodies compromised out of respect and belief that it was the right step in a multi-cultural state or rather out of lack of choice in the given time and situation, needs to be looked into further. What can be argued quite certainly, however, is that the Austrian school system was becoming increasingly confessional by the 1930s and the level of confrontation had just not yet reached the point, at which it would be recognizable on an official level, as it would soon become.

The Sabbath at Public Schools

The Sabbath was another potentially confrontational case in public schools. However, it was handled quite peacefully by state authorities and the IKG. A decree of the Ministry of Education in 1876 ordered schools to be considerate of the Israelite commandment to refrain from writing, drawing and handiwork on the Sabbath when organizing class schedules and ruled that any direct or indirect force to transgress this commandment should be refrained from.[21] This decree was still valid in the 1930s. That does not, however, mean that it was always adhered to. The Lower Austrian Education authority confirmed that Jewish orthodox organizations had complained to the IKG and the Vienna School Board, claiming that Jewish children were forced to write on Saturdays.[22] The Vienna School Board was always ready to confirm the validity of the de-

[20] IKG to Stadtschulrat für Wien, Z. 7361 ex 1933; protocol books of the IKG plenary meetings A/W 71.20, CAHJP.

[21] K.k. Ministry of Education, 1876 January 31, Z. 1208; referred to in letter from K.k. Niederösterreichischer Landesschulrat to headmasters of all secondary schools and all district school inspectors, 1911 November 14, A/W 1556, CAHJP.

[22] K.k. niederösterreichischer Landesschulrat to headmasters of all secondary schools and all district school inspectors, 1911 November 14, A/W 1556, CAHJP.

cree, but while in 1911 k.k. governor of Lower Austria Richard von Bienerth-Schmerling reminded all secondary school headmasters and district representatives to ensure consideration of the Sabbath,[23] in 1930 the Vienna School Board declined to do so, claiming that there was no need to, as class schedules were considerate of the Sabbath.[24] But also among Jewish representatives, apart from orthodox circles, the observance of the Sabbath was generally not seen as a pressing issue. Just as the majority of Viennese Jewry was not religiously observant and many parents did not mind if their children wrote on the Sabbath,[25] the IKG did not invest a lot of effort in publicly objecting to apparent infringements of the Sabbath at schools. On the contrary, although the Sabbath is considered strictly religiously speaking no less important than other Jewish holidays, the IKG did not request it to be one of the days, on which Jewish children should be exempt from school, as it did with other major holidays.[26] The IKG, and even most other orthodox organizations, regarded it as inevitable, that Jewish children would have to attend public schools on Saturdays and accepted the compromise that they would not have to write. Strictly religious organizations pressed for the implementation of this decree more strongly than the IKG itself.

Head Covering

Another decree, of which schools had to be reminded, concerned the head covering of Jewish boys during religious instruction. In 1921, a teacher for Jewish religious instruction handed in a petition to the state education authority in the name of the teachers at the federal secondary school in the second district of Vienna requesting a uniform decision concerning the head covering of Jewish boys during religious education classes.[27] According to the petition, this issue had caused quite a bit of confusion as in 1906 the IKG had ordered to let boys wear a head covering during religious instruction if their parents wished so, and a year later the Lower Austrian Education authority had apparently decided that boys should not be

---

[23] K.k. niederösterreichischer Landesschulrat to headmasters of all secondary schools and all district school inspectors, 1911 November 14, A/W 1556, CAHJP.

[24] Stadtschulrat für Wien to IKG, 1930 April 30 , protocol books of the IKG plenary meetings A/W 71.20, CAHJP.

[25] Rettet den Sabbath für die Jugend, in: Jüdische Presse, Wien, Bratislava, 1935 June 28, 1.

[26] Bezirksschulrat, 1891 November 22 , A/W 1556, CAHJP.

[27] Teachers at the federal school of the second district of Vienna to Landesschulrat, 1921 exact date?, protocol books of the IKG's school commission meetings (Sektion II) , A/W 1518.8, CAHJP.

allowed to wear a head covering. However, in 1911, the state education authority again referred to the order of the Jewish community to let students wear a head covering during religious classes if their parents wanted them to do so. Some teachers therefore introduced the obligation to wear a head covering during their class, but in other classes the teachers themselves apparently did not wear a head covering and the order lead to a split between the more or less religious pupils as well as to disciplinary problems, as the teacher, who submitted the petition, stated in his letter to the state authorities: "Apart from the fact, that exceptional regulations seriously endanger the discipline – they say that in schools, where individual pupils are allowed to cover themselves, they hide each other's caps to fool around – it can impossibly be the aim of the decree to make room for ambivalence in class through two different customs, nor even less to position the religious education teacher behind individual religiously devoted pupils."

The letter shows that teachers for religious instruction did not always wear a head covering, an interesting fact keeping in mind that the Jewish community was at least partly responsible for choosing teachers. Teachers teaching Jewish religion at public schools therefore did not necessarily have to be religiously observant according to all aspects of orthodox Jewish law. This tendency seems to be consistent with the fact that writing on the Sabbath was not a major concern of the IKG. There are two possible explanations for such a tendency. Either the Jewish community was trying to avoid confrontations with the schools and state authorities or individual adherence to religious law was not seen important enough to interfere, quite possibly it was not seen by the Jewish leaders, many of whom were not religiously observant themselves, as a public issue or the responsibility of the IKG.

The cases above, repeatedly show that although there were several issues which could have caused friction in IKG–state relations, it usually did not require too much effort to reach compromises in matters concerning religious customs, at least on the official level. Jewish Orthodox associations might not have agreed with all official IKG policies, but they did have their own private primary school, which was closed on the Sabbath and received substantial grants from the IKG on a regular basis.

The Parallel Class Crisis, the Jewish Primary School and the Road to Segregation

As minimal as confrontation between the state authorities and the IKG on school matters had been until the mid–1930s, at least on an official level, as large the friction became after the implementation of the new Austrian Constitution in May 1934.[28] The Constitution incorporated the third Concordat, concluded by Federal Chancellor Engelbert Dollfuß on 5 July 1933, which granted the Church major influence, particularly in school matters.[29] Amongst others it increased religious instruction for Catholic children and prepared the grounds for a confessional Catholic school system with Catholic state schools.

The *Parallelklassenverordnung*

On 18 September 1934 the IKG received notification of an order published three days earlier by the Vienna School Board under the title "parallel class division of pupils at secondary schools and teacher training institutions", which stated that on 4 July 1934 the Ministry of Education had ordered for practical reasons that parallel classes were to be organized in a way that united non-Catholic pupils in one class and separated them from the Catholic class.[30] The leaders of the IKG were outraged as nobody had consulted with them on the matter. By the time they received notification the order was already in place. However, it was not entirely unexpected. Rumors on the plans had prompted leaders of the IKG to turn to the Ministry of Education in June. Nevertheless, the IKG had been left out of the decision-making about the division of parallel classes and realized in September that the order was already being implemented. In addition, the IKG learned without any official notification, that as a result of the parallel class order children were not only being separated in secondary schools, but also in primary schools. In many cases the implementation of the order went even further, when children were separated according to confessions within one class even if there was no need for a parallel class considering the number of pupils.[31] Jewish children were forced to switch schools in order to attend non-Catholic classes, separate specifically Jewish classes were created at some schools and Catholic classes at other schools. Jeanette Weiss, headmaster of a school in the second Viennese district in the *Kleine Pfarrgasse,* was forced into retirement after all Jewish children had been sent to attend another

---

[28] Verordnung der Bundesregierung vom 24. April 1934 über die Verfassung des Bundesstaates Österreich, Bundesgesetzblatt (hereafter BGBl.) 1934 I. Nr. 239, http://www.verfassungen.de/at/oesterreich34.htm, 2010 February 27.

[29] Concordat between the Holy See and the Rep. of Austria of 1933 July 5, Art. 6, http://www.concordatwatch.eu/showtopic.php?org_id=921&kb_header_id=1811, 2010 February 27.

[30] Speech by IKG president Dr. Desider Friedmann, including attached copies of relevant documents, 1934 September 26, protocol books of the IKG plenary meetings A/W 71.20, CAHJP.

[31] Neue Freie Presse, Wien, 1934 September 25.

school in the *Kleine Sperlgasse*.[32] Furthermore, in the *Sophien-Gymnasium*, the headmaster had been removed from his position for belonging to the Social Democratic Party and the new headmaster, who had been dismissed from another school for National Socialist involvements, was put in his place to manage the school, where half of the pupils were Jewish.[33] IKG president Desider Friedmann pointed out that the implementation of the parallel class was not conform with § 36–38 of the 1905 School and Education decree, according to which children were to be admitted to the school responsible for the area where they lived and therefore should not be forced to attend schools further away only because they were Jewish.[34] Furthermore, Friedmann underlined that the IKG had not received any explanations concerning reasons for the order from state authorities. The community leaders clearly refused to accept the official claim that classes were divided for practical–reasons, especially because Jewish community leaders would have been willing to solve any technical problems concerning religious instruction classes if they had been contacted. Any practical problem seemed to them proportionately minor considering the disadvantages of the class divisions, which, as Friedmann noted in an open plenary session of the IKG executive committee, would "cause and strengthen feelings of inferiority among Jewish youth" and therefore the IKG could "not agree to a spatial segregation of our children from the children of other confessions."[35] Friedmann continued: "I think that I do not have to elaborate why certain sensitivity exists specifically in current times among Jewish circles. You will agree that from such a spatial distancing a transition to discrimination can be found very easily." His speech clearly reflected the already very tense and increasingly anti-Semitic atmosphere in Austrian society.

In 1898 a very similar decree had also caused a lot of unease among IKG representatives, who in those days complained about a planned confessional division to the Minister of Education Count Artur Bylandt-Rheidt After an examination of the case it was decided that pupils were only allowed to be separated according to confessions if the technical difficulties concerning the class schedule of religious instruction could not be solved otherwise.[36] In general, therefore, the 1898 order had not been implemented.

---

[32] IKG, 27 Sept. 1934, A/W 1528, CAHJP

[33] IKG, 1934 September 26, A/W 1528, CAHJP.

[34] Verordnung des Ministeriums für Kultus und Unterricht, 29. September 1905, http://alex.onb.ac.at/cgi-content/anno-plus?apm=0&aid=rgb&datum=19050004&seite=00000406&zoom=2, 2010 February 27.

[35] Dr. Desider Friedmann at the IKG plenary session, 1934 September 26 , protocol books of the IKG plenary meetings A/W 71.20, CAHJP.

[36] Ibid.

In 1934, on the other hand, exaggerated implementation of the order had already begun before the IKG was even notified. While using the same means of protest as in 1898, appealing to state authorities that the order was illegal, IKG leaders did realize that this time the opponent was more than a decree, namely a changing tendency in Austria's political sphere. In his speech at the IKG plenary session, where the parallel class order was discussed, Leopold Plaschkes, member of the executive committee, outlined: "What is happening here is to be valued as a collapse of a tendency, the liberal tendency, which unites Christian and Jewish children in order to decrease anti-Semitism".[37] Liberal tendencies had not succeeded in combating anti-Semitism and the Ministry of Education was accused of enforcing it further with an order that was conceived as a humiliation and insult, not only by the IKG, but by many Jewish parents who had turned to the IKG for help. Plaschkes admitted that no laws had been passed directly to discriminate against Jews, but an administrative practice of public authorities, which excluded Jews from certain professions and economic circles, this time had resulted in Jewish children having to leave schools, switch schools and being herded in Jewish classes, causing the IKG to be up in arms against the parallel class order.

The Jewish Primary School

At the same time as confessional classes in public schools caused strong sentiments and opposition, the majority of the IKG, with the backing of many parents, was planning the establishment of its own Jewish primary school. Critics within the IKG, such as representatives of the non-Zionist *Union Österreichischer Juden* represented by Jakob Ornstein, believed that the establishment of a Jewish school contradicted the fight against confessional division at public schools as it was just another type of segregation.[38] However, to most IKG representatives, confessional classes at public schools were an entirely different matter than confessional schools. While Catholic children were separated from Jewish children in public schools with the aim to provide them a better Catholic education, the separated Jewish children on the other hand did not receive better Jewish education in public schools. The only difference was a sense of being separated. In his speech at the IKG plenary session, executive committee member Robert Stricker clarified that the Jews wanted "no *Judenklassen*, no Jewish Ghetto, but a Jewish schooling system with absolute equal status, included into the framework of

---

[37] Dr. Leopold Plaschkes at the IKG plenary session, 1934 September 26, protocol books of the IKG plenary meetings A/W 71.20, CAHJP.

[38] Dr. Jakob Ornstein at the IKG plenary session, 1934 September 26, protocol books of the IKG plenary meetings A/W 71.20, CAHJP.

the state, with Jewish influence and not as a private matter of the Jews, but a Jewish school system, which is cared for in a material and moral way by the state just as the other school system. We demand a religious-national education of the youth without Ghetto and without restriction."[39] Executive committee member Jakob Ehrlich spoke along the same lines to point out that fighting against confessional separation at public schools and establishing a Jewish primary school did not contradict each other: "If Jews unite in freedom in order to promote Jewish purposes, then such a union, which was formed out of free choice, in order to promote estimable aims, will be able to respect itself and will also find the respect of the non-Jewish world. But, if a separation is implemented against our will, which possibly serves a foreign interest, but definitely not ours, the memory of Jewish Ghettos of the past will be called up."[40]

In November 1934 the school commission of the IKG discussed the option to file a petition to state authorities concerning the establishment and financing of Jewish primary schools. The majority of IKG leaders believed that the state was responsible for financing Jewish schools. In March 1935 the school commission discussed sending a petition to the state authorities to make clear that "not the IKG, but actually the state would be obliged to establish Jewish schools."[41] Furthermore, "if the state makes its school system German-Christian, then the Jews also want their own school system. But the state also has the obligation to care for the Jewish school."

Not all members of the commission agreed whether to approach the state and therefore no decision was made at that plenary session whether to turn to the state for financial support. Apart from the *Union Österreichischer Juden*, also some Orthodox circles opposed the establishment of an IKG managed primary school. They believed such a school would not put enough emphasis on religious values, but instead would focus on Zionist ideology, conforming to the ideals of the leading party of the community. Articles published during the debates about the parallel class order in the Orthodox Jewish newspaper *Jüdische Presse* express not only sharp criticism of the planned IKG primary school, which was seen as irreligious and at the same time a competitor for the Orthodox Talmud Torah primary school, but also support for the confessional classes at pub-

---

[39] Oberbaurat Ing. Robert Stricker at the IKG plenary session, 1934 September 26, protocol books of the IKG plenary meetings A/W 71.20, CAHJP.

[40] Dr. Jakob Ehrlich at the IKG plenary session, 1934 September 26, protocol books of the IKG plenary meetings A/W 71.20, CAHJP.

[41] IKG, protocol book of school commission, 1935 March (exact date?), Sektion II, A/W 1518.8, CAHJP.

lic schools.[42] While the IKG leadership fought against the parallel class order, some orthodox circles regarded it, just like state authorities, as a first step towards creating more religiously observant confessional schools. State authorities were aware of inner-Jewish conflicts and at several occasions the IKG leadership corresponded with Austrian politicians to convince them that their views and demands represented the large majority of Viennese Jewry and not those of the *Jüdische Presse*, whose publications on the matter they saw as damaging to Jewry in general.[43]

Despite the debates on the Jewish primary school, the IKG opened the gates of their new primary school in September 1935 and the Austrian state school inspector and district school inspector for the second Viennese district came to congratulate the IKG in the name of the Viennese mayor and the president of the Vienna School Board.[44]

Towards Complete Segregation

When in January 1938 count Georg Thurn-Valsassina, leader of the *Vaterländische Front's* youth division suggested to organize Jewish youth in a separate sub-division because of differences in religious education, the IKG officially welcomed this step, while the *Union Österreichischer Juden* strongly opposed it as anti-Semitic segregation.[45] In the same month, the *Jüdische Presse* published in a small notification the details of an upcoming ban on Jewish religious education at public schools, introduced by the Ministry of Education. Such a move would have changed the IKG's education policy in the extreme as their main activity had been focused on exactly those classes. However, the IKG leadership did not have a lot of time to contemplate about that matter, because less than two months later Austria was annexed to the German *Reich* and shortly thereafter the Nuremberg race laws were introduced resulting in a complete segregation of Jewish children into Jewish schools, at times several age-groups in one class. Children had to walk long and dangerous ways to their new schools; the number of Jewish children allowed to attend secondary education in Jewish schools was significantly restricted. Jewish schools later served as accumulative stations for Jews before they were deported.

---

[42] Jüdische Presse, 1934 September 14, 1934 October 5, 1934 October 12.

[43] IKG to the Federal government, ministry of education and mayor of Vienna, 1934 October 8, Z.7219 ex 1934, A/W 1528; note of a meeting of the IKG executive committee with State Secretary Dr. Pernter, 1934 September 27, A/W 1528; IKG to Adass Jisroel, A/W 1528, CAHJP

[44] Report of IKG on the inauguration of the Jewish primary school 1935 September 25, A/W1652.6, CAHJP

[45] Jüdische Wochenschrift, 1938 February 4.

By 1942 Jewish children did not attend schools. Most of them had either fled or were deported. When there were hardly any Jews left in Vienna, previously Jewish schools were again used for Christian children.[46]

Conclusion

Jewish education during the interwar period was strongly connected to state policies and laws concerning religious instruction in general for all churches and religious organizations. Not only did the Jewish community take on Jewish education as one of its main responsibilities because state law required this, but the state also enforced the attendance of religious instruction. Furthermore, although the law of inter-denomination was set up to enhance the freedom of religion, its restrictions also served as a tool to prevent conversions of Jewish children by their parents. When in line with the law, the Austrian state authorities cooperated fully with the IKG and ordered parents to leave their children in the IKG to receive Jewish religious instruction, even if they themselves had left the Jewish religion. Without state law and cooperation with state authorities in enforcing this law, the IKG could not have set up a compulsory public system for religious instruction and a large number of Jewish children would not have received any religious education.

Not only did state policies guarantee that all Jewish children received Jewish religious instruction, but it also ensured the right of Jewish children to keep basic laws of the Sabbath by not having to write, draw or do handiwork on Saturdays. Jewish boys were generally allowed to wear a head covering at religious instruction classes. When it came to compulsory prayers in class for Catholic children, state authorities consulted with the IKG to find the most acceptable solution for classes attended also by Jewish children. The IKG, on its side, did not make strong efforts to enforce the Sabbath laws or the head covering at public schools. Although they did not promote confessional prayer in class, they had no objections to Jewish children staying in class while Christians were praying according to their customs.

The Jewish values and identity the IKG leadership wanted to convey to the Jewish children was not necessarily a religious one. They themselves were mostly not religiously observant apart from an orthodox minority, which had its own orthodox primary schools and other educational institutions. The emphasis of the official IKG leadership was put on culture, history, language and cus-

---

46 Hedwig Millan, "Jüdische Schüler an den Wiener Pflichtschulen vom März 1938 bis 1942", www.david.juden.at/kulturzeitschrift/70–75/73–millian.htm, 2010 February 27.

toms in order to participate in services at the synagogues. This tendency was in line the aim to be considered equal, with equal rights to other confessions. The curriculum was quite universal, with a Jewish emphasis, but based on values the non-Jewish society could identify with. The aim was to stay Jewish, but in a way which was very similar to any other confession. In practice this worked quite well as long as Austrian state policy regarded education an inter-confessional matter.

From the mid-1930s however, after the implementation of the third Concordat and the new Constitution, this approach changed drastically, Austria became increasingly confessional, education increasingly Catholic. When Jewish children were to be separated from Catholic children the Jewish community leaders changed their approach to the state as the state had changed its approach to them. Cooperation and compromise had turned into conflict. The values of universality and equality the Jewish community wanted their children to grow up in vanished. In the light of rising tension and anti-Semitism the IKG also turned to a further segregation of choice and established its own primary school, while still hoping that state policies causing segregation in public schools could be overturned. The question of segregation and integration around the state policy of separation at public schools and the Jewish primary school also caused a lot of inner-Jewish tension between orthodox, Zionist and non-Zionist parties. But, there was not much time left for engaging in discussions and searching for solutions. The annexation of Austria by the German *Reich* brought along a new policy of total segregation and finally the abolishment of any kind of public education for Jewish children in Vienna.

Michael S. Maier
(University of Vienna)

Defeated Masculinity: Transformations of Masculinity in the Narrated Life Histories of Two Former Austrian Wehrmacht Soldiers (1945–1960)

War and Gender

Due to their far-reaching consequences, modern wars, in particular those that end in a military defeat, are considered a major cause of social upheavals and processes of change, which also affect the construction of gender and gender relations to a great extent. With regard to World War II, we can observe an intensification of doing-gender processes during the war and the immediate post-war period: On the one hand, the total war fostered the forming of dichotomic gender categories and gender-related experiences, based on the traditional binary between a male fighting front and a supportive, predominantly female home front, with the associated image of the waiting woman who depends on male protection. On the other hand, the valid order of the sexes was disrupted by the reality of wartime and the extraordinary conditions caused by war, since both sexes were forced to undertake new duties and roles outside the traditional gender norms, for example, when women on the civilian front began to replace men in traditionally male professions.[1] As a consequence, with the homecoming of the veterans after the war, it was necessary to renegotiate the troubled gender hierarchy and, at the same time, to reformulate both individual and national ideals of masculinity. In the defeated countries of Austria and Germany, these processes of social transformation became most evident, for these two countries were the ones "most deeply involved in the gender crises of the twentieth century concerning war, militarism, and fascism, in which exceedingly violent models of masculinity came to the fore."[2]

Whereas, surprisingly enough, until now men after war have been largely ignored as a research topic by traditional military his-

---

1 Johanna Gehmacher – Maria Mesner, Land der Söhne. Geschlechterverhältnisse in der Zweiten Republik, Innsbruck/Wien/Bozen 2007, 37; Introduction, in: Margaret Randolph Higonnet – et al. (Eds.), Behind the Lines. Gender and the Two World Wars, New Haven/London 1987, 1–17. For the relationship between war and gender, see in more general terms: Joshua S. Goldstein, War and Gender. How Gender Shapes the War System and Vice Versa, Cambridge 2001.

2 Robert W. Connell, Der gemachte Mann. Konstruktion und Krise von Männlichkeiten (3rd Ed.), Wiesbaden 2006, 14.

tory, the Austrian and German "homecoming melodrama" in the outcome of World War II[3] became a major concern of gender and women's history in the 1980s and 1990s, when feminist historians started to examine the lifeworlds (*Lebenswelten*) of women in the war and early post-war era. In addition to the research on the essential reconstruction and family work done by women during the first years of hardship after the war, one of the main focuses of these surveys was the history of the personal relationships of these women with the returning *Wehrmacht* soldiers as well as their sexual fraternizations with soldiers of the Allied occupying forces.[4] The previously mentioned studies as well as recently completed studies regarding the national, moral, and social reintegration of World War II veterans in East and West Germany,[5] the medical-psychiatric examination of these war-damaged men,[6] and the continuing effects of war comradeship on veterans' unions after 1945[7] stress the significance of the category "gender" for the

---

3 Irene Bandhauer-Schöffmann, Heimkehrer, in: Historicum. Zeitschrift für Geschichte 15/Sommer 96, Linz-Puchenau 1996, 29.

4 For the gender-specific impact of World War II and National Socialism on post-war Austria, see, e.g., Irene Bandhauer-Schöffmann - Claire Duchen (Eds.), Nach dem Krieg. Frauenleben und Geschlechterkonstruktionen in Europa nach dem Zweiten Weltkrieg, Herbolzheim 2000; Irene Bandhauer-Schöffmann - Ela Hornung (Eds.), Wiederaufbau weiblich. Dokumentation der Tagung „Frauen in der österreichischen und deutschen Nachkriegszeit", Wien/Salzburg 1992; Ela Hornung, Warten und Heimkehren. Eine Ehe während und nach dem Zweiten Weltkrieg, Wien 2005; Ingrid Bauer, Welcome Ami Go Home. Die amerikanische Besatzung in Salzburg 1945-1955. Erinnerungslandschaften aus einem Oral-History-Projekt, Salzburg/München 1998; Erika Thurner, Nationale Identität und Geschlecht in Österreich nach 1945, Innsbruck/Wien/München 2000. For an overview on the immediate German-German post-war period, see: Hanna Schissler (Ed.), The Miracle Years. A Cultural History of West Germany, 1949-1968, Princeton 2001; Klaus Naumann (Ed.), Nachkrieg in Deutschland, Hamburg 2001.

5 For these aspects, see the recently published US-American monographs by: Robert G. Moeller, Protecting Motherhood. Women and the Family in the Politics of Postwar West Germany, Berkeley 1993; idem, War Stories. The Search for a Usable Past in the Federal Republic of Germany, Berkeley 2001; Frank Biess, Homecomings. Returning POWs and the Legacies of Defeat in Postwar Germany, Princeton 2006.

6 See Christiane Winkler, Männlichkeit und Gesundheit der deutschen Kriegsheimkehrer im Spiegel der Ärztekongresse des „Verbands der Heimkehrer", in: Martin Dinges (Ed.)., Männlichkeit und Gesundheit im historischen Wandel ca. 1800 - ca. 2000, Stuttgart 2007, 157-173; Svenja Goltermann, Die Gesellschaft der Überlebenden. Deutsche Kriegsheimkehrer und ihre Gewalterfahrungen im Zweiten Weltkrieg (2nd Ed.), München 2009.

7 See Thomas Kühne, Kameradschaft. Die Soldaten des nationalsozialistischen Krieges und das 20. Jahrhundert, Göttingen 2006.

stabilization of post-war societies (*"Kriegsfolgengesellschaften"*[8]) and the processes of social reconstruction in Austria and the two German successor states of the "Third Reich". In many respects, the research on gender-historical implications of modern wars intersects with the emerging field of "New Military History" (*Neue Militärgeschichte*), which is interested in innovative scholarly approaches such as the nexus between military, war, gender, and nation, or the demilitarization of militarized societies, and, in connection with that, the transformations of masculinity after the end of wars.

The present essay[9] takes up this new perspective in military history and deals with the metamorphoses and social (re)constructions of individual male identities of former Austrian *Wehrmacht* soldiers and prisoners of war[10] in the aftermath of World War II. I will therefore focus on the transformation of a military manhood shaped by National Socialism to a civilian masculinity and also examine the reconstruction of masculinity – the so called "remasculinization"[11] of the post-war society – after the loss of the war. Using two exemplary biographical case studies, I will illustrate how in the individual male perception (military) masculinity plunged into a "crisis" with the end of World War II (or how it is interpreted as such in the narrated life histories) and, in a second

---

8 Klaus Naumann, Einleitung, in: idem, Nachkrieg, 9.

9 The following remarks are partially based on preliminary results of my ongoing dissertation, dealing with the transformations of masculinity in the narrated life histories of former Austrian *Wehrmacht* soldiers. For this purpose, I have conducted 25 narrative-biographical interviews with former World War II participants (most of them born in the 1920s), including several interviews with female war veterans, wives of veterans and individuals who experienced the homecoming of their father as a child.

10 In total, more than 1.3 million Austrians – nearly 41 percent of the whole male population – served in the German armed forces from the time of the Anschluss in March 1938 until the end of the war. During World War II ca. 242.000 soldiers of Austrian origin were killed and ca. 600.000 were taken as prisoners of war by the Allied armies; Rüdiger Overmans, Deutsche militärische Verluste im Zweiten Weltkrieg (2nd Ed.), München 2000, 219/Chat 26, 263/Chat 51; Harald Knoll, Kriegsgefangenschaft und Heimkehr, in: Stefan Karner – Gottfried Stangler (Eds.), "Österreich ist frei!" Der Österreichische Staatsvertrag 1955. Beitragsband zur Ausstellung auf Schloss Schallaburg 2005, Horn/Wien 2005, 133.

11 The term "remasculinization" dates back to a study by Susan Jeffords on the rehabilitation of masculinity after the US defeat in the Vietnam war and is defined by her as "a regeneration of the concepts, constructions, and definitions of masculinity […] and a restabilization of the gender system within and for which it is formulated."; id., The Remasculinization of America. Gender and the Vietnam War, Bloomington 1989, 51.

step, how male gender identities in the immediate post-war period were reconstructed or renegotiated in the private domain.[12]

Homecoming as a Turning Point in the Biographies of Men

National Socialism and World War II were experienced as a violent collective trauma by millions of members of the war generation and became an inextinguishable part of their biographies. The mass experience of total war both on the front line and at the home front as well as the following search for "normality" after the end of the war produced a deeply private dimension of experience within the public space and virtually led to a melding of the private and the public realms.[13] In order to uncover a subjective perspective on history, oral history, especially in the form of narrative interviews,[14] has been established in historical scholarship as a reliable biographical method, which also provides a unique opportunity to look into constructions and structures of gender that are often hidden yet relevant to everyday life.[15] Thus, biography researcher Bettina Dausien assumes that in an autobiographical interview the narrator "not only (re)constructs his life history,

---

[12] Currently, the crisis paradigm in the history of masculinities is under fire because the term "crisis" suggests an ahistorical norm of masculinity, which is incompatible with the premise of gender as a permanent process of negotiation. Jürgen Martschukat and Olaf Stieglitz have argued that a contemporary crisis of masculinity sometimes can be seen as a "strategy of male self-victimization", in order to restabilize the threatened hegemony; id., Männer und Männlichkeiten in der Geschichte Nordamerikas: Eine Einleitung, in: idem (Eds.), Väter, Soldaten, Liebhaber. Männer und Männlichkeiten in der Geschichte Nordamerikas. Ein Reader, Bielefeld 2007, 19. See also the volume of L'Homme regarding the „Krise(n) der Männlichkeit" as a gender-historical concept: L'Homme. Zeitschrift für Feministische Geschichtswissenschaft 19/2, Köln/Weimar 2008.

[13] Richard Bessel, "Leben nach dem Tod" – Vom Zweiten Weltkrieg zur zweiten Nachkriegszeit, in: Bernd Wegner (Ed.), Wie Kriege enden. Wege zum Frieden von der Antike bis zur Gegenwart, Paderborn et al. 2002, 245.

[14] See Gabriele Rosenthal, Erlebte und erzählte Lebensgeschichte. Gestalt und Struktur biografischer Selbstbeschreibungen, Frankfurt am Main/New York 1995; Reinhard Sieder, Erzählungen analysieren – Analysen erzählen. Narrativ-biografisches Interview, Textanalyse und Falldarstellung, in: Karl R. Wernhart – Werner Zips (Eds.), Ethnohistorie. Rekonstruktion und Kulturkritik. Eine Einführung (2nd Ed.), Wien 2001, 145–172.

[15] For the value of oral history for gender history, see May B. Broda, Erfahrung, Erinnerungsinterview und Gender. Zur Methode Oral History, in: Marguérite Bos – Bettina Vincenz – Tanja Wirz (Eds.), Erfahrung: Alles nur Diskurs? Zur Verwendung des Erfahrungsbegriffs in der Geschlechtergeschichte. Beiträge der 11. Schweizerischen HistorikerInnentagung 2002, Zürich 2004, 159–171.

but at the same time also his gender identity. The telling of a life history is therefore a certain 'construction medium' for both categories, for biography and gender."[16]

Without a doubt, World War II ranks among the most formative and biographically most far-reaching events in the lives of the surviving, now aged former *Wehrmacht* soldiers and war veterans.[17] Thus, in contrast to the more continuous and private experiences of women at the home front, the end of the war was experienced by the World War II veterans as a biographical turning point and a disruption of their military life construction. The narrative-biographical interviews in my analysis illustrate the fragility and instability of male gender identities in the life-historical transition period from war to peacetime,[18] culminating in the biographical key event of the homecoming, as the following narrative example of the *Wehrmacht* veteran Erwin H., who returned from American and French war captivity in October 1945, proves:

> *"Well, my biggest disappointment was not the war, was not the captivity, but it was the coming home. This was, well, the biggest disappointment of my life. (...) The hope that we would be welcomed at our homecoming by white-dressed flower girls, was, of course, that we would only receive a stamp on our discharge papers at the office at Meidling station, well, was very big, right? Well, we thought, as young boys, we all, well, had completely, we all thought, well, no, when we came home then, then there would be, yes, there would, yes, everybody would be in the streets and they would say: Now finally the boys are coming home, right? Healthy and alive and so forth, right? But no, you! On the contrary, right? He said 'what are you doing, what are you making...' Well, this, this... My mother, actually, with her words 'what are you doing here', right? She put more or less the whole thing in a nutshell, right? (smiles) We were not welcomed at all!*

---

16 Bettina Dausien, Biografie und Geschlecht. Zur biografischen Konstruktion sozialer Wirklichkeit in Frauenlebensgeschichten, Bremen 1996, 5; see also: Sylka Scholz, Männlichkeit erzählen, in: Christine Burckhardt-Seebass – Sabine Allweier (Eds.), Geschlechter-Inszenierungen. Erzählen – Vorführen – Ausstellen, Münster 2003, 75–89.

17 For the gender-specific difference of male and female war biographies, see Irene Bandhauer-Schöffmann – Ela Hornung, Von Mythen und Trümmern. Oral History-Interviews mit Frauen zum Alltag im Nachkriegs-Wien, in: id. (Eds.), Wiederaufbau, 24–54; Karin M. Schmidlechner, Geschlechtsspezifische Erinnerungen an den Zweiten Weltkrieg, in: Barbara Hey – Cécile Huber – idem (Eds.), Krieg: Geschlecht und Gewalt, Graz 1999, 149–159.

18 See Jörg Echternkamp, „Kameradenpost bricht auch nie ab ..." – Ein Kriegsende auf Raten im Spiegel der Briefe deutscher Ostheimkehrer 1946–1951, in: Militärgeschichtliche Zeitschrift 60/2, München 2001, 438.

> *We were not welcomed! There were so many, so many, so many freed forced laborers there, there were enough men there. We lousy, ragged, and verminous figures, reduced to a skeleton, we were, certainly only troublesome, only further eaters who probably would have, well, consumed the few remaining resources, right? Well, it... Looked at in that light, we could have gone away again. Well, I'm wondering anyway that they had let us pass the border, right? Because you all have served in the German army, well, go back again. Well, in Germany they had hugged us and kissed us and in Austria they had... Yes, just that they didn't give us a kick in our ass. Well, but the disdain was physically noticeable, right?"*[19]

In this interview segment, the 1924-born Erwin H., who had served from January 1943 until the end of the war as a military engineer in the *Wehrmacht*, follows the narrative pattern of the "fallen war hero". He contrasts his expectations about his homecoming with his real experiences: Instead of being welcomed as a bright young hero in a military parade by "white-dressed flower girls", (having an explicit sexual connotation), he had "the biggest disappointment of his life". This rejection, which culminates in the interview text in the words of his mother, namely, what he was doing there, is perceived by the narrator as a betrayal of him and his comrades by the Austrian post-war society. The "young boys", as Erwin H. speaks of himself in order to imply his innocence, are subsequently presented as physically damaged victims of war and compared by the narrator to the Nazi victim group of the liberated forced laborers, seemingly ranking higher in the hierarchy than the homecoming *Wehrmacht* soldiers. The war-marked body ("reduced to a skeleton") of Erwin H. here serves as the most visible sign of his demasculinization.

Parallel to Erwin H., the vast majority of the interviewed veterans perceived the military defeat, the war captivity, and the often disappointing homecoming experiences as diminishment of their masculinity. The self-positioning of my interview partners as war victims in connection with the perception of a male identity crisis in the narrated life histories allowed these men to ignore questions regarding their individual involvement in the Nazi *Vernichtungskrieg* (war of extermination) in the interviews as well as in their civilian post-war lives. Gabriele Rosenthal considers this "de-thematization" of the National Socialist crimes and the associated

[19] Due to the translation and in order to ensure better readability, I have cleaned up and simplified the original German interview texts. All recorded interviews and their transcripts are in the possession of the author.

promotion of the myth of the "clean *Wehrmacht*" to be a constitutive element of the war narrations of former *Wehrmacht* soldiers and sees in it a narrative strategy for the biographical "normalization of the Nazi past", even though certain aspects of the war experiences could never be dealt with.[20]

The militarization and nationalization of men since the nineteenth century was radicalized under the Nazi dictatorship, in an intensity not known by other modern non-fascist masculinities in Europe and overseas at that time.[21] The virile fanaticism of the Nazi ideology heightened military masculinity to the universal life principle of the National Socialist "*Volksgemeinschaft*" (people's community) and glorified the *Wehrmacht* soldiers as racially superior war heroes. With the total defeat in World War II and the walk into war captivity, the male soldierly existence of the members of the German armed forces laid in ruins before them:

> *"The Russians only said one thing again and again: We would have to pay reparations for twenty years. And this was a terrible thing. (...) Indeed, for myself, I didn't believe that. Indeed, in my romantic state of mind ... Romantic state of mind, why? I had married in the year forty-four, before the capture, as I told you. I was so in love, and I was so happy that I had found a person, that I couldn't stop thinking of her. I had to think of her all the time. And I had to think about our home all the time. And to bear in mind what was going on with our child, if the child was coming? If... What child we would have? And what was she experiencing at home? We didn't know that. The Russians came into our barracks and said (shouts): 'Vienna kaput! Vienna kaput!' In other words, they had conquered Vienna. Oh god, no! And then, what would happen to my daughter? What was going to happen to us? Such were my thoughts, yes? (takes a deep breath)"*[22]

---

20 Gabriele Rosenthal, Erzählbarkeit, biografische Notwendigkeit und soziale Funktion von Kriegserzählungen. Zur Frage: Was wird gerne und leicht erzählt, in: Karin Hartewig (Ed.), Der lange Schatten. Widerspruchsvolle Erinnerungen an den Zweiten Weltkrieg und die Nachkriegszeit aus der Mitte Europas. 1939–1989. BIOS Sonderheft 1993, 18; see also: Ela Hornung, Trümmermänner. Zum Schweigen österreichischer Soldaten der Deutschen *Wehrmacht*, in: Wolfgang Kos – Georg Rigele (Eds.), Inventur 45/55. Österreich im ersten Jahrzehnt der Zweiten Republik, Wien 1996, 232–250; Gertrud Kerschbaumer, Täteranteile und Opfermythen in den Lebensgeschichten ehemaliger Kriegsgefangener der GUPVI, in: Gertraud Diendorfer – Gerhard Jagschitz – Oliver Rathkolb (Eds.), Zeitgeschichte im Wandel. 3. Österreichische Zeitgeschichtetage 1997, Innsbruck/Wien 1998, 369–375.

21 For the construction of fascist masculinity, see George L. Mosse, Das Bild des Mannes. Zur Konstruktion der modernen Männlichkeit, Frankfurt am Main 1997, 203–233.

22 The interview with Albert B. was conducted together with his wife Trude.

Albert B. had married his wife Trude in Vienna towards the end of the war and, after his capture on the Eastern front, was being held in Soviet war captivity until September 1947. In his captivity narrative he portrays himself as a new family man und draws a very personal picture of his internment, wavering between his love to Trude and his concerns about his family at home. Generally speaking, in many ways the masculinity embodied by Albert B. in his war biography differs from the heroic-martial Nazi ideal of military masculinity: On the one hand, his military career in the *Wehrmacht* was characterized by conflicts with his superiors and a principal denial of military service, on the other hand, he tried to volunteer for an elite German paratrooper (*Fallschirmjäger*) unit and has also preserved positive memories of his service in the *Wehrmacht*. Biographical case studies such as Albert B. underline the repressiveness and complexity of a militarized hegemonic model of masculinity for the construction of gender in the National Socialist era, even though, in reality, only few men met the requirements of the hyper-masculine Nazi warrior ideal.[23]

The present interview extract reaches a dramatic climax when Albert B. imitates the yelling of the Soviet guards alluding to the conquest of Vienna: The painful worries – the home city, with his wife and the newborn child, was now in the hands of the enemy – touch on a central point in the male-soldierly self-conception, namely, the social construction of the male fighter and guardian, mainly created by the introduction of compulsory military service in the nineteenth century, which consolidated the dual concept of soldierly man and peaceful woman. In this context, Albert B.'s time in war captivity can be read as a humiliation of his (military) masculinity: Like all Austrian and German men, Albert B. had failed to defend his homeland and his family and was now, as a prisoner of war in the custody of the former enemy, not able to fulfill his role as protector of his people.

My request in the interview if Albert B. was plagued by doubts due to the long separation from his wife provoked a narrative about an event in the prisoner-of-war camp, which, as will be shown, implies a deep sexual uncertainty of the defeated men:

> *"I was in the room of the shoemaker; there we sat together and sewed. The tailor and Hermann, who was sewing, were sitting behind me, right? And then we were simply talking. Then they said: 'Oh well, what do you think? Because in Austria, there are now four different types of occupation soldiers' (very excited) 'What do you think? Do you think that your wife, when you are away? If*

---

[23] For the inhomogeneity and spectrum of military concepts of masculinity in the Nazi era, see Maria Fritsche, Feige Männer? Fremd- und Selbstbilder von Wehrmachtsdeserteuren, in: Ariadne. Forum für Frauen- und Geschlechtergeschichte 47, Kassel 2005, 54–61.

that, that, do you believe that?' (halting) 'That she will not run away with a soldier of the occupation forces? She is young, isn't she? Nineteen years, right?' (calmer) I said, 'she doesn't do that.' I said, 'that is impossible', I said. 'I trust her!' I said, 'I don't believe that this will happen.' And, at the same time, it happened that Hermann, who was sitting in the back, got a letter saying: (imitates a different voice) 'Dear Hermann, I inform you that what you... What was once your woman is now mine.' He had that then... He also thought about home, right? And then he got a letter from that Primitiverl (idiot) writing to him in that way: 'I, I have, this is now my woman, over.'"

In this re-enactment of an everyday dialogue in the Soviet internment camp, the fidelity of Albert B.s' wife, who is implicitly accused of having a sexual relationship with a solider of the occupying armies at home, is called into question by his fellow prisoners. The victorious Allied soldiers appear here as potential rivals and as sexual threat for the defeated and captured former *Wehrmacht* soldiers. Ingrid Bauer and Renate Huber argue that after the military defeat many Austrian men perceived the sexual liaisons of the local women with their former enemies as a dismantlement of their last position of power – the national-patriarchal ownership of "their" women; the scholars speak in this context of a "double defeat" of Austrian masculinity.[24] In the concrete interview text, Albert B.'s masculinity, now reduced to his male gender identity as husband and father, is at stake: Although the narrator repeatedly assures that he believes in the fidelity of his wife, his defensive speech to his comrades also indicates the vulnerability and insecurity of his masculinity in the war captivity situation. The final episode about his fellow Hermann, who had been informed about the loss of his wife by a letter, stresses the serious sexual threat for the detained veterans and leads to solidarity with the cheated comrade, whereas at the same time he strongly condemns the behavior of the rival. It is remarkable that masculinity is here constructed by the narrator in terms of his faithful, waiting wife at home and is put under pressure by the victorious soldiers of the occupying armies.[25]

---

[24] Ingrid Bauer – Renate Huber, Sexual Encounters across (Former) Enemy Borderlines, in: Günter Bischof – Anton Pelinka – Dagmar Herzog (Eds.), Sexuality in Austria. Contemporary Austrian Studies, vol. 15, New Brunswick 2007, 66, 85.

[25] See the numerous contributions of Ela Hornung on the omnipresence of the gender arrangement of the homecoming man and the waiting woman in the immediate post-war period, which, according to Hornung, played an important role for the reconstruction of the gender relations after World War II; see, for e.g., idem, Heimkehrer und wartende Frau. Zur Symptomatik eines Geschlechterverhältnisses nach dem Zweiten Weltkrieg in Österreich, in: Bandhauer-Schöffmann – Duchen, Krieg, 67–84.

In summary, it can be said that National Socialist manhood lost its hegemonic status with the breakdown of the Nazi regime and the superior masculinity of the soldiers of the occupying armies challenged the demilitarized Austrian (and German) post-war masculinity.[26] The historical turning point between war/front/captivity and post-war/home/family led to a collective breakdown of the male identity of former *Wehrmacht* soldiers and necessitated a biographical reorientation – a process that was closely linked to the adaptation of a new or modified concept of masculinity.

The Post-War Reconstruction of Male Identity

For hundreds of thousands of returning Austrian soldiers at the beginning of the Second Republic it was necessary, after the traumatic war and experiences of captivity, to find back into a "normal" life and to re-establish a place within the fast-changing post-war society. In the concrete case of Albert B., the homecoming turned out to be a happy family reunion, which marked for him the beginning of a new chapter in his life:

> *"We were so happy, though. I can't find words to describe it. It, It, it gave us the basis to stay together for sixty years. Anyway, it was so wonderful. Certainly, we had to get to know each other. This should not be forgotten. Indeed, we didn't know each other. We knew each other through letters; we knew each other through writing letters. Therein we said everything; what we wanted to be and what we wanted to do, right? But how and what one or the other one wanted, we didn't know at all. We also had to become accustomed to each other. My wife was very proud of her small hood, yes? And she was so busy with the child and later with the children, yes? When the second one was there, when the second child, it was here in this small house where we, where she brought it into the world, and I was present, right? I was present at the birth, right? And she held my hands and, as often happens, she bit my hand. Of course, when it hurt, right? (very emotional) And I was present, right? And then I saw it, how my child came into the world. Yes, and then when it was over after three years, she said: 'You are a man; you have to be able to build a house.' I said: 'I'm a Taschelpicker, I'm a leather worker, I can't...' 'Yes, you have to be able to build the house. Everybody is building a house.' Well, all right, I got started."*

---

[26] See also Christoph Kühberger, Gescheiterte Männer? Über den Bruch der idealtypischen nationalsozialistischen Männlichkeit unter der amerikanischen Besatzung, in: Stefan Zahlmann – Sylka Scholz (Eds.), Scheitern und Biografie. Die andere Seite moderner Lebensgeschichten, Gießen 2005, 191–206.

In the above-quoted very dense interview extract, Albert B. combines several elements, which are to some extent far apart in time, shedding light on the reconstruction of his male identity after his coming home. At the beginning, the narrator describes typical experiences of "wartime marriages": Due to the absence of men, most of the couples who had married during the war were not able to start a regular family life, but they first had to search for a new basis for their relationship after the reunion. What is remarkable here is that Albert B. associates his new role as a husband directly with his fatherhood and with his feeling of becoming a father for the second time. Having got to know his firstborn daughter not until his return from Soviet war captivity, his life took on greater importance after the birth of his second child about a year after his coming home (as expressed by him in a very emotional narrative). In the following reconstructed dialogue – one of the few passages of the interview in which masculinity is addressed directly – Albert B. is confronted with the desire of his wife Trude, who is appealing to his "masculine" abilities, for a new home. The house, which was built by their own hands during several years of work, is given much space in the couple's account on the post-war era and can be seen in both the history of the family and that of the Second Republic in general as a factual metaphor for the socio-economic consolidation and the reconstruction of the order of sexes after World War II, with men as the builder and women responsible for reproductive work.[27]

Overall, the early period of the relationship between Albert and Trude B. after their reunion was – without being able to go into details here – characterized by the negotiation of the role allocation within the family. After his homecoming in autumn 1947, Albert B. met a strengthened and independent woman, who, as Trude B. points out in the interview, felt that her role should not only be confined to "the kitchen and children". On the long run, their shared life history was characterized by the shifting of matrimonial

[27] The metaphor of house building was also used by Federal President Körner in 1955, on the occassion of the tenth anniversary of the Second Republic, as a symbol of the post-fascist reconstruction consensus; "The house of the new Austria was built during ten years of hard, self-sacrificing, collectice work. (...). In spite of some differences in opinion, we, again and again, managed to agree on the construction plan, for building was more important than disputing."; quoted in: Wolfgang Kos, Eigenheim Österreich. Zu Politik, Kultur und Alltag nach 1945 (2nd Ed.), Vienna 1995, 152. Until today, in the Austrian post-war society the single-family house represents, according to Ernst Hanisch, "one of the greatest construction works of the Republic with regard to its civil society as well as the values of the small family with its traditional gender roles."; Ernst Hanisch, Männlichkeiten. Eine andere Geschichte des 20. Jahrhunderts, Wien/Köln/Weimar 2005, 104.

power relations, which resulted – after "some serious conversations" – in the final re-establishment of Albert B. as head of the family and the retreat of his wife to the "female sphere" of household and education.

The biographies of veterans in my interview sample clearly emphasize the relevance of such a re-familialized concept of masculinity, which is linked to matrimony and fatherhood, for the re-masculinization of former *Wehrmacht* soldiers, even though not all men were able to fulfill their roles as husbands and fathers. In contrast to those men who had married before or during the war, for many of the solitary and often younger veterans the starting of a family was a major concern after the "lost years". The "golden age of the family" in the years between 1955 and 1965 cannot hide the fact, however, that – to a large part – families still had to cope with the consequences of the war: On the one hand, experiences of war were under a taboo in many families, on the other hand, male hegemony over women and children could not be enforced to the same extent as it had been possible before the war. In this context, scholars refer to the "facade-families" of the 1950s and 1960s, whose intra-familial tensions at the level of gender were in sharp contrast to the "sacred" ideal of the family that was propagated.[28]

Whereas war and captivity, as the fate of a whole generation, and homecoming, as the outstanding event in individual biographies, provided a broader framework for narration, it was much harder for veterans to verbalize their experiences of what Vera Neumann termed the "privatization of the consequences of the war"[29] and the process of social reintegration.[30] A major characteristic of (life-historical) memories of the early post-war years is a particular focus on the professional biography, which is marked, as Siegfried Mattl has argued for the later 1940s and, in particular, for the 1950s, by the "heroization of everyday life" and a "fetishization" of work and production. According to contemporary clinical psychiatry, those veterans whose male identities were most strongly affected were the ones who aspired to become "men of action" in the upcoming "economic miracle" in order to compensate their experiences of degradation resulting from the loss of the war.[31] It is telling that in most of the life histories under con-

---

[28] Ingrid Bauer, Frauen, Männer, Beziehungen. Sozialgeschichte der Geschlechterverhältnisse in der Zweiten Republik, in: Johann Burger – Elisabeth Morawek (Eds.), 1945–1955. Entwicklungslinien der Zweiten Republik, Wien 1995, 107.

[29] Vera Neumann, Nicht der Rede wert. Die Privatisierung der Kriegsfolgen in der frühen Bundesrepublik. Lebensgeschichtliche Erinnerungen, Münster 1999.

[30] See similar results in: Kerschbaumer, Täteranteile, 372f.

[31] Siegfried Mattl, „Aufbau“ – eine männliche Chiffre der Nachkriegszeit, in: Bandhauer-Schöffmann – Hornung, Wiederaufbau, 16, 19.

sideration the narrative of homecoming is immediately followed by the supra-segment "return to employment". This is also true for Albert B., who was able to take up employment as early as a few days after his coming home:

> *"Of course, I was very, very happy, but very weak. Still very weak. Nonetheless, I had to go to diverse administrative offices. I didn't look good. My face was covered with boils. I had barber's itch. It was even wet. It looked terrible. And my wife didn't care about it; she was nevertheless completely... Yes, she was glad that I was there. The first days were very happy, until we found to each other again. Until we were completely happy again. Until the fear, the great fear that was still inside me was gone, right? More or less vanished. But I realized that I had to do something! Certainly, we had nothing, right? My wife had received a widow's pension so far, because I was counted as dead. And then the widow's pension was, certainly, paid out once again, and then there was nothing more. Yes, I had to work. I had to look for a job. That was clear to me. I could have had four weeks of vacation; I refused. After fourteen days, I had a long list of potential jobs; I chose the nearest one, which was in the 10th district. A factory. There was a job vacancy. I went there. That was the nearest place. And there I started to work. On 26 September I had come home and on 4 or 5 March, around that time, I already worked as a journeyman, because before I had only been a learned apprentice having passed journeyman's examination, nothing else."*

In the first part, Albert B. describes his poor physical and mental condition after his return home and refers to "the great fear" by which the first days in the bosom of his family were overshadowed. But, as he argues, he could not afford weakness in the face of losing the family's only source of income, the widow's pension of his wife, and the dire financial situation made it necessary for him to take the initiative ("But I realized that I had to do something!"). Without taking the four weeks of vacation to which he would have been entitled as a veteran, Albert B. immediately sought employment and soon found work as a journeyman in a factory, albeit only because of his state as a former prisoner of war, as he later explains. He was employed by that company, which was specialised in the production of bags, for eleven years, until he became factory manager at another leather manufacturing company, whose success was significantly influenced by his innovative product developments. Experiences of professional advancement after the war are a characteristic of the narrated life stories of Albert B. and other men interviewed about the post-war period who moved up from virtually nothing, allowing to comprehend Austria's economic recovery after World War II also in terms of individual (professional) biographies.

The identity-establishing factor of work becomes even more obvious in the example of Erwin H., who was completely disappointed by his return to Austria. After giving a short account of how he met his later wife after the war, he soon starts to recapitulate his employment career in his narrative, from which I would like to quote an extract:

> *"I married my wife in 1946, and now I have been married to her for fifty-seven years. We have five children together, five girls, nine grandchildren, and two great-grandchildren. Well, a respectable family. (...) In the meantime, I joined the state vocational school and continued my studies, my ongoing, again. (...) Well, I was matriculated in 1947. I graduated from there with distinction. My further education was, well, really handicapped by my marriage and subsequently also by the second child, who came into the world in 1950. However, my boss, the architect (anonymized), for whom I had worked since 1946, assured me I could, parallel to my employment, begin my studies. (...) At this time I was already paid a decent hourly wage. I have just looked it up; it was 1.90 schillings per hour. Well, my earning was comparable to a middle-ranking state official, and I saw no reason to deepen my knowledge, for it seemed impossible to me to work, with or without degree, as an architect (...) Thus, I was a workhorse. I worked, parallel to my studies, on Saturdays, when there were only four hours. So I went to work early. Otherwise, I did all the office work after school. (...) Was sitting there the whole night at the drawing board and was plotting."*

At the beginning of this interview extract, Erwin H. builds a bridge between the year 1946 and the present, making himself out as a respectable family man with a considerable number of descendants. The close biographical relation of family and employment is, again, evident in the narration: Not without pride, the narrator refers to the resumption of his education, which had been interrupted by the war, and his graduation in 1947. In the following segment, he explains why he then chose not to study architecture, arguing that his salary was already comfortable at that time, thus relativizing the potential "stigma" of not having a university degree. Consequently, Erwin H.'s narrative is characterized by a fetishization of his work performance: he portrays himself as a "workhorse", giving an account of how he was able to cope with a considerable number of working hours, even though he was a family man and had to shoulder the double burden of work and school.

Even though the lives of the men in my interview sample were quite different from one another, in all post-war biographies under consideration certain concepts of masculinity are manifested that can be related to traditional patterns of male identity such as dominance, strength, rationality, authority, or productivity. Certainly, after 1945 the framework for the construction of masculinity changed from a military to a civilian one: soldierly values lost their importance for the production of gender, and with the return of veterans from war, the biographical construction of masculinity shifted to the private sphere, particularly to the roles of husband, father, and male breadwinner, or, more general, to the place of employment. Thus, in the short term, World War II and its effects seemed to have shaken the foundations of hegemonic bourgeois masculinity only to a limited extent. But yet, as a consequence of the loss of respect for the military, the spaces changed where masculinity could be acquired and the hegemonic model of masculinity, though not undisputed any longer, could exercise its power on women and, in particular, on the juvenile masculinities of the following generation.

Final Remarks

Even though the reconstruction of individual cases can reflect the heterogeneity of male experiences at the end of World War II only to a certain extent, and gender historians recently began to focus on longer-term developments of concepts of masculinity,[32] my biographical analyses illustrate the historical and cultural variability of masculinity, experiencing a change from the ultra-masculine, hard-bodied ideal of the Nazi front-line soldier to a "civilized" or demilitarized model of masculinity after the loss of the war. The transformation from soldier to civilian (husband) in Austria as well as in Germany in the second half of the 1940s was accompanied by the restoration of patriarchal order in the reunited families.[33] In this context, Pierre Bourdieu referred to the "inertia of the [sexual] habitus", which, even in times of upheaval, supports conservative gender ideologies and strengthens gender asymmetries.[34] The gender backlash after the social turmoil caused

---

[32] For the last century, see Martin Lengwiler, In kleinen Schritten: Der Wandel von Männlichkeiten im 20. Jahrhundert, in: L'Homme. Zeitschrift für Feministische Geschichtswissenschaft 19/2, Köln/Weimar 2008, 75–94.

[33] Reinhard Sieder, Sozialgeschichte der Familie, Frankfurt am Main 1987, 241.

[34] Pierre Bourdieu, Die männliche Herrschaft, in: Irene Dölling – Beate Krais (Eds.), Ein alltägliches Spiel. Geschlechterkonstruktionen in der sozialen Praxis, Frankfurt am Main 1997, 171; see also Inge Stephan, Im toten Winkel. Die Neuentdeckung des „ersten Geschlechts" durch men's studies und Männlichkeitsforschung, in: Claudia Benthien – idem (Eds.), Männlichkeit als Maskerade. Kulturelle Inszenierungen vom Mittelalter bis zur Gegenwart, Köln/Weimar/Wien 2003, 20f.

by World War II[35] reproduced traditional family structures and institutionalized the heterosexual nuclear family.[36] The displacement of the social effects of war and National Socialism into the private sphere of the family is remarkable in so far as in the post-war period the family, according to Robert Moeller, constituted "the only community to which Germans [and Austrians] could be committed without any pressure of justification".[37] Thus, there is some evidence that after 1945 the hegemonic model of masculinity in Austria and (West) Germany as well as in other countries marked by fascism was freed from its hyper-militaristic core and integrated into a bourgeois post-war concept that was much more adjusted to the emerging Western consumer society.[38]

When looked at from the perspective of biography, the (allegedly) apolitical concept of family father and male breadwinner separated the former *Wehrmacht* soldiers from their military past under National Socialism and provided, after the often devastating experiences of war and homecoming, the framework for a reconstruction of masculinity in which traditional male norms and values could be re-established on the basis of a civilian masculinity. Wolfgang Schmale argues that the concept of hegemonic masculinity, which is associated with the emergence of bourgeois society and the introduction of compulsory military service in the nineteenth century, did not collapse until the movement of 1968, creating the space for new alternatives that were, especially among the youth movements, drifting farther and farther away from

---

[35] The majority of gender historians believe that World War II and its consequences caused over a longer period of time – with the generation of the "war children" – a change in gender relations; see Irene Bandhauer-Schöffmann, Hat der Zweite Weltkrieg die Geschlechterverhältnisse verändert? Ein Vergleich zwischen Österreich und Slowenien, in: Tina Bahovec (Ed.), frauen.männer, Klagenfurt 2007, 396f.

[36] See Maria Mesner, Die Neugestaltung des Ehe- und Familienrechts. Re-Definitionspotentiale im Geschlechterverhältnis der Aufbau-Zeit, in: zeitgeschichte 24, 5/6, Innsbruck 1997, 186–210; Sieglinde Rosenberger, Frauenpolitik: Moderne zwischen Megatrends und Backlashes, in: Österreichische Zeitschrift für Politikwissenschaften 24/1, Wien 1995, 39f.

[37] Robert G. Moeller, Heimkehr ins Vaterland: Die Remaskulinisierung Westdeutschlands in den fünfziger Jahren, in: Militärgeschichtliche Zeitschrift 60/2, München 2001, 415.

[38] See Wolfgang Schmale, Geschichte der Männlichkeit in Europa (1450–2000), Wien/Köln/Weimar, 236f. For Germany, see also: Frank Biess, Männer des Wiederaufbaus – Wiederaufbau der Männer. Kriegsheimkehrer in Ost- und Westdeutschland, 1945–1955, in: Karen Hagemann – Stefanie Schüler-Springorum (Eds.), Heimat – Front. Militär und Geschlechterverhältnisse im Zeitalter der Weltkriege, Frankfurt am Main 2002, 356–361.

militarism.[39] However, for many of the surviving members of the *Wehrmacht* generation the experiences of World War II have remained an integral part of their male identity, as is evident from the fierce reactions of Austrian and German war veterans to the *Wehrmacht* exhibition (*Wehrmachtsausstellung*) in the mid-1990s, which not only deconstructed the myth of the "apolitical soldier", but also questioned the biographical self-perception of the military past of a whole generation.

---

39 Schmale, Geschichte, 242f.

Maximilian Graf
(University of Vienna)

Austria and the German Democratic Republic 1949–1972 Diplomatic and Political Contacts in the Period of Non-recognition

Introduction

Even twenty years after the revolutions of 1989, the fall of the Berlin Wall and the subsequent process of German reunification, completed on 3 October 1990, very little research has been done on the relations between Austria and the German Democratic Republic (hereafter GDR). Above all, there is a lack of studies based on archival sources.[1] Christoph Boyer's articles on economic relations[2] as well as the papers on the Austrian position towards the revolution of 1989 in the GDR and the reunification

---

1 Based on sources from the Stiftung Bruno Kreisky Archiv, Vienna: Stefan Gron, "Partner DDR"? Zur Entwicklung der bilateralen Beziehungen zwischen Österreich und der DDR, MA thesis, Vienna 2005; Selected works published before 1989: Alfred Ableitinger, Österreichisch-Deutsche Nachkriegsbeziehungen seit 1945, in: Robert A. Kann - Friedrich E. Prinz (Eds.), Deutschland und Österreich. Ein bilaterales Geschichtsbuch, Wien/München 1980, 199–219; Hans-Jürgen Fink, Österreich, in: Hans-Adolf Jacobsen - Gert Leptin - Ulrich Scheuner - Eberhard Schulz (Eds.), Drei Jahrezehnte Außenpolitik der DDR. Bestimmungsfaktoren, Instrumente, Aktionsfelder, München/Wien 1979, 526–529; Andrea Rögner-Francke, Die Beziehungen zwischen der DDR und Österreich, in: Hans-Joachim Veen - Peter R. Weilmann (Eds.), Die Westpolitik der DDR. Beziehungen der DDR zu ausgewählten westlichen Industriestaaten in den 70er und 80er Jahren, Melle 1989, 133–189; Engelbert Washietl, Österreich und die Deutschen, Wien 1987.

2 On economic relations see Christoph Boyer, Economic relations between Austria an the Soviet zone of occupation of Germany/German Democratic Republic, 1945–1973, in: Gertrude Enderle-Burcel - Piotr Franaszek - Dieter Stiefel - Alice Teichova (Eds.), Gaps in the Iron Curtain. Economic relations between neutral and socialist countries in Cold War Europe, Kraków 2009. and the papers by Christoph Boyer, Maren Seliger and Roman Stolzlechner in: Gertrude Enderle-Burcel - Dieter Stiefel - Alice Teichova (Eds.), „Zarte Bande. Österreich und die europäischen planwirtschaftlichen Länder - „Delicate Relationships". Austria and Europe's Planned Economies (=Mitteilungen des Österreichischen Staatsarchivs, Sonderband 9), Wien 2006; on relations between the Communist Party of Austria (KPÖ) and the Socialist Unity Party of Germany (SED) see Josef Ehmer, KPÖ und SED. Ein ambivalentes Verhältnis, in: Wolfgang Neugebauer (Ed.), Von der Utopie zum Terror. Stalinismus-Analysen, Wien 1994, 171–181.

of Germany by Michael Gehler[3] are surely the most notable exceptions.

This paper, based on the latest available archival documents from the Foreign Ministries of both Austria and the GDR, as well as from the East German Socialist Unity Party (hereafter SED) archives, will focus on diplomatic and political contacts in the period of non-recognition, from 1949 to 1972. Almost no research has been done on this topic.

Only on the Austrian interpretation of the work of the Austrian Delegation in West Berlin, which played an important role in contacts in the period of non-recognition, has some research based on Austrian sources already been done. The Austrian delegation in Berlin served a diplomatic purpose, being responsible for Austrians living in Berlin and in East Germany.[4] Finally, Matthias Pape wrote a short summary of the diplomatic contacts between Austria and the GDR in Moscow, based primarily on the documents found in the estate of the former Austrian Political Representative and Ambassador in Moscow Norbert Bischoff.[5]

In considering relations between Austria and the GDR from 1949 to 1972, one must of course keep in mind the political situation of both countries after 1945/49 and 1955 in the international context of the Cold War and especially, the relationship of both countries to the Soviet Union (hereafter USSR) and the Federal Republic of Germany (hereafter FRG).

---

[3] On Austian – (East) German relations in 1989/90 see Michael Gehler, Österreich, die DDR und die Einheit Deutschlands 1989/1990, in: Zeitschrift für Geschichtswissenschaft 57/5, Berlin 2009, 427–452 and Idem, Eine Außenpolitik der Anpassung an veränderte Verhältnisse: Österreich und die Vereinigung Bundesrepublik Deutschland–DDR 1989/90, in: Idem – Ingrid Böhler (Ed.), Verschiedene europäische Wege im Vergleich. Österreich und die Bundesrepublik Deutschland 1945/49 bis zur Gegenwart. Festschrift für Rolf Steiniger zum 65. Geburtstag, Innsbruck/Wien/Bozen 2007, 493–530.

[4] Gron, "Partner DDR"?, 36–39; Klaus Fiesinger, Ballhausplatzdiplomatie 1945–1949: Reetablierung der Nachbarschaftsbeziehungen und Reorganisation des Auswärtigen Dienstes als Formen außenpolitischer Reemanzipation Österreichs, München 1993, 364–368; Hans J. Thalberg, Von der Kunst, Österreicher zu sein. Erinnerungen und Tagebuchnotizen, Wien/Köln/Graz 1984, 231–261; Rudolf Agstner, 130 Jahre Österreichische Botschaft Berlin. Von der Moltkestraße zur Stauffenbergstraße. Handbuch der Vertretungsbehörden von Österreich (–Ungarn) in Deutschland seit 1720, Berlin/Wien 2003, 192–199.

[5] Matthias Pape, Ungleiche Brüder. Österreich und Deutschland 1945–1965, Köln/Weimar/Wien 2000, 253–260.

Preliminary Remarks

Annotations on Austrian and East German Foreign Policy after 1945/49

After World War II, Austria and Germany came under quadripartite Allied control and occupation. But soon their fate differed. While the Allies of the anti-Hitler coalition decided to re-establish Austria as a sovereign state, Germany gravitated towards division thanks to the circumstances of the Cold War.[6]

Despite Allied control and occupation Austria succeeded in re-establishing its own foreign policy relatively soon.[7] Due to the second Allied Control Agreement, which came into effect in 1946, Austria was allowed only to maintain diplomatic relations with United Nations member states. Therefore it was impossible to establish official relations between Austria and the GDR until the signing of the Austrian State Treaty in May 1955, which finally marked the complete restoration of Austrian sovereignty.[8]

On the other hand, the GDR was founded on 7 October 1949, and only on 25 March 1954 would it receive "expanded sovereign rights", then renewed by the treaty on friendship and cooperation between the GDR and the USSR on 20 September 1955. Nevertheless, the GDR never became completely independent from the USSR.[9]

Actually, the so called "Basic Law", the provisional constitution and founding document of the FRG and promulgated on 23 May 1949, made clear that the government of the FRG saw itself as the sole legitimate representation of the German people, even though it also was not sovereign or independent of Allied control. This position was confirmed by the West German Chancellor Konrad Adenauer after the foundation of the GDR. Following the foundation of the GDR, the FRG started a successful campaign to contain the GDR. Until 1955, no non-communist state had officially rec-

---

6 Christoph Kleßmann, Die doppelte Staatsgründung. Deutsche Geschichte 1945–1955, Bonn 1986; For the most recent overview on the period 1945 to 1949 see: Hans-Peter Schwarz: The division of Germany 1945–1949, in: Melvyn P. Leffler – Odd Arne Westad (Eds.), The Cambridge History of the Cold War, vol. 1: Origins, Cambridge 2010, 133–153.

7 For an overview on Austria's first steps towards its own Foreign policy see Fiesinger, Ballhausplatzdiplomatie.

8 Gerald Stourzh, Um Einheit und Freiheit. Staatsvertrag, Neutralität und das Ende der Ost-West-Besetzung Österreichs 1945–1955, Wien/Köln/Graz 2005, 34–57.

9 On the first years of East German Foreign Policy see Ingrid Muth, Die DDR-Außenpolitik 1949–1972. Inhalte, Strukturen, Mechanismen, Berlin 2001. The most recent study on East German Foreign Policy: Hermann Wentker, Außenpolitik in engen Grenzen. Die DDR im internationalen System 1949–1989, München 2007.

ognized the GDR, and the FRG had abstained from diplomatic relations with those Communist states maintaining diplomatic relations with the GDR. Only after Adenauer's visit to Moscow, in September 1955, did diplomatic relations between the FRG and the USSR begin. Moscow thus became the first capital to host an East and a West German Ambassador.

This shift in West Germany policy needed to be justified and led to the formulation of the "Hallstein Doctrine". At the end of 1955, the diplomatic representatives accredited in the FRG were informed in the course of an "Ambassadors conference" about the new situation – that Moscow would be an exception also in the future. The "Hallstein Doctrine" was therefore often interpreted as a strict rule by which the FRG would abort diplomatic relations with any state recognizing the GDR or simply moving close to recognition. But the "Hallstein Doctrine" turned out to be no doctrine at all. Often it seemed to be no more than an accumulation of emergency measures. Nevertheless, especially the West (including Austria) supported the FRG's policy of non-recognition. In the so called "Third World", the FRG was successful in containing the GDR as long as was desired, in most cases by making use of its economic leverage.[10]

Official relations between Austria and the GDR 1949–1972

In looking at this political situation, it was impossible to establish bilateral relations between Austria and the GDR until the signing of the Austria State Treaty in May 1955. Nevertheless, some economic ties developed in the first half of the 1950s. Until 1953, trade between the two countries was settled by means of compensation, running more or less on a private level. The Administration of Soviet Assets in Austria (USIA) was another important trading partner. In December 1953, the Austrian Federal Chamber of Commerce (*Bundeskammer der gewerblichen Wirtschaft*) and the GDR Chamber of Foreign Trade (*Kammer für Außenhandel der DDR*) signed a first agreement on an annual trade volume[11] In October 1954, the GDR Chamber of Foreign Trade opened a trading mission (*Vertretung der Kammer für Außenhandel der DDR*) in Vienna, which basically served as a quasi-Embassy. Similar East German

---

[10] On the Hallstein Doctrine see: William Glenn Gray, Germany's Cold War. The Global Campaign to Isolate East Germany, 1949–1969, Chapel Hill 2003 and Werner Kilian, Die Hallstein-Doktrin. Der Diplomatische Krieg zwischen der BRD und der DDR 1955–1973. Aus den Akten der beiden deutschen Außenministerien, Berlin 2001.

[11] Christoph Boyer, Economic relations between Austria an the Soviet zone of occupation of Germany/German Democratic Republic, 1945–1973, in: Gertrude Enderle-Burcel – Piotr Franaszek – Dieter Stiefel – Alice Teichova (Eds.), Gaps in the Iron Curtain. Economic relations between neutral and socialist countries in Cold War Europe, Kraków 2009, 192–194.

quasi-representations had been set up in many other countries without official diplomatic ties to the GDR during the 1950s. Despite persistent East German efforts, Austria refused to set up an equivalent mission in East Berlin until 1970. Only in that same year did the East German mission receive the right to issue visas. Likewise, Austria did not sign an official inter-governmental treaty on trade until the diplomatic recognition of the GDR – on 21 December 1972 – the day the German-German Basic Treaty was signed. Economic relations remained on the level of agreements between the chambers, and the trade volume remained negligible.[12]

Despite its neutral status, Austria followed the West German policy of non-recognition towards the GDR. The Austrian position was determined by its western orientation and the much more important bilateral and economic ties with the FRG. Although in the case of the GDR, Austria played its oft-practised role as diplomatic "ice breaker" for Socialist countries only after the diplomatic recognition,[13] it otherwise sometimes pushed the limits of the West German "Hallstein Doctrine". For example, the Foreign Ministry of the FRG never really trusted the Austrian laissez faire attitude towards the East German trade mission in Vienna. When Austria allowed the GDR to open a travelling office (*Verkehrsvertretung*) in Vienna in 1960, Bonn protested harshly.[14] The same reaction occurred – with far more international attention – in 1963, when Austrian Airlines and Interflug (an East German state-owned airline) organized a regular direct flight between East Berlin and Vienna. Giving in to protests by the Western Allies (against a breach in their monopoly on aviation with West Berlin) and the FRG, Austrian authorities quickly put an end to what became known as the "Interflug affair" by quickly stopping those direct flights. Austrian Airlines had to recognize that this kind of cooperation between East and West

---

12 Stefan Gron, "Partner DDR"?, 20–26.

13 Wolfgang Mueller, Peaceful Coexistence, Neutrality, and Bilateral Relations across the Iron Curtain: Introduction in: Arnold Suppan – Wolfgang Mueller (Eds.), Peaceful Coexistence or Iron Curtain? Austria, Neutrality, and Eastern Europe in the Cold War and Détente, 1955–1989, Vienna 2009, 7–29, 19–20, 27; On Austria's role as "ice breaker" in the case of the GDR see also Andrea Rögner-Francke, Beziehungen, 133–189, 147.

14 Aktenvermerk, Gegenstand: Verkehrsvertretung der DDR in Wien, Wien 1960 August 4, Österreichisches Staatsarchiv (hereafter ÖStA), Vienna, Archiv der Republik (herafter AdR), Bundesministerium für Auswärtige Angelegenheiten (hereafter BMfAA), Wpol 1960, Fremdenverkehr Deutschland-Ost, GZ. 146.778-Wpol/60, Zl. 146.207-Wpol/60.

had touched upon one of the most delicate problems of the Cold War – the Berlin question.[15]

After the Second Berlin Crisis and the Cuban Missile Crisis – the stormy beginning of the 1960s – a period of détente gradually emerged in East–West relations. These changes made the FRG's "*Neue Ostpolitik*" possible, which led to an improvement in German–German understanding, and finally to widespread international recognition of the GDR. The history of aviation connections between Austria and the GDR gives quite a symbolic picture of emerging détente in that period of Cold War history. What seemed impossible in 1963 had already become reality in 1970. A regular direct flight was established and aviation was extended in April 1972, even before the diplomatic recognition of the GDR.[16] However, an inter-governmental aviation treaty (for many reasons) was not signed until 1980.[17]

First "diplomatic contacts" after the foundation of the GDR (1949–1955)

Soon after the foundation of the GDR, first contacts between Austria and the GDR developed. These contacts continued to exist after the signing of the Austrian State Treaty and the declaration of permanent neutrality in 1955. When the GDR came into existence, the Austrian Delegation in West Berlin maintained ties with the Soviets in East Berlin, and initiated unofficial contacts with the newly established Foreign Ministry of the GDR (hereaf-

---

15 Stefan Gron, "Partner DDR"?, 26–30. For a summary based on West German sources see: Rolf Pfeiffer, Eine schwierige und konfliktreiche Nachbarschaft – Österreich und das Deutschland Adenauers 1953–1963, Münster/Hamburg/London 2003, 187–192.

16 Summary on the aviation links between Austria and the GDR dated 21 December 1976, Bundesarchiv -Abteilung DDR (BArch-DDR), Berlin, DM 1/16981. For a short summary see Engelbert Washietl, Österreich und die Deutschen, 140, 145–146.

17 Governmental Treaty on Aviation between Austria and the GDR signed on 11 November 1980, BArch-DDR, DM 1/16981. The main reason for the delay was "the Austrian demand to be granted fly-over rights for Austrian Airlines in the flight corridor via Prague to Berlin-Tegel (West), a demand that was left long unanswered by the GDR. Actually, it was not in the competence of the GDR to grant fly-over rights to Berlin (West) since it had no control over air traffic corridors – this was a prerogative of the USSR – and a favorable decision for Austria would have been a precedent case. Thus, the 1980 air traffic agreement only served to elevate the existing arrangement [...] to the state level." Friedrich Bauer, Austria and the German Democratic Republic, 1972–1990, in: Arnold Suppan – Wolfgang Mueller (Eds.), Peaceful Coexistence or Iron Curtain? Austria, Neutrality, and Eastern Europe in the Cold War and Détente, 1955–1989, Vienna 2009, 412–434, 414.

ter MfAA). Naturally, contacts between the East German representatives and the Austrian representatives in Moscow emerged. Contacts to the GDR were about to follow in several other Socialist countries in Europe.

Since it is impossible to cover all kinds of contacts in this short space, I am going to focus on those contacts in Berlin and Moscow; most of them concerned consular and humanitarian affairs, which, together with East German attempts to gain diplomatic recognition, were important matters of negotiation between Austria and the GDR. The archival record on consular and humanitarian affairs is often incomplete. But it is possible to draw a fairly accurate picture.

The Austrian Delegation in West Berlin

As early as August 1945, Austria was represented in Berlin by an "Austrian Bureau". Since September 1945 the bureau was headed by Wilhelm Buchare, an Austrian who had lived in Berlin since 1927 and acted as the "Austrian Repatriation Committee for Germany in Berlin". Sometime in 1946, it seems that the official name changed from "bureau" to "delegation". In 1946 the delegation moved from Berlin-Zehlendorf to Berlin-Dahlem. Until 1947, the repatriation committee acted more or less on its own initiative. It organized special trains for Austrian refugees, prisoners of war (hereafter POWs) and others to return to Austria.[18]

On 16 May 1947, the Austrian Minister of the Interior Oskar Helmer appointed Alexis Altschiller as Commissioner for Repatriation (*Beauftragter für Repatriierungsangelegenheiten*) in the American Sector of Berlin.[19] Nevertheless, the delegation was not only responsible for Austrians who lived in the American sector. For whatever reason, Austria was not able to set up a consulate in the Soviet Zone of Occupation in Germany (SBZ). The Austrian Delegation in West Berlin thus became the default address for Austrians living in the SBZ as well. In 1949, the number of Austrians living in the SBZ and in the Soviet sector of Berlin was about 20,000.[20]

From 24 June 1948 to 12 May 1949, the Soviets blocked the railway- and road-access of the Western Allies to their sectors in Berlin. The Western Allies responded by organizing an airlift in order to supply their half of the city, at least until Stalin decided to

[18] Vgl. Fiesinger, Ballhausplatzdiplomatie, 364–365.

[19] Vgl. Agstner, 130 Jahre, 192.

[20] Vgl. Fiesinger, Ballhausplatzdiplomatie, 364.

end the blockade.[21] Naturally, the Berlin Blockade complicated the work of the Austrian delegation. In February 1949, Altschiller informed the Federal Chancellery, Foreign Affairs (hereafter BKA, AA) that since the beginning of the Berlin Blockade in the spring of 1948, repatriation transports by train were no longer possible. Only a certain number of repatriates had been able to get out by plane.[22] Another report from April 1949 refers to 60 to 80 persons approximately every six weeks being able to fly to Lübeck on the basis of an arrangement with the British occupation forces. The report further states that this was the only way to bring Austrian citizens out of the "Eastern Zone".[23] Both reports draw a rather dark picture of the living conditions of Austrians in the Eastern part of Germany. Besides the financial burdens resulting from the payments for transportation of the repatriates by plane, problems pertaining to transportation of their belongings and problems with the protection of Austrian assets in the SBZ were reported.

After the foundation of the GDR on 7 October 1949, the Austrian Delegation reported on the new political situation in East Germany.[24] The provisional East German People's Chamber even invited the delegation to attend its sessions on 11–12 October. After consultations with the Americans, however, Altschiller and his office manager, Gustav J. Seewald, abstained from a visit because there was no special order from the Austrian government in this respect.[25]

At the end of November 1949, the MfAA informed its State Secretary, Anton Ackermann, about the first contacts with Seewald. The documentation indicates that the talks had been strictly private and unofficial. In the question of repatriation, the GDR had signalled that problems could be solved on the basis of reciprocity.

---

[21] On the Berlin Blockade see: Helmut Trotnow – Bernd von Kostka, Die Berliner Luftbrücke. Ereignis und Erinnerung, Berlin 2010 and Volker Koop, Kein Kampf um Berlin. Deutsche Politik zur Zeit der Berlin-Blockade 1948/1949, Bonn 1998; On Allied plans for a similar blockade of Vienna see: Erwin A. Schmidl, „Rosinenbomber" über Wien? Alliierte Pläne zur Luftversorgung Wiens im Falle einer sowjetischen Blockade 1948–1953, in: Idem (Ed.), Österreich im frühen Kalten Krieg 1945–1958. Spione, Partisanen, Kriegspläne, Wien/Köln/Weimar 2000, 171–192 and Richard Hufschmied, Wien im Kalkül der Alliierten (1948–1955). Maßnahmen gegen eine sowjetische Blockade, Wien/Graz 2002.

[22] Altschiller to Secretary General Wildner, Berlin 1949 February 26, ÖStA, AdR, BMfAA, II-pol 1949, Deutschland 6, GZ. 83.020-pol/49, Karton 101.

[23] Vgl. Agstner, 130 Jahre, 193.

[24] Seewald to Secretary General Wildner, Berlin 1949 October 10, ÖStA, AdR, BMfAA, II-pol 1949/Deutschland 3, GZ. 88.220-pol/49, Karton 100. (Many reports followed during the weeks after the foundation of the GDR.)

[25] Seewald to BKA, AA, Berlin 1949 October 18, ÖStA, AdR, AA, II-pol 1949, Deutschland 2, GZ. 88.384-pol/49, Karton 99.

The main problem was that for the GDR, business needed to be run officially, mediated by official contacts with the MfAA. Interestingly, Seewald told one of his interlocutors that the Austrian government was undoubtedly committed to establishing normal diplomatic relations with the GDR. He, nonetheless, highlighted the difficulties caused by the Western Allies, which were – at least at that moment – tying the hands of his government.[26]

In October 1950, the MfAA summarized the activities of the Austrian Delegation. Apart from the list of contacts mentioned above, the MfAA reported on the activities of the Austrian Property Management Ltd. (*Österreichische Liegenschaftsverwaltung GmbH*), which was also located in the residence of the Austrian Delegation. Additionally the Austrian Property Management Ltd. held an Administrative Office–East (*Verwaltungsbüro – Ost*) in the Soviet sector of Berlin. This office contacted the MfAA to find out which documents were needed to reach the release of Austrian properties. The MfAA referred to the normal diplomatic path and no further requests followed.[27] Greta Kuckhoff of the Economic Division at the MfAA (*Hauptabteilung Wirtschaftspolitik im MfAA*) proposed to the Vice Chairman of the Council of Ministers, Walter Ulbricht, that negotiations with non–friendly states should not be held.[28]

The last report of the delegation in the year 1951 clearly shows how the GDR decided to handle the case. East German administrative bodies increasingly insisted on the normal diplomatic channels. Due to the lack of an official link with the MfAA, the Austrian authorities thus began to look for another channel. The solution was a simple one. The Austrian applicants had to hand in notarized credentials (*notariell beglaubigte Vollmachten*), authorizing members of the delegation to apply for and to receive documents in the MfAA. Thus, the representatives acted directly on behalf of individuals and not as representatives of their country. By 1951, the number of Austrians living in the GDR and in East Berlin had diminished to approximately 17,000.[29]

On 1 February 1952, the Austrian Delegation was put under the authority of the BKA, AA.[30] Since November 1952, the delegation was headed by Consul Franz Hoinik.[31] After a period of uncer-

---

26 Memo by Kegel on a visit by Seewald at the MfAA, 1949 November 30, Politisches Archiv des Auswärtigen Amtes (hereafter PA, AA), Berlin, Ministerium für Auswärtige Angelegenheiten der DDR (hereafter MfAA), A 16542, Bl. 171–173.

27 Short summary on the Austrian Delegation, dated October 1950, PA, AA, MfAA, A 15154, Bl. 1–2.

28 Kuckhoff to Ulbricht, Berlin 1950 October 4, BArch, DC/20/3875, Bl. 8–14.

29 Vgl. Agstner, 130 Jahre, 194–196.

30 Vgl. Fiesinger, Ballhausplatzdiplomatie, 368.

31 Vgl. Agstner, 130 Jahre, 196.

tainty with regards to Austrian citizens from the GDR, Hoinik noted in March 1953 that emigration of Austrians citizens was usually permitted within a few months, as long as the formalities were fulfilled. These formalities did not really constitute a problem, but exporting the belongings remained difficult. Temporary departures for visits in Austria were only permitted in rare cases and mostly for members of the so-called technical intelligence, scientists, entrepreneurs or people who were part of political life.[32] In other words: mostly for communists.

Documentation on contacts concerning daily consular work rarely exists or is still not declassified in the Archives, but in my interpretation the continuous existence of those contacts is proven by the following example. In January 1955, Hoinik visited the Soviet Embassy in East Berlin and appears to have asked for a meeting with a leading member of the MfAA, instead of the regular meetings in the Consular Division. He was told to ask the Chief of Protocol in the MfAA Ferdinand Thun, to whom he was already known, for an appointment.[33] On 14 January Hoinik met Thun in the MfAA. He wanted to speak confidentially about questions concerning travel between Austria and the GDR. At the beginning of the negotiations, Hoinik said: "The point of view of the governments is one thing, the necessities of life, another." Further, he said that he probably did not need to explain whether he shares the views of his government on the issue of mutual recognition. In medias res, Hoinik pointed out that an Austrian visa was absolutely necessary for all kinds of travel to Austria. He emphasized that the Austrian handling of GDR passports, against some claims that the recognition of the GDR passport was inadmissible, was very liberal (visas were issued directly into the GDR passport and no provisional travel documents from the Allied Travel Office were needed). Concerning delays in visa affairs, Hoinik stressed that he already had intervened in the "Foreign Ministry". Thun recognized that Hoinik's visit was dealing only with consular matters. He thus organized an appointment in the Consular Division of the MfAA.[34] There are no documents available on these negotiations.

In summarizing the contacts of the Austrian Delegation with the MfAA before the signing of the Austrian State Treaty in 1955, a few

---

32 Amtsvermerk, Gegenstand: Verkehr österreichischer Staatsbürger i. d. DDR mit der österr. Delegation, Wien 1953 May 13, ÖStA, AdR, BMfAA, II-Pol 1953, Deutschland 3, GZ. 320.617-Pol/53, Karton 232.

33 Memo by Thun on a phone call by the head of the Protocol Division of the Embassy of the USSR, Berlin 1955 January 13, PA, AA, MfAA, A 16542, Bl. 209–210.

34 Memo on the visit by Hoinik at the Protocol Division of the MfAA, Berlin 1955 January 14, PA, AA, MfAA, A 16542, Bl. 211–212.

conclusions can be drawn. After the foundation of the GDR in 1949, the delegation continued to serve as the only Austrian address for the Austrians living in the GDR. In making informal contacts with the MfAA, delegation members tried to improve the situation of Austrian citizens. It seems that leaving the GDR permanently was no problem, but that leaving temporarily was only possible for certain people. Efforts concerning Austrian assets seemed to be rare. Even though Austria followed a strict policy of non-recognition, it acted in a very liberal manner concerning the question of visas for East Germans. Some statements of the Austrian representatives even went beyond the official policy of non-recognition. The members of the Delegation tried to improve their contacts with East German officials, who proved helpful in humanitarian affairs.

Contacts in Moscow

Beginning in December 1946, Norbert Bischoff served as Austria's diplomatic representative in Moscow. Until 1953, he was accredited as Political Representative, and afterwards, until 1960, as Ambassador. He was a personal confidant of Federal Chancellor Julius Raab (1953–1961) and an important figure in achieving the Austrian State Treaty. His political reports from Moscow often differed from the reports written by other Austrian representatives accredited in the capitals of the Western Allies or in West Germany. He opposed the single-minded Western orientation of Austria and tried to create understanding for Soviet foreign policy through his reports. However, although his efforts were met with little enthusiasm at the Ballhausplatz, his knowledge and his good relationship with Raab kept him in his position. Nonetheless, Bischoff remains an enigmatic figure. At the end of his diplomatic mission in 1960, he was quite frustrated. Some rumours emerged that Bischoff himself had become a victim of Soviet propaganda.

Of course, his position, which differed from the official policy of the Ballhausplatz, also influenced his approach to the GDR and his contacts with East German representatives. By 1949, the first contacts had developed.[35]

Since the GDR was not recognized by Austria, the East German ambassador did not visit or sent a letter of introduction to the Austrian representation when he started his mission in Moscow. But

---

[35] On Bischoff see Pape, Ungleiche Brüder, 253–260; Viktor Matejka, Anregung ist Alles. Das Buch Nr. 2, Wien 1991, 85, 142; Oliver Rathkolb, Die paradoxe Republik. Österreich 1945–2005, Wien 2005, 177; Günter Bischof, Austria in the First Cold War, 1945–1955. The Leverage of the Weak, Basingstoke 1999, 72, 134, 143, 155; Rudolf Agstner - Gertrude Enderle-Burcel - Michaela Follner (Eds.), Österreichs Spitzendiplomaten zwischen Kaiser und Kreisky. Biographisches Handbuch der Diplomaten des Höheren Auswärtigen Dienstes 1918 bis 1959, Wien 2009, 133–135.

this does not mean that no contacts emerged. Already in December 1949, at a reception held by the Foreign Minister of the USSR in Moscow, Andrei Ia. Vyshinsky, Bischoff met the East German Representative Rudolf Appelt, who immediately introduced him to the East German Foreign Minister, Georg Dertinger. This purely courteous meeting did not touch on political issues. In his report to Vienna, Bischoff pointed out that his "purely private" acquaintance with Appelt could, if necessary, serve as unofficial contact with the East German government.[36] Indeed, several talks with Appelt were about to follow. In March 1950, Appelt informed Bischoff that Dertinger regretted that, for obvious reasons, no detailed talks had been possible in December. Appelt also touched on the economical and cultural developments in the GDR. He especially pointed out the success of the youth movement and the increasing importance of the GDR in comparison to the FRG.[37] In May Bischoff wrote a very similar report about another meeting with Appelt. This time the Austrian representative commented on Appelt's glorifying remarks in a sarcastic way: "Obviously the Ambassador is pleased with himself and the world".[38] Whilst Bischoff's report focused on Appelt's remarks on developments in the GDR, Appelt reported about the same meeting that Bischoff's purpose was to talk about the POW-question, a topic that remained unmentioned in Bischoff's report. According to Appelt's memo, Bischoff informed him about his proposal to approach the Soviet government in favour of Austrian POWs. He consulted Appelt because he was not sure if the number of 5,000 Austrian POWs located in the Soviet Union and given by the Austrian government was accurate. His insecurity resulted from the number of 13,000 German POWs given by the Soviets. In his opinion, the relation between the number of Austrians and the number of Germans was not correct. Appelt – of course – verified the Soviet figures.

Appelt's report continues by mentioning a conversation about the situation in Austria and the GDR. After remarking that Bischoff showed keen interest in the developments in the GDR, Appelt gave an accurate summary about Bischoff's views on Austria. In Bischoff's interpretation, in 1950 there was no prospect of a State Treaty because of the disagreements between the occupation pow-

---

36 Political Representative Bischoff to Foreign Minister Gruber, Moscow 1949 December 28, ÖStA, AdR, BMfAA, II–Pol 1950, Deutschland 2, GZ. 120.333–Pol/50, Zl. 75/P, Karton 134.

37 Political Representative Bischoff to Foreign Minister Gruber, Moscow 1950 March 27, ÖStA, AdR, BMfAA, II–Pol 1950, Deutschland 2, GZ. 123.148–Pol/50, Zl. 36/P, Karton 134.

38 Political Representative Bischoff to Foreign Minister Gruber, Moscow 1950 May 12, ÖStA, AdR, BMfAA, II–Pol 1950, Deutschland 2, GZ. 124.550–Pol/50, Zl. 51/P, Karton 134.

ers. Although there were some problems caused by the existence of four occupation zones in Austria, he described the situation as bearable. But, he also pointed out that the situation was hindering either the formation or increase of an Austrian national consciousness. In Bischoff's opinion, the economic situation was consolidated by the European Recovery Program (hereafter ERP), although the immediate goal of the ERP – the economic independence of the participating countries – was not going to be reached. Bischoff seemed to believe that Austria was not going to be able to stand on its own feet financially after the end of the ERP in 1952, but he was convinced that another more viable program would follow.[39]

In the archival sources from Vienna and Berlin, there are no more documents to be found on relevant diplomatic contacts in Moscow until 1954. But, as the following documented contact concerning humanitarian concerns will show, Austria sought unofficial direct contact to the GDR.

On 11 February 1954, Attaché Gerhard Gmoser of the Austrian Embassy visited the GDR's Embassy. The aim of his visit was to talk about Austrian citizens imprisoned in the GDR. More specifically, Gmoser wished to address the question of 100 to 150 Austrians who had been imprisoned as members of the German Wehrmacht in 1945. In order to fulfil the mandate of his government, he asked to examine the question of release and repatriation of these Austrian citizens by the responsible East German authorities. Gmoser requested that the matter should be seen from the standpoint of humanity. His East German interlocutor Christoph Seitz assured him that he would inform the responsible authorities and promised to report to the Austrian Embassy on the outcome.[40]

Whilst a decision was being made in East Berlin regarding the Austrian request, the Kremlin in March 1954 declared the GDR to be a sovereign state. On this occasion, the head of the Austrian Representation in Bonn, Adrian Rotter, reported on 3 April about forthcoming East German attempts to gain recognition by Western

---

[39] Handwritten memo by Appelt on conversation with Bischoff on 11 May 1950, PA, AA, MfAA, A 12885, Bl. 1–3. The subsequent approach of the Political Representation of the Austrian government in the USSR on 28 July 1950 was adressed to the Deputy Foreign Minister of the USSR Andrei A. Gromyko (Zl. 3753-PrM/1950). A later report by Bischoff to Foreign Minister Gruber, on 15 October 1950 shows that he still disagreed with the Ministry of the Interior over the numbers of Austrian POWs located in the USSR (Zl. 89/P.) Documents will be published in: Julia Köstenberger – Wolfgang Mueller – Aleksandr Tschubarjan (Eds.), Österreichisch-sowjetische Beziehungen. Dokumente. Vienna: ÖAW, to be published 2010.

[40] Memo by Seitz (Embassy Moscow) on a conversation with Gmoser, Moscow 1954 February 11, PA, AA , MfAA, A 205, Bl. 7–8.

countries.[41] Rotter's report was forwarded to Austrian representations in several European capitals. The instruction by the BKA, AA stated that contacts between the GDR and other countries, especially any signs of a forthcoming recognition of the GDR as a sovereign state, should be followed carefully and communicated to Vienna.[42] The numerous reports, which followed in April 1954, assured the BKA, AA that the GDR was not going to be recognized by any Western European country.

At the end of April, the East German government instructed its Embassy in Moscow to inform the Austrian Embassy under what circumstances the government of the GDR was willing to talk about questions concerning the relations between Austria and the GDR.[43] The East Germans proposed that beside the POW–question, many other questions should be negotiated between authorized representatives of the governments of Austria and the GDR in Berlin. Bischoff immediately informed his government and asked for further instructions.[44]

After a few days delay the political division of the BKA, AA dealt with the East German proposal. Thereupon the Ballhausplatz immediately telegraphed Bischoff and stated that the visit of the Ambassador of the GDR, on which Bischoff reported, was very similar to the attempts of the GDR to gain de facto–recognition in many other countries since the Soviets had granted them expanded sovereignty. Vienna thus assumed that negotiations would be important for the GDR as a precursor for de facto–relations. Far-reaching concessions in cases of imprisoned Austrians and in economic matters were expected. It was clearly stated, however, that with respect to the relations with the FRG, even de facto–relations would be impossible at that moment. At the most, the Austrian Delegation in Berlin should be entrusted with specific and limited contacts in urgent cases. This was a strategy which had been pursued for years with varying, mostly limited success. Bischoff was instructed by the BKA, AA to stay receptive in the event of similar

---

[41] Ambassador Rotter to Foreign Minister Figl, Bonn 1954 April 3, ÖStA, AdR, BMfAA, II–Pol 1954, Deutschland 2, GZ. 142.904–Pol/54, Zl. 64–Pol/54, Karton 271. On the GDR's attempts and the FRG's countercampaign see William Glenn Gray, Germany's Cold War, 21–27.

[42] Amtsvermerk, Gegenstand: Frage der Aufnahme dipl. Beziehungen der Weststaaten zu der DDR, Vienna 1954 April 13, ÖStA, AdR, BMfAA, II–Pol 1954, Deutschland 2, GZ. 142.904–Pol/54, Karton 271.

[43] Kluge (MfAA) to Embassy Moscow, Berlin 1954 April 26, PA, AA , MfAA, A 205, Bl. 3.

[44] Ambassador Bischoff to BKA, AA, Moscow 1954 April 30, ÖStA, AdR, BMfAA, II–Pol 1954, Deutschland 2, GZ. 143.435–Pol/54, Karton 271.

cases in the future.[45] Nevertheless, Bischoff kept his direct contacts with Appelt.

After a decision by the West German Federal Administrative Court (*Bundesverwaltungsgericht*) on 30 October 1954, stating that Austrians who became German citizens on 13 March 1938, and who continued living in Germany after 1945 must be regarded as Germans, the East German Chairman of the Council of Ministers, Otto Grotewohl, issued a declaration on 19 November. He stated i. a. that the forced award of German citizenship does not apply to Austrians living in the GDR.[46] This governmental declaration was handed over to Bischoff who answered Appelt on 27 November that he had handed over this "important text" to his government.[47] This correspondence proves that Bischoff had kept his direct contacts with Appelt. The conflict on the question of citizenship stressed the relationship between Austria and the FRG until May 1956.

After the State Treaty negotiations between the Soviets and the Austrian governmental delegation in Moscow in April 1955, some additional reports were sent from Moscow to Berlin. The embassy reported on the reception of the Austrian delegation at the airport, where the GDR representatives were present. Bischoff expressed his thanks for that gesture several times.[48] On 7 May, Bischoff visited the East German Embassy. After conveying wishes for the recovery of the ill Ambassador Appelt (who died later that year), he expressed thanks for an invitation to the GDR's annual festivities. In the same breath, however, he stated that he could not accept the invitation. A short conversation on the Austrian State Treaty and the German question was followed by the East German remark that relations between Austria and the GDR concerning visa-questions should be normalized as a result of the new situation in Austria. Bischoff remained receptive, remarking that he is not informed about details, but he suggested that relations should be organized as they were arranged with the other "people's democracies". The report finally pointed out that Bischoff was driving without a flag on

---

45 Amtsvermerk, Gegenstand: Fühlungnahme des Botschafters der DDR in Moskau, Vienna 1954 May 4, ÖStA, AdR, BMfAA, II–Pol 1954, Deutschland 2, GZ. 143.435–Pol/54, Karton 271.

46 Gron, "Partner DDR"?, 9–11.

47 Gyptner (HA II) to State Secretary Handke, Berlin 1954 December 7, PA, AA, MfAA, A 17492, Bl. 1; Bischoff to Appelt, Moscow 1954 November 27, PA, AA, MfAA, A 17492, Bl. 2.

48 Seitz (Embassy Moscow) to MfAA, Moscow 1955 April 20, PA, AA, MfAA, A 205, Bl. 9–10.

the hood of his car. Without a doubt, he thereby wanted to underline the unofficial character of his visit.[49]

Whilst the relationship between Austria and the FRG was heavily burdened after the signing of the Austrian State Treaty, the GDR welcomed it publicly as a possible example for the solution of the German question. East German politicians and the media did so, not only because of the position of the USSR and the GDR's opposition to the position of the FRG. Another factor may have been that there was little hope to be recognized diplomatically by neutral Austria.[50]

On 19 July, a diplomat of the East German Embassy visited Ambassador Bischoff. In their conversation, the East German informed Bischoff – referring to statements made by the Vice Chairman of the Council of Ministers Walter Ulbricht – about the willingness of the GDR to talk about the normalization of its relations with Austria. Bischoff showed interest and promised to talk to Federal Chancellor Raab on this subject during his upcoming holidays. He justified his planned approach with the argument that a telegram to his government would have had much less of a chance of success. Subsequently, even if Bischoff really tried to influence Raab's position towards the GDR, his efforts remained without success.

During the conversation with the East German representative, Bischoff noted especially the importance of solutions in consular affairs and the elevation of the trade treaty between the Chambers to governmental level. Another important topic brought into the conversation by the GDR was the question of the shipment of mineral oil. Bischoff annotated that just a short time ago the production was completely under Soviet control and made clear that it would take some time for Austria to get an overview of the production figures. At the end of the East German memo on the conversation, the East German Embassy gave a brief interpretation of Bischoff's personality and political position. In its opinion, Bischoff was surely going to work – within his possibilities – on this matter. But he would not take a too strong position in favour of the GDR. In its view, Bischoff had a "tendency to make his own politics and put himself in the centre of interest without compromising himself."[51]

---

[49] Memo on a visit by Bischoff, Moscow 1955 May 10, PA, AA, MfAA, A 205, Bl. 11–13.

[50] Stourzh, Einheit, 478–483; Gron, "Partner DDR"?, 16–19.

[51] Memo on a conversation with Bischoff, Moscow 1955 July 19, PA, AA, MfAA, A 205, Bl. 21–22.

Bischoff, in keeping with his position towards official Austrian foreign policy, held quite intense contacts with the East German representatives. Even in the POW-question he tried to hold negotiations with the East Germans before he talked to the Soviets. Nevertheless, no official contacts between Austria and the GDR emerged from Bischoff's GDR-contacts in Moscow. The intervention in 1954 on behalf of Austrians imprisoned in the GDR failed because the East German side demanded official talks.

Diplomatic contacts of non-recognition 1955–1972

Even though Austria was not about to recognize the GDR, contacts in Berlin and Moscow continued after the signing of the Austrian State Treaty and the declaration of permanent neutrality in 1955. The tasks of the delegation in West Berlin remained pretty much the same. Naturally they were complicated by the Berlin Crisis, especially after the erection of the Berlin Wall.

The Austrian Delegation in West Berlin – a representation towards the GDR?

From 1956 to 1958, the Austrian delegation in West Berlin was headed by the general consul Ernst Luegmayer.[52] In 1957, a discussion ensued at the BKA, AA about the status of the delegation in Berlin. It was stated that an official recognition of the delegation could only be reached by the three Western commanders of Berlin and not by all four commanders of Berlin, because the "Russians" constantly declared themselves not competent. They constantly referred to the government of the GDR. In fearing that a de jure recognition of the Austrian delegation would inevitably lead to the problem of a discussion about the recognition of the GDR it was recommended within the BKA, AA to continue business according to the status quo.[53] But problems resulting from this status remained under discussion.[54] Finally, in 1958, an investigation of the subject was made. The handling of the problem by other countries was studied and the tasks of the delegation were made clear. Firstly, the Austrian delegation should work as a political listening post. Secondly it was responsible for consular affairs concerning West Berlin, and thirdly, it should protect the interests of Austrians in

---

52 Vgl. Agstner, 130 Jahre, 201.

53 Amtsvermerk, Gegenstand: Österreichische Delegation Berlin; Frage der de jure-Anerkennung und Beziehungen zur DDR, Vienna 1957 May 6, ÖStA, AdR, BMfAA, II-Pol 1957, Deutschland-Ost 2, GZ. 219.787-Pol/57, Karton 427.

54 Amtsvermerk, Gegenstand: Österr. Delegation in Berlin; Frage der de jure Anerkennung, Vienna 1957 August 13, ÖStA, AdR, BMfAA, II-Pol 1957, Deutschland-Ost 2, GZ. 223.237-Pol/57, Karton 427.

the GDR as long as the status of non-recognition remained untouched.

When general consul Hans J. Thalberg took over Luegmayer's position as head of the Austrian delegation in West Berlin, in 1958, the BKA, AA quickly found a solution for the problem of non-recognition of the Austrian delegation. Thalberg sent letters to each of the commanders of the four occupying powers in Berlin (an accreditation letter to the Western ones and a personal letter to the Soviet commander), informing them officially that he was the new head of the Austrian delegation in Berlin, and also requesting an exact date for a first visit.[55] According to Thalberg's memoirs, this procedure was possible because Austria, like Switzerland and Sweden, kept alive the fiction of the four-power status and had set up a mission sui generis simply called "delegation". His successors were only accredited by the three Western commanders because the Soviets had increasingly removed themselves from the four-power arrangement during the Berlin crisis.[56] The delegation maintained its contacts with the MfAA, mostly in the matter of consular affairs. Because of Austrian handling of GDR-passports, as mentioned above, GDR citizens were able to travel without travel documents issued by the Allied Travel Office in West Berlin. In return, Austrian citizens in the GDR were treated with more consideration, and were able to leave the GDR relatively easily whenever they wished to do so. If the GDR hindered departures of Austrian citizens, the Austrian delegation responded simply by delaying the issuance of visas to GDR citizens. This procedure worked – more or less – without any severe complications, even though there never was an official agreement on such a practice,[57] which was adhered to (almost) until the recognition of the GDR.[58]

Humoristic diplomatic approaches to the policy of non-recognition in Moscow

Contacts between Austrian and East German diplomats in Moscow continued after 1955, as they did in several other Socialist countries' capitals such as Budapest, Prague and Warsaw. The GDR was seeking international recognition, while Austria continued its policy of non-recognition. Even Bischoff continued not to attend official East German events. But in the diplomatic corps, diplomats of both countries met frequently. Two quite funny epi-

---

[55] Agstner, 196–197.

[56] Thalberg, Kunst, 233.

[57] Thalberg, Kunst, 246–247.

[58] General consul Hoess to BMfAA, Berlin 1972 February 18, ÖStA, AdR, BMfAA, II-Pol 1972, DDR 9/5, GZ. 152.618-6/72, Karton Pol-72/15.

sodes illustrate that there was also a humoristic approach to the policy of non-recognition, even though diplomatic relations were not about to be established.

On 5 October 1957, the East German Ambassador in Moscow, Johannes König, met Bischoff at an event in the Czechoslovak Embassy. The news of the Soviet satellite "Sputnik", which had been launched on that day, constituted the main topic of conversation between the diplomats present at the Czechoslovak Embassy. Bischoff humorously made the remark that the protocol of the Foreign Ministry of the USSR should reserve a seat for the ambassadors in the next satellite. König answered with another teasing remark that he had already reserved such a seat. Bischoff gave the appear ance that he was taking König seriously and asked: "Really?" König answered: "Of course not. The GDR does not have the ambition to build the first embassy on the moon." Hereupon the Polish Ambassador interjected: "No, it [the GDR, M. G.] would prefer to set up an embassy in Vienna."[59]

Another episode happened about two years later. When the Austrian diplomat Otto Eiselsberg met his East German colleague Thun in December 1959 at a movie-night in the Romanian Embassy, he informed him that he had bought a new opera guide published in the GDR in 1951. Eiselsberg stated that the opera guide was detailed and well-presented, but he also noted that the guide included "*alte Anschlusstendenzen*" ("annexion tendencies"). When Thun asked how he should understand that remark, Eiselsberg explained that Austria as a country was not included in the guide, but that the Austrian composers were listed under "Germany". In contrast, Switzerland was listed separately. Eiselsberg further said that he did not want to discuss the case of Beethoven, over which there is never going to be a consensus, but Haydn definitely was Austrian. In a humorous way, he concluded: "If the opera guide were published in West Germany, we would have to protest. There is something positive about the fact that we do not have diplomatic relations – we are not able to protest."[60]

Early Political Contacts – "Unofficial Talks" with Vice–Chancellor Bruno Pittermann

Bruno Pittermann was an important politician of the Socialist Party (hereafter SPÖ) in post-war Austria. When Vice-Chancellor and Chairmen of the SPÖ Adolf Schärf was elected president of the re-

---

[59] Memo on a conversation with Ambassador Bischoff, Moscow,1957 October 8, PA, AA, MfAA, A 15154, Bl. 9–10.

[60] Memo on a conversation with Eiselsberg, Moscow 1959 December 15, PA, AA, MfAA, A 12835, Bl. 1–2.

public in 1957, Pittermann assumed Schärf's duties. From 1959 until 1966, Pittermann was in charge of Austria's nationalized industries.[61] From 1952 to 1972, he represented Austria at the European Council in several functions.[62] Apart from these functions, Pittermann is definitely not known as an important factor in Austria's foreign policy.

As early as 1960, a first contact between Pittermann and East German officials took place. In May, the Minister for Foreign and Inner-German Trade, Heinrich Rau, visited Austria. Although this was not an official visit, Pittermann received him in his office at the Federal Chancellery as the official responsible for Austria's nationalized industries. The content of the conversation went beyond the topic of trade relations between East German foreign trade companies and Austria's nationalized industries. Moreover, they discussed political and bilateral matters. Back at home Rau informed leading East German politicians about the meeting with Pittermann,[63] which was definitely not in line with Austria's policy of non-recognition towards the GDR.

In 1961, the head of the East German trade mission in Vienna, Karl Keilholz, met with Pittermann. Their conversation took place in the Austrian parliament and chiefly focussed on economic relations. During that meeting, Keilholz passed along to Pittermann an invitation to the Leipzig Spring Fair from minister Rau himself. Pittermann thanked him for the invitation, but made it quite clear that he was not going to accept it because of his relations with his West German "friends", especially with Willy Brandt.[64] During a meeting between Pittermann and Keilholz on 16 July 1962, the Vice Chancellor informed his East German interlocutor about some aspects of the conversations of Chancellor Alfons Gorbach (Austrian Peoples Party, hereafter ÖVP) during his visit in the USSR. According to the memo written by Keilholz, detailed talks concerning the German question had been held in Moscow, during which Nikita S. Khrushchev had recommended to the Austrian Chancellor that the GDR be recognized. Concerning the relations between Austria and the GDR, Pittermann said that they should proceed step by step toward normalization. He further noted that an immediate recognition of the GDR would cause many problems which

---

[61] Verein für Geschichte der Arbeiterbewegung (Ed.), Bruno Pittermann. Ein Porträt, Wien 1995, 6.

[62] Iibidem., 14–18.

[63] Rau to Winzer, Berlin 1960 May 18, PA, AA, MfAA, A 17.812, Bl. 56–60 and Rau to Grotewohl, Berlin 1960 May 18, BArch-DDR, DC 20/15229, Bl. 1–5.

[64] Memo on conversation Keilholz with Pittermann, Vienna 1961 February 2, PA, AA, MfAA, A 12.851, Bl. 143–145.

would not be in the interest of either side.[65] Information on the conversation with Pittermann was given to the members of the politburo on 6 August 1962.[66]

Two years later, in 1964, Pittermann's GDR-contacts intensified. On 26 May, he spoke with the new head of the East German trade mission, Paul Knoblauch. It is interesting to note that on that day, Pittermann served as the replacement for the Austrian Foreign Minister Bruno Kreisky. One of the aims of the East Germans was to find out whether Pittermann and other Austrian politicians were willing to hold talks with GDR-politicians. Pittermann recalled his conversation with Rau in 1960 and signalled that he was willing to hold such talks as long as political conditions would be respected. On the question of whether Kreisky would also accept such talks, Pittermann refused to give a clear answer.[67] Thus, although a conversation with Kreisky never took place before the recognition of the GDR, Pittermann's contacts continued to exist.

On 6 July, Pittermann invited Knoblauch to an event on the occasion of the visit of a Romanian governmental delegation in Vienna.[68] It was the first time that an East German commercial counsellor was officially invited to an Austrian government banquet. No conversation with Pittermann took place on that evening. In Knoblauch's opinion, Pittermann was too busy and had no time for such a conversation;[69] another reason may have been that Pittermann did not want to talk to an East German "representative" in public.

On 16 July, Pittermann met Knoblauch on the premises of the SPÖ in the parliament. Pittermann declared his willingness to hold talks with the GDR at Brno in mid-September, during the Brno Fair. During the conversation, he handed over a letter that contained the proposal to release imprisoned members of the SPÖ to the GDR government.[70] His letter, which included a list of names, was transmitted to the MfAA. State Secretary Otto Winzer informed the Minister for State Security, Erich Mielke, about Pitter-

---

[65] Memo on conversation Keilholz with Pittermann, Vienna 1962 July 16, PA, AA, MfAA, A 12863, Bl. 151.

[66] Information to the members and candidates of the politburo, Vienna 1962 August 6, Stiftung Archiv der Parteien und Massenorganisationen der DDR – Bundesarchiv (SAPMO-BArch), Berlin, DY 30/J IV 2/2J/845.

[67] Conversation Knoblauch with Pittermann, Vienna 1964 May 26, PA, AA, MfAA, A 12885, Bl. 35–38.

[68] Invitation for Knoblauch, PA, AA, MfAA, A 12878, Bl. 164.

[69] Report by Knoblauch to Ministry for Foreign and Inner-German Trade, Vienna 1964 July 7, PA, AA, MfAA, A 12878, Bl. 165.

[70] Conversation Knoblauch with Pittermann, Vienna 1964 July 16, PA, AA, MfAA, A 12878, Bl. 166–169.

mann's willingness to improve the relations between Austria and the GDR and asked him to supply information on the persons who were on that list.[71] The outcome of Pittermann's initiative is unclear. Additional research in the sources of the East German Ministry for State Security should, nonetheless, reveal more information.

Because of Pittermann's willingness to hold talks with the GDR, the politburo decided on 15 September that the conversation in Brno should be held by one of its own members, Bruno Leuschner. The directive for the conversation formulated the main goals of the GDR. The greatest attention should be paid on the development of the bilateral relations. Furthermore, the position of the SPÖ towards inter-party-contacts to the SED had to be evaluated.[72]

Despite all efforts, the planned conversation in Brno did not take place since Pittermann, as a result of the "Olah-crisis", was indispensable in Vienna.[73] Instead of the meeting in Brno, Pittermann proposed a meeting in Vienna on 9 October. It was decided at the MfAA that State Secretary Winzer should hold the talks with Pittermann on the basis of the directive that had passed the politburo in mid-September.[74] During the meeting, which took place at the Federal Chancellery, nothing concerning the bilateral relations between Austria and the GDR was agreed upon. According to Winzer's memo, Pittermann favoured meetings with GDR officials in Socialist countries, for example in Prague, instead of meetings in Vienna. To Pittermann's question about progress concerning his intervention on behalf of imprisoned members of the SPÖ, Winzer answered that they probably had been granted amnesty on the occasion of the fifteenth anniversary of the GDR on 7 October 1964. At the end of the conversation, Pittermann recalled once again his meeting with Rau in 1960, adding that in those days such a meeting "was still revolutionary".[75] Winzer's memo was then communi-

---

[71] Winzer to Mielke, Berlin 1964 July 23, PA, AA, MfAA, A 15.798, Bl.. 29–32.

[72] Politburo meeting (Protocol no. 34/64), 1964 September 15, SAPMO-BArch, DY 30/J IV 2/2/949, Bl. 4 and SAPMO-BArch, DY 30/J IV 2/2A/1051, Bl. 22–31.

[73] On the "Olah-crisis" (the SPÖ Minister of the Interior Franz Olah was involved in a financial scandal and was dismissed from his post) see: Manfred Lechner, „..Jener dessen Namen unter den Lebenden nicht genannte werden mag.". Der „Fall Olah" – Ein Megaskandal der Zweiten Republik?, in: Michael Gehler – Hubert Sickinger (Eds.), Politische Affären und Skandale in Österreich. Von Mayerling bis Waldheim, Thaur/Wien/München 1996. 419–436.

[74] Krolikowski to Stoph, Berlin 1964 October 1, PA, AA, MfAA, A 15.798, Bl. 33.

[75] Conversation Winzer with Pittermann, 1964 October 9, PA, AA, MfAA, A 18.002, Bl.. 2–12.

cated to leading East German politicians such as Walter Ulbricht, Willi Stoph, Herrmann Axen, Erich Apel and Julius Balkow.[76]

Between the 1966 elections – when the ÖVP won an absolute majority – and the formation of the single-party Austrian government on 19 April, Herbert Plaschke (a senior official in the MfAA) went on a mission to Vienna. There, he first met with Pittermann. During their conversation the Chairman of the SPÖ analyzed the results of the elections and reported on his expectations for the upcoming formation of the government. Because of the result of the elections, another aim of Plaschke's mission was to establish first contacts with the ÖVP. This was accomplished through a conversation with the chief of Chancellor Klaus's cabinet, Franz Karasek. Plaschke concluded in his report about the mission that given the new circumstances, the relations between Austria and the GDR would not improve, but not worsen either. He clearly pointed out that the new contacts with the ÖVP should be developed and that the contacts with the SPÖ should be strengthened.[77]

Both Karasek and the former Foreign Minister Karl Gruber (1945–1953) were candidates for the position of Foreign Minister during the formation of the Austrian government in 1966. Due to different opinions on this question within the ÖVP, the post was granted to a compromise candidate, Lujo Tončić-Sorinj. Instead, Karasek became permanent under-secretary in the Foreign Ministry, and Gruber became state secretary at the Federal Chancellery.[78]

After the formation of the new Austrian government, the GDR established several contacts with the Austrian Foreign Ministry, but a meeting between the actual East German Foreign Minister Winzer and the new Austrian Foreign Minister was rejected by the Austrian Foreign Ministry for obvious reasons.[79]

Hermann Axen's visit to Austria in 1966

Despite the refusal of the ÖVP-government to allow any contacts between members of the government and GDR-officials, the candidate of the politburo and architect of East German foreign policy in

[76] The note on [the conversation with] Pittermann was sent to Ulbricht, Stoph, Axen, Apel and Balkow on 16 October 1964, PA, AA, MfAA, A 18.002, Bl. 1.

[77] Report by Plaschke about his mission to Vienna 7–11 March 1966, PA, AA, MfAA, A 12878, Bl. 178–188.

[78] Reinhard Meier-Walser, Die Außenpolitik der monocoloren Regierung Klaus in Österreich 1966–1970, München 1988, 51–52.

[79] Amtsvermerk, Gegenstand: DDR – persönliche Besprechung mit Dr. Plaschke, Wien, 1966 July 21, ÖStA, AdR, BMfAA, II-Pol 1966, DDR 2, GZ. 41.116-6(Pol)/66, (P), Karton 1037; First contacts in the Foreign Ministry in Vienna had taken place in 1964.

the 1960s, Herrmann Axen, went to Austria on 30 September 1966. His trip was sanctioned by Walter Ulbricht. Axen was supposed to hold a "political conversation" offered by Pittermann, who was now free of any governmental responsibility. Furthermore, he was supposed to try to establish contact with the new ÖVP-government. Because all former attempts to get in touch with the ÖVP-government had failed, Plaschke contacted the legal advisor of State Secretary Gruber who managed to arrange a conversation with Gruber at the Federal Chancellery. Moreover, because "the enemy" should not be informed in advance, Axen picked up his visa for Austria at the Austrian Embassy in Budapest. (Normally visas were picked up at the Austrian Delegation in West Berlin.)

During the meeting, Gruber introduced Axen to the State Secretary at the Foreign Ministry, Carl Bobleter. After opening remarks by Axen on the relations between Austria and the GDR and on Austrian neutrality, which in his opinion demanded the recognition of both German states, Gruber answered that Austria was not ignoring the political realities. It simply sought to avoid taking any risks regarding Austria's relations [with the FRG, M. G.]. Axen countered that the FRG's "Hallstein doctrine" was the real problem. No immediate results emerged from the conversation, but Gruber expressed assurance that contacts should be maintained. However, Gruber still requested that discretion be maintained about the contact.[80] Axen reported on his conversations in Vienna during the politburo meeting on 11 October; his recommendations for further dealings with Austria were approved. In particular, his recommendations constituted a continuation of recent attempts to increase contacts with the ultimate goal of achieving diplomatic recognition.[81]

Increasing contacts prior to the recognition of the GDR

Contacts with diplomats in the Austrian Foreign Ministry and with Pittermann were maintained through the following years.[82] Despite all efforts by East German representatives in Vienna and elsewhere, Austria refused to recognize the GDR. The ÖVP-government and the SPÖ-governments after 1970, led by Chancellor Kreisky, welcomed the developments of détente and West Germany's "Neue Ostpolitik". But none of them wanted to endanger

---

[80] Report by Axen on conversations in Vienna and Budapest, Berlin 1966 September 30, SAPMO-BArch, DY 30/11434 and SAPMO-BArch, DY 30/IV 2/2.035/107.

[81] Politburo meeting (Protocol no. 41/66), 1966 October 11, SAPMO-BArch, DY 30/J IV 2/2/1080, Bl. 6, Appendix: Bl. 63.

[82] See for example the documentation on the contacts in 1967 in: PA, AA, MfAA, C 141/70, Bl. 1–14.

the dialogue between East and West Germany by recognizing the GDR too early.[83]

Another conversation with Pittermann in 1971 showed quiet clearly that the SPÖ-government, with regard to the friendship between the SPÖ and the West German Social Democratic Party (SPD) and especially with its chairman, the West German Chancellor Willy Brandt, was not going to recognize the GDR.[84]

On 7 July 1972, Foreign Minister Winzer met with the Austrian Foreign Minister Rudolf Kirchschläger at the Polish Embassy in Vienna. The conversation lasted for several hours, but again no agreement was reached regarding the recognition of the GDR. Kirchschläger informed Winzer that Austria was going to act in consultation with other neutral countries such as Switzerland, Sweden and Finland.[85]

When it was certain that the German-German Basic Treaty would be signed on 21 December 1972, delegations of both countries met in Vienna between 5 and 7 December. They held negotiations about a precise date on which diplomatic relations should be established. Finally, 21 December was fixed as the most appropriate date. On 6 December Kirchschläger informed the public about the forthcoming recognition of the GDR.[86]

Conclusion

Although Austria from the beginning officially supported the West German claims to an exclusive mandate for the entire German people, it nevertheless developed diplomatic and political contacts to the GDR without officially recognizing the East German state. From the foundation of the GDR in 1949 until the signing of the Austrian State Treaty in 1955, official relations between Austria and the GDR were even impossible due to the provisions of the second Allied Control Agreement. Nevertheless, the Austrian delegation in West Berlin continued its work on behalf of Austrians living in East Germany. Therefore the delegation maintained the contacts to the Soviets it had developed since 1945, and established contacts with the MfAA.

Concerning contacts in Moscow, the "Bischoff-factor" should not be underestimated. His early contacts with GDR officials ap-

83 Gron, "Partner DDR"?, 41–42.

84 Note on a conversation with Pittermann, Vienna 1971 February 24, PA, AA, MfAA, C 597/76, Bl. 39–41.

85 Information about the conversation of Winzer with Pittermann, 1972 July 7, PA, AA, MfAA, C 597/76, Bl. 39–41.

86 Gron, "Partner DDR"?, 42–43. Bauer, Austria, 412–434, 414.

pear not at all unusual, but it is surprising that he contacted the East German Ambassador in connection with the POW-question. Surely this was one of his own initiatives on which he may have deliberately not reported to Vienna. However, it seems that the Ballhausplatz too considered Moscow to be the right place to talk to the GDR concerning POW matters. The 1954 POW-initiative suggests this interpretation.

As the GDR in Berlin in many cases insisted on the usual diplomatic channels, the Austrian initiative in Moscow was answered with the offer to hold inter-governmental negotiations on the POW- and other questions. Such negotiations would have been tantamount to recognition of the GDR; for this reason Vienna refrained. Contacts to the GDR were supposed to be avoided as far as possible, East German overtures were also supposed to be reported immediately. Anyhow, Bischoff kept his direct contacts, but even he never attended official East German events either before or after the signing of the Austrian State Treaty. Meetings between Austrian and East German diplomats in the diplomatic corps were unavoidable, and sometimes even had a humoristic shape.

In Berlin the system of relatively well-known barter (the issuance of visas in return for the departure of Austrians) existed until Austria diplomatically recognized the GDR in 1972. At least on the work of the Austrian delegation in West Berlin, the FRG was informed and never protested against. West German protests occurred more often when Austria moved too close to the limitations set out by the "Hallstein Doctrine" (for example by allowing the GDR to open a travelling office in Vienna in 1960 or during the "Interflug affair" in 1963). However, the current state of research suggests that the FRG did not know about the early political contacts between Austria and the GDR. The meeting between Pittermann and Rau truly can be described as revolutionary, especially because it happened during the Berlin Crisis. Over the following years Pittermann regularly talked with leading members of the East German trading mission. He even handed out invitations to official events and offered further political talks with East German politicians.

The 1966 visit by Axen in Vienna has to be seen in this tradition. His visit to Austria after being invited by Pittermann even got Axen admitted to the Federal Chancellery and a conversation with state secretary Gruber right at the start of the ÖVP single-party government. However, despite these apparent East

German successes and some, more intense diplomatic and political contacts after the FRG implemented its "*Neue Ostpolitik*", Austria continued its policy of non-recognition of the GDR until the signing of the German–German Basic Treaty.

Josef Švéda
(University of Alberta)

Czech Communist and Post–Communist Heroes in the Twentieth Century

There are many historical figures which are adulated and glorified in all countries across the globe. Heroes are usually connected to certain historical events: great victorious battles and wars which also fit into the contemporary ideological situation. This paper shall focus on Czech heroes produced in the twentieth century. Some of them are no longer popular in the modern Czech Republic. Especially the idols of the communist era lost their glory; they were violently removed from the national pantheon and substituted by others. I would like to pay special attention to the new Czech post–communist heroes who appeared after 1989.

Czech history in the twentieth century is usually seen as full of ruptures which are miraculously circled around the number eight. It was in 1918 when the independent Czechoslovak Republic was established, in 1938 when it was "betrayed" in Munich (as Czechs put it) and its border regions given to Hitler for the promise of peace, in 1948 when the Communists seized power, and in 1968 when the project of "socialism with a human face" was crushed by the armies of the Warsaw Pact. The only exception to the rule is the "Velvet Revolution" of 1989. Each of these changes of the political regime brought about a radical change of writing history. Those historical persons glorified as heroes in the previous epoch were defamed and their statues were removed. New historical figures became prominent and were praised as heroes. And so after the 1918 "national revolution" the Czech nationalists tore down the statues and portraits of not just the Emperors Josef II and Francis Josef I, but also Marshal Count Joseph Radetzky. As Nancy Wingfield put it: "There was no place in Czech history for a figure that was so much part of recent Austrian history, so Radetzky did not join other earlier Czech military heroes in the national pantheon of the First Republic".[1] Instead new heroes of the "legendary" battle of Zborov known as the "the Legionnaires", who fought against the Habsburg empire in World War I, were praised.[2] Even a public holiday was instituted on 2 July for the Czechs (not the ethnic

1 Nancy Wingfield, Flag Wars and Stone Saints: How the Bohemian Lands Became Czech, Harvard 2007, 151.

2 Robert B. Pynsent, The Literary Representation of the Czechoslovak 'Legions' in Russia, in: M. Cornwall, R.J.W. Ewans (Eds.), Czechoslovakia in a Nationalist and Fascist Europe 1918–1948, Oxford 2007, 63.

Germans and Magyars) to celebrate them. New statues were raised, new history was written, and films about the glorious struggle for independence were shot. All these cultural products were meant to play an active role in representing – but as Scott Spector put it – also enforcing and sometimes constituting – visions of society and history.[3] This of course can be said about all the changes in Czechoslovakia in the twentieth century.

Another massive emergence of new heroic figures began straight after World War II. These were the resistance fighters who bravely fought against the Nazi invaders. But at this time they were divided into two groups: communist and non-communist. It is no surprise that it was the communist heroes who became prominent after the 1948 communist takeover. The communist resistance was presented as the only effective force struggling with the Nazi occupiers. The most famous communist resistance hero, Julius Fučík, will be examined in this paper and compared to the post-communist heroes, who emerged after 1989.

Czechoslovak communists tried to erase the memory of the legionnaires and the political leaders of the First Republic. However, they used the nationalist agenda for their own purposes. The figures of the Hussite movement, such as the military leader Jan Žižka, remained in the national heroic inventory, but they were presented also as socialist heroes rather than just the nationalist ones. The communist cultural theorist Zdeněk Nejedlý praised the era of national revival, Slavic brotherhood, and the Soviet Union. The great communist icons were adulated, "a colossal statue of Comrade Stalin leading a vanguard of peasants and workers was solemnly unveiled on Letná plain, on the very spot that Tomáš Garrigue Masaryk had once selected as the national *Sokol* exercise ground".[4] The communist leaders Lenin, Stalin and Gottwlad were presented to the nation as role models. The short period of liberalization in 1968 was then substituted by the "normalization" and the statues of Lenin and others were raised again.

The last political change, the 1989 Velvet revolution, has thus far brought about a complete revision of the national heroic pantheon again. Today, on the one hand, one can see a revival of the interwar era political figures such as the first "President-Liberator" Tomáš Garrigue Masaryk who, as Wingfield put it, again acquired his near-mythical status.[5] We also witness praises of the Czechoslovak Legions and a re-emergence of the non-communist resistance fighters in World War II. On the other hand, there are attempts to in-

---

[3] Pynsent, Literary Representation, 190.

[4] Mary Heimann, Czechoslovakia: The State That Failed, Yale 2009, 205.

[5] Wingfield, Flag Wars, 298.

stall new heroes to the Czech heroic inventory who fought against communism. In the Czech Republic the most prominent are the Mašín[6] brothers. The attempt to create these new anti-communist heroes can be well illustrated by a speech of the Czech Prime Minister Mirek Topolánek in September 2007. "Every epoch needs its heroes. Every epoch has its heroes. There are heroes of yesterday, thanks to whom we can feel so safe today: the heroes of the Czechoslovak Legions [...], the Second World War heroes from the Battle of Britain [...], the heroes of the anti-communist resistance like the Mašín brothers [...]. We need heroes as our models. We need to perceive them not as some statues on a pedestal but as one of us. Only in this way will we be able to ensure the appearance of the heroes of tomorrow. The country which does not have its heroes and models, and which has no will to defend its values, to defend its citizens, is a lost country."[7] Topolánek mentions Czech heroic figures that are prominent today – members of the Czechoslovak Legions and World War II fighters from the Western Front. However, he also mentions a new heroic couple – the Mašín brothers. They are part of what Czech historians today call the "third resistance".

The Mašín brothers were not unknown to the Czech public before 1989. The story has been tackled by writers and film-makers in communist Czechoslovakia from the 1960s onwards. Here, the Mašíns are also characters in popular tales, though they are on the other side of the axiological axis as they are the villains. These narratives were published as detective stories based on real events, where the Mašíns played the role of the criminals. Even a superficial reading (and watching) of these detective stories, however, reveals that they are somehow different from other stories of this genre. There are no main figures of a detective and the Mašíns are in the very centre of the narrator's attention being depicted as anti-heroes. They also appear as characters in one episode of a famous television series *Major Zeman's Thirty Cases* entitled *Fear.* The series depicts the life and career of a fictitious character, Detective Jan Zeman. The stories are loosely based on historical events (criminal cases) from Czechoslovak history. The eponymous character Jan Zeman is fictional and there are no direct references to historical persons. Again, they are represented as insane killers. After 1989, the discourse radically changed and the Mašíns were installed in the Czech heroic pantheon. Unlike the nationalist and communist mythologies, the post-communist

---

6 The name "Mašín" is pronounced as "Mah-sheen".

7 Speech of MirekTopolánek delivered in Ostrava on 15 September 2007), Simple Heroism, http://www.vlada.cz/scripts/detail.php?id=25127, 2010 February 26. Translated by the author.

discursive formations have not been scrutinized. This paper aims to be a pioneering inquiry into this matter.

The Mašín Brothers

The Mašín brothers' story actually begins with their father Josef Mašín Sr. who fought for the independent Czechoslovakia in the Legions in World War I. He received many medals for bravery. He was also a member of the Czech home resistance group "The Three Kings" which was fighting against the Nazis. This group conducted many sabotage activities (even a bomb attack in Berlin) and transmitted coded messages to London. Eventually in 1941, the group was destroyed and Josef Mašín was captured and executed. After World War II he was praised as a national hero by non-communists. The narratives create a causal link between the Mašín brothers and their "heroic" father. It is suggested that they also resisted against "evil and injustice" just like their father.

Straight after the 1948 communist takeover, we are told, the Mašín brothers (Ctirad and Josef) and their friends decided to fight against the communist regime. They established a resistance group and conducted several acts of violence. In September 1951 the group raided two police stations in order to get weapons. Two policemen were killed, one at each police station. On 2 August 1952 two members of the group (Josef Mašín, Václav Švéda[8]) robbed a car transporting the salary for the Kovolis company employees. They claimed they did that in order to get money for their resistance activity. They seized 800.000 crowns and killed a paymaster Josef Rošický. They also conducted some other sabotage activities. On 7 September 1953 Václav Švéda and Ctirad Mašín burned 17 hay stacks in the area of the Moravian town Pivín.

Finally, they decided to leave Czechoslovakia in 1953, bound for West Berlin. On 4 October 1953 Josef Mašín, Ctirad Mašín, Milan Paumer, Zbyněk Janata and Václav Švéda crossed the Czechoslovak East German border hoping to get to West Berlin. They tried to hijack a car but were not successful. Then they were hunted by more than 20 000 East German and Soviet troops. In several clashes, they killed three East German policemen but they always managed to escape even when they were surrounded in a forest. Two of the group, Zbyněk Janata and Václav Švéda were captured. On 1 November 1953 the rest of the group finally got to West Berlin. Later, they went to the USA and joined the U.S. army.

This is the story produced by Czech official historians and novelists. We can see that it fits perfectly into the post-communist Czech mythology. Josef Mašín Sr., the national hero of both world

[8] He is not my relative.

wars, has been revived. He epitomizes the struggle for "freedom" of Czech nation. After the 1989 revolution, there was a significant change in the discourse which can be characterized by the revival of the Czech non-communist World War II heroes and Josef Mašín Sr. is one of them. His heroic deeds are still interpreted in a strictly nationalist manner. He is one of the Legionnaires who bravely fought against the Habsburg Empire. This perspective still sticks to the nationalist interpretation of history. It sees the "national struggle" as a key element of history and the independent nation state as its supreme goal. What is left out (except of other things) is the perspective of the ethnic Germans living in Bohemia who did not welcome establishing Czechoslovakia with such enthusiasm. This nationalist perspective divides the protagonists of this story into two irreconcilable camps: the Czechs who are "suffering" under the Habsburg Empire in the First World War and under Nazi rule in World War II. The ultimate enemies are the Austrians and the Germans, and Josef Mašín senior fights bravely against them. There is a clear-cut axiological axis, which attributes the positive qualities to Czechs and the negative ones to Germans and Austrians. The same applies to the Mašín brothers' story. They symbolize the struggle against the communists and should not be forgotten. As Václav Veber, a Czech historian put it: "But we should be able to give an impartial, exact image of what these courageous fighters, this pride of the Czech nation did in their struggle against communism, so that they would help all of us to save face and instill hope of a renewed wholesome life. These heroes belong in textbooks. Until they have been included in them, our account of those times will be incomplete, unsatisfactory and distorted."[9]

It is also interesting to note that this quote is from a volume of articles called *For Freedom and Democracy* which focuses on the crimes of communism. We can see here the use of an accusative phrase with a preposition "for" (in Czech "*za*") implying "a struggle for" something. This idiom was widely used in the slogans and titles during the communist era – "For World Peace", "For Bolshevik Orientation of KSČ",[10] "For Marxist Linguistics" etc. Vladimír Macura points out that this seemingly neutral idiom is heavily burdened with meanings. It presents reality as a dynamic process with an explicitly ideological perspective.[11] In this case it is a struggle for "freedom" and "democracy" rather than communism or Marxism.

---

[9] Lukáš Babka – Václav Veber (Eds.), Za svobodu a demokracii III. Třetí (protikomunistický) odboj, Hradec Králové 2002, 18. Translated by Jan Čulík.

[10] KSČ – Komunistická strana Československa (Communist Party of Czechoslovakia)

[11] Vladimír Macura, Šťastný věk (a jiné studie o socialistické kultuře), Praha 2008, 40.

This implies that the Mašín brothers' activity really is a struggle for these noble ideas. Such apprehension of history is not rare among Czech historians today. A prominent role in promoting this "heroic" image of the Mašíns plays *The Institute for the Study of Totalitarian Regimes* (now criticized even by the former dissidents like Václav Havel). However, historians are not the only promoters of what could be called the Mašín myth. It is also various newspaper articles, documentary films and non-fiction novels. The Czech-American author Jan Novák wrote what he called a "truthful novel" *So Far So Good* [*Zatím dobrý*][12] which again represents the Mašíns as heroic freedom fighters. It was published in 2004, won prestigious prices, and happened to be one of the most successful novels of the post-communist era. However, as opposed to this "official" heroic image, the Czech public seems to be rather split into two camps. The Mašín brothers' actions are still regarded as controversial in today's Czech Republic by many and are a topic of continuous public debate. Those who defend the group's activities claim that armed resistance against the communist regime was justifiable. Those who criticize them claim that they were no more than murderers because they cruelly killed six people (including one unarmed and tied policeman). In 2008, a heated public debate started again after the Mašíns got a medal for their anti-communist resistance from the Prime Minister Mirek Topolánek.

The Communist Hero Julius Fučík

The Mašín brothers replaced a prominent hero of the communist era Julius Fučík who became a famous icon especially after 1948 when the communists put forward their interpretation of history. It is fruitful to compare the semiotic processes employed in both of these myths. Julius Fučík was a communist journalist and writer executed by Nazis for his resistance activity. In jail he wrote a piece called Reportage: *Written from the Gallows* [*Reportáž psaná na oprátce*][13] describing his struggle with the Nazis and the brutal interrogations which he had to go through. He was executed but the text was smuggled out of prison and was published after the war. The communists used the text as a prime symbol of their heroic resistance against Nazis and created the Fučík myth.

The cult of Fučík was directed at youth, the new people of the socialist paradise and was organized on a large scale. "The government awarded Fučík the posthumous title National Hero, Young Pioneer troops, local Komsomol organizations, schools, streets,

---

[12] Jan Novák, Zatím dobrý. Mašínovi a největší příběh studené války, Brno 2004. (All the quotes from this book are translated by Jan Čulík)

[13] Julius Fučík, Reportáž psaná na oprátce, Prague 1945. English edition: Julius Fučík, Notes from the Gallows, New York 1948.

mines and a huge park in Prague were named after him."[14] The Fučík cult in the 1950 Czechoslovakia was perceived as somehow natural. Fučík represented an ideal which also formed a set of rules how to act and behave. This model was about to produce generations of new people.[15] As the Soviet writer Peter Ojfa claims: "Today we need thousands, millions of heroes of a Fučík type – all people around the world because to be a hero like this means to be a whole, honest, pure man, genuine communist."[16] His remarks strikingly correspond to the aforementioned Topolánek's opinion on the Mašín brothers. Both authors agree that the heroes they praise are examples worthy of following.

However, there are significant differences between the structures of the two myths. The Fučík myth was constructed in the era of Stalinism. This period is usually perceived as a time of the ultimate terror, the Gulags, and political trials. However, this picture would not be complete without mentioning the opposite feature of the time: the happiness and joy which accompanied building the "new world". Once an ardent communist poet, later a critic of Stalinism, Milan Kundera commented on this in an interview: "The totalitarianism of the '50's was not just oppression alone. It was not by means of its execution posts that it attracted the masses, the young, the intelligentsia. It was by its smile. We tend to forget this today; we are ashamed of this. We no longer say: the bloody totalitarianism of the '50's had a poetry that we succumbed to. If we blame it on the Gulag, we feel pardoned. If we speak of the poetry of totalitarianism, we remain implicated in the scandal."[17]

The Fučík myth in the 1950s was indeed lyrical in nature. The predominant literary genre which glorified him was poetry not prose. Milan Kundera himself was one of the promoters of the Fučík cult. In his epic poem *The Last May* [*Poslední máj*][18] describes an episode from *Reportage* where the "Gestapo man leads Fučík up the Petřín hill in Prague, as Satan led Jesus to temp him. Kundera's Fučík is a man of light like Christ, and, more important, a man of love like Christ."[19] Kundera here creates a biblical parallel. The Gestapo investigator wants Fučík to testify and betray his communist colleagues. He shows him nature in spring, a beautiful girl, young

---

14 Robert B. Pynsent, Questions of Identity: Czech and Slovak Ideas of Nationality and Personality, London 1994, 208.

15 Macura, Šťastný věk, 90.

16 Ibid.

17 Alain Finkielkraut, Milan Kundera Interview, in: Cross Currents: A Yearbook of Central European Culture 1, Ann Arbor 1982, 23.

18 Milan Kundera, Poslední máj, Prague 1955.

19 Pynsent, Questions, 208.

free singing boys but all of these things – spring, love, freedom – are for Fučík just an appeal to further resistance. The hero thus wins over the tempter and, although he is back in his prison cell, he is not alone, but he knows that he is a part of a "mass of comrades".[20] One can thus see that the hero's struggle is internal. He does not fight Gestapo with guns (like the Mašíns), but rather with his spirit. Fučík was a lyrical hero in nature.

Another feature of the Fučík myth which corresponds with the contemporary "lyrical era" was his youth and beauty. Although in the time of his imprisonment he was already in his forties, Fučík was depicted as a young hero. His idealized picture was made by Max Švabinský and widely circulated. Fučík is represented as a "beautiful" and "charming" hero. His face was "supremely sublime, beautifully damascened" or "one of the most beautiful". No less important than hero's beauty was a motive of joy, happiness, and smile.[21] The contemporary poets were praising Fučík for helping to make the "new communist world" possible.

Petr Steiner observes that Fučík's *Reportage* bears a strong resemblance to the the New Testament: "For *Reportage* replicates more than just isolated words of Christ. Its affinity with the Bible is much more thorough."[22] Likewise, Vladimír Macura remarks that the Fučík myth comported with ancient mythic cultures and manifests "clear features of solar and calendar myths".[23] Both authors thus conclude that the Fučík's text is deeply rooted in mythical universe. The same can be said about the Fučík cult which was created after World War II. But the mythical background was used for the actual political purposes. Petr Steiner claims that Fučík's *Reportage* could be regarded as a Marxist romance: "History, according to Marx, follows this romantic plot quite closely, though its hero is not one but many: the entire working class."[24] In Fučík's narrative, there are also many heroes, ordinary people, workers and comrades who should not be forgotten. This is another important feature of the Fučík myth. He is not depicted as a single and unique hero who would fight the Nazi occupiers alone but he is posited as a part of a broader collective of communists. There is a clear paradox in this mythical structure: on the one hand, Fučík is depicted as a unique persona, and a role model which we all should follow and on the other hand he is "one of us", simple and ordinary people. And so many poems stress that Fučík is "simple man" and "hu-

---

20 Macura, Šťastný věk, 98.

21 Ibid., 94–95.

22 Petr Steiner, The Deserts of Bohemia. Czech Fiction and its Social Context, Ithaca 2000, 136.

23 Macura, Šťastný věk, 97 quoted from Pynsent, Questions, 208.

24 Steiner, Deserts, 119.

mane" but at the same time he is raised on a pedestal. This antinomy does not disturb the myth. On the contrary, any manifestation of equality moves the socialist hero away from the others. The principle of hierarchy is not in balance with the principle of equality.[25] Fučík shares this attribute with the cult of the great communist leaders Lenin, Stalin and Gottwald. The Marxist notion of equality and social determination of the individual is crucial here. The individual action is limited by the "objective" historical conditions. Fučík's struggle is meaningful because he is a part of a broader collective. The Marxist romance can have its happy ending: "The inescapable proletarian revolution will eventually come to wrest away the mean of production from those who usurped them and abolish all private property. And since the division of humankind into antagonistic classes was begun by a skewed distribution of surplus, in a classless society people will be rewarded solely on the basis of their natural needs. Only then will initial harmony return, albeit on a dialectically higher level."[26] This ideological structure was predominant in the 1950's Czechoslovakia. The heroes were lowered down to the masses but this did not diminish their greatness. The Mašín brothers as we shall see are represented in a different mode.

Robert Pynsent regards the Fučík cult as a part of long Czech tradition of martyrdom started in the tenth century by king Wenceslas: "The Fučík legend also keeps to our martyrdom model. Fučík goes voluntarily into a dangerous situation (underground anti-German activity); he is betrayed by friends (mainly Mirek); he writes letters home (in this case the text of his memoirs); and he is killed."[27] Fučík is simply read as another martyr, the myth which is forming the Czech national consciousness. However, although one can see certain parallels between Fučík and some Czech martyrs, this thesis seems to be rather simplified. As it is clear from the previous analysis, Fučík was not simply a martyr, but rather a true hero fighting the Nazis. His simple but courageous nature served as an example for the young generations. He was not celebrated because he sacrificed his own life, but because he fought the Nazis. Vladimír Macura stresses that the fact of the hero's death was overshadowed by enthusiasm, smile and joy. It was almost forbidden to mourn for the Fučík's death. Instead, one should look for a prospect of a near happy future.[28]

Fučík was not just a national hero. The Fučík cult was created as a political instrument, as a proof that the communists were the

---

25 Macura, Šťastný věk, 104.

26 Steiner, Deserts, 120.

27 Pynsent, Questions, 207–208.

28 Macura, Šťastný věk, 95–96.

only effective force able to fight the Nazis. Therefore, as Petr Steiner argues, it added "a significantly new ideological spin to the old game. Julius was not just a lonely patriot bravely confronting a numerically superior foreign power but the personification of the communist movement fighting a rear-guard battle after the cowardly bourgeoisie had delivered the nation into the Nazi yoke."[29] This reading of the cult is more precise as it takes into account not just the "questions of identity" of the Czech nation, but also the other important contemporary ideological structure – not only the national, but also the communist one. The political situation in 1989 brought about new heroic figures. Some of them are martyrs like Jan Palach, a young student who set himself on fire in 1969, or Milada Horáková who was sentenced to death in the 1950s political show trial. But there are also new heroes like dissident Václav Havel who became president in 1989 or the Mašín brothers who resisted to the communists "with guns in their hands". The semiotic processes which are used in all of these mythical structures are to a high degree the same. The Mašín myth is worth examining as it well illustrates not only the similarities but also differences which were brought about by the discursive shift after 1989.

The Mašín Romance

The Mašíns' narrative representations tell about of their adventures and struggle against the communists. It is called "the greatest story of the Cold War" or "the story that could have changed the course of the Cold War".[30] So the Mašíns are not portrayed as lyrical heroes as Julius Fučík once was; they are men of action. They have all the necessary predispositions to be heroes. Their heroism originates from their early childhood, they dream about fighting for freedom and their country. When the time comes and ruthless Communists are terrorizing peaceful citizens, they are ready to launch a full-scale campaign and, with the help of the Americans, save the Czechs. They are similar to James Bond who is "the Cavalier entrusted with a mission."[31] "Bond indubitably represents Beauty and Virility as opposed to the Villain, who appears often monstrous."[32] The same qualities are possessed by the Mašín brothers and their adversaries respectively.

---

[29] Steiner, Deserts, 20.

[30] The title of Jan Novák's novel can be translated as *So Far So Good: The Mašíns and the Greatest Story of the Cold War. Barbara Masin's historical book is called Gauntlet: Five Friends, Twenty Thousand Enemy Troops, and the Secret That Could Have Changed the Course of the Cold War.*

[31] Umberto Eco, The Narrative Structure in Fleming, in: B. Waites, T. Bennet (Eds.), Popular Culture: Past and Present, London 1982, 260.

[32] Ibidem, 246.

The Mašín brothers' quest is a continuation of their father's freedom struggle. They are predetermined for their mission by their "noble" origin. Their father was a "knight" of both World Wars. He fought against the Austrian empire for the independent Czechoslovak state in World War I and against the Nazis in World War II and his heroism is indisputable. Ctirad and Josef Mašín are his sons and they are closely connected to their father. The reader is always reminded about a genetic correspondence between them and the ethos of Mašín family: "Did they have heroism running through their veins?"[33] Barbara Masin quotes the Mašín brothers' uncle Ctibor who writes to them: "'You have in your blood all the essential characteristics of good soldiers and patriots.'"[34] Barbara Masin's father Josef also reminds her about the heritage of the family: "'Be proud of the Masin [sic!, recte: Mašín] name. And always remember that the Masins fought for freedom.'"[35]

This implies that their "godlike" origin obliges them to fulfill their father's moral mandate. The father's legacy functions in the narrative structure as a trigger and, at the same time (on the mythical level), it illustrates the exclusive origin of the heroes which predetermines them to act. This means that the brothers are also in a very close mental relationship (which binds them to their father). Although the qualities of the brothers differ slightly, they share the same courage and abilities and "against outside threats they presented a united front."[36]

The Mašíns are born into this world with their quest, which is to fight against the evil embodied in the communist regime in the same way their father struggled against the Nazis. They are different from the others because they do fight. This is another quality which makes the Mašíns resemble the mythical heroes. The hero is active; he cannot passively wait until evil wins. His task is to step out of the lot of the ordinary and act – unlike the rest of the society. As Barbara Masin put it "Nobody in Czechoslovakia, it seemed, was doing anything to reverse the Communists' hijacking of the government – except the Masin brothers. [They were, like their father, fighters, not victims]."[37] The others (the rest of the enslaved citizens) just accepted their sad fate. The Mašíns' peers were

---

33 Novák, Zatím dobrý, 22.

34 Masin, Gauntlet, 53.

35 Ibid., 3.

36 Ibid., 55.

37 Ibid., 100. (The sentence in the brackets is included in the Czech language edition of the book not in the English language edition: Barbara Masin, Odkaz: Pravdivý příběh bratří Mašínů, Prague 2005, 121.)

just "commiserating with each other in hushed voices"[38] but they had no courage to do anything to change the situation. This creates a void, an empty space which is filled by the heroes. The Mašíns do have all the qualities the hero needs to have. They are brave, strong, they "run like Zátopek"[39] and shoot like "Finnish snipers"[40] and their main possession is their moral superiority. We can see here a clear contrast to Julius Fučík who was represented as a single unit within a broader collective of comrades.

A mythical hero is allowed to lie, to kill and to steal because he is pursuing higher, sublime values. So even the Mašín brothers have to lie (in order to lure the policeman out), they hijack cars, rob the vehicle with the money. They can also slit the throat of a policeman. The men they killed or injured could not have been innocent because they were the armed enforcers of the brutal communist regime. However, the Mašín brothers realize that "if you are fighting for individual human life and dignity, you must do so with as much concern for innocent lives as humanly possible."[41] In order to identify with the hero, the reader must be sure that he really is a positive figure. For example, when the hero kills someone, the narrator explains why he has to eliminate this man by proving that he is a villain. The reader is assured that he was the enemy and that the heroes knew this.

The Mašín brothers' narrative representations are thus grounded in a mythical universe in the same way as the communist hero Julius Fučík. While Fučík's romance is based on Marxist ideas, the Mašín brothers fight for democracy – in these narratives it is liberal democracy. Their actions are interpreted as a war against communism. The narratives offer an easily legible black and white world. This narrative scheme is an integral part of the European cultural tradition, it is present in all mythological systems. Tales of heroes and their extraordinary deeds have been part of Western culture since antiquity. The narrative representations of the Mašín brothers belong to a narrative structure which Northrop Frye called romance. According to Frye, the other basic literary forms are tragedy, comedy, and satire. The romance is characterized as follows: "The complete form of the romance is clearly the successful quest, and such a completed form has three main stages: the stage of the perilous journey and the preliminary minor adventures; the crucial struggle, usually some kind of battle in which either the hero or his

---

38 Ibid., 100.

39 Emil Zátopek was a Czech athlete best known for winning three medals in long-distance events at the 1952 Summer Olympics in Helsinki.

40 Novák, Zatím dobrý, 523.

41 Masin, Gauntlet, 67.

foe, or both, must die; and the exaltation of the hero."[42] Frye's observations were originally applied to fiction. Hayden White in *Metahistory* (1978) adopted this distinction and used it when analyzing historical narratives. The historian confronts the chaos of events already constituted and chooses elements of a particular story. He has to subordinate other events which he does not consider as relevant: "This process of exclusion, stress, and subordination is carried out in the interest of constituting *a story of a particular kind*. That is to say, he 'emplots' his story."[43] The romantic thinkers and their reflections on history "turned upon their apprehension of the historical field as a 'Chaos of Being' which they then proceeded to comprehend respectively as simply a chaos, a plenum of creative force, and a field of struggle between heroic men and history itself." [44] The operation of emplotting reality is thus not reserved solely for fictional narratives.

The plot analysis of the narratives shows that they perfectly fit into the category of romance. There is a discernible conflict – the communist 1948 coup, the death struggle which is victorious. The Mašíns and Milan Paumer get to the West, winning over their foes – almost thirty thousand troops who hunt them across East Germany and try to kill them. The Mašíns' activity was a part of a campaign against communism led by the USA. In the end, the war is successful as communism disintegrates; that is the final "catharsis". The plot structures of the Mašín brothers' representations are similar to romance. Romance is also characterized by a clear-cut division between good and bad. The previous observations disclosed the sharp division between the positive and negative characters. In both narratives, the axiological axis is extremely polarized. The reader gets an image of a clearly divided world where the forces of good (the USA) struggle against evil (the Soviet Bloc). This division participates in creating a mythical universe. In the Mašín romance, it is the USA which represents the idyllic world. It is a promised land where people live happily and freely as once Soviet Union for Julius Fučík and his comrades. The Mašíns wanted to join the Americans and help them liberate the world from communist oppression: "Pepa and Radek concluded that a few hard-hitting sabotage actions could unleash the power of rumour and bring about popular rebellion to coincide with the expected American invasion."[45]

---

42 Northrop Frye, The Anatomy of Criticism: Four Essays, Princeton 1957, 187.

43 Hayden White, Metahistory: The Historical Imagination in Nineteenth-Century Europe, Baltimore 1973, 6.

44 Northrop Frye, The Secular Scripture: A Study of the Structure of Romance, Cambridge, Mass.; London 1976, 149.

45 Masin, Gauntlet, 113.

Americans are the ultimate hope and the prospective saviours of the Czechs in the same way as once Soviet Union was for Julius Fučík. The Mašíns hoped that their sabotage activities would coincide with the American invasion. They wanted to induce a massive uprising. Their heroic deeds which seem to be supernatural are praised by the ordinary people who think that these actions have been carried out by their potential miraculous saviours, the Americans: "'Parachutists from the West are attacking SNB policemen!' 'It is the first sally of the Third World War!' 'The Americans are coming!' 'The Americans will save the Czechs!'"[46] Or as Jan Novák has it: "'American partisans with flame–throwers ride about there, but none of them have been caught! No one saw them arrive, no one saw them leave, it is as if they had wings.'"[47] Their deeds seem to be almost magical. The rumour spreads across "the enslaved nation", hyperbolizes their abilities and raises the heroes to a divine pedestal. This also proves that public opinion is clearly on the heroes' side and that people are waiting for someone to rescue them. After the Mašíns and their friends cannot operate in Czechoslovakia anymore, they want to continue with their liberating mission abroad and so they join the U.S. Special Forces.

The romance also includes the necessary counterpart to the "paradise" which is the land behind the Iron Curtain, the cruel world of communism: "The other is a world of exciting adventures, but adventures which involve separation, loneliness, humiliation, pain, and the threat of more pain. I shall call this demonic or night world. Because of the powerful polarizing tendency in romance, we are usually carried directly from one to the other."[48] Czechoslovakia after the communist coup is a land where the heroes operate, yet it is still their home, they have their friends and family there. Everything changes after they cross the border with East Germany. This is the real zone of danger where they are left alone and have to make their way to the West. It is full of traps and unpredictable events. They lose two of their friends and after many adventures they finally reach the "island of freedom" – West Berlin. The Soviet Bloc is a dark place ruled by a cruel dictator, Joseph Stalin, where people are executed for no reason, millions are dying in the Gulag, the system gets rid of its own representatives, and the individual human being means nothing. It is where evil comes from and stretches its clutches in order to swallow the free world.

The Mašín brothers' narrative representations have a coherent plot and closure. Historical reality is emplotted in the mode of romance. However, as Hayden White put it: "real life can never be

[46] Masin, Gauntlet, 76.

[47] Novák, Zatím dobrý, 332.

[48] Frye, The Secular Scripture, 53.

truthfully represented as having the kind of formal coherency met with in the conventional, well-made or fabulistic story."[49] This coherence and unity presented by a single voice has its ideological implications: "The narrative is not merely a neutral discursive form that may or may not be used to represent real events in their aspect as developmental processes but rather entails ontological and epistemic choices with distinct ideological and even specifically political implications."[50] There are some ambivalent facts in the story which distort the heroic image and disrupt the coherency of the narratives, but they are ignored, suppressed or explained implausibly. For example, the armed struggle of the Mašíns did not begin until 1951. It was after the 1948 communist takeover when they applied to study in a Military Academy not before. Their applications were rejected because of their "bourgeois origins". However, one might ask a question: Had they been accepted, would they have fought on the communist side in event of a Third World War? This question is never asked. Instead, this fact is ignored, simply stated but not commented or some authors like Barbara Masin claim that the Mašíns wanted to "attack the system from within".[51] This version is possible but not supported by any clear historical evidence so it happens to be solely a speculation. This fact is thus clearly in contrast with the claim that the Mašíns started their resistance against the communists soon after the communist takeover in 1948. The romance stays coherent and the Mašín brothers retain their heroic image.

Liberal Romance

The Mašín romance fits into the post-communist ideological situation. Communism was condemned as a "totalitarian" ideology and liberal democracy and capitalism are presented here as a functional mode of organizing society. The Mašíns fought for the "American ideals" which are presented as universal. The heroic qualities they used in their freedom struggle are also indispensable in the "free market jungle". Josef Mašín retires as a millionaire. Although coming to the USA with five dollars in his pocket, he was able to make his fortune. His brother also started his own business. When he had trouble, he did not give up, but fought the circumstances so that he

[49] Hayden White, The Content of the Form: Narrative Discourse and Historical Representation, Baltimore 1987, ix.

[50] Hayden White, The Content of the Form: Narrative Discourse and Historical Representation, Baltimore 1987, ix.

[51] Barbara Masin, Gauntlet: Five Friends, Twenty Thousand Enemy Troops, and the Secret that Could Have Changed the Course of the Cold War, Annapolis 2006, 60.

could become a "real" American.[52] Their heroic nature not only gives them the chance to merely survive under any circumstances, but to be the best. What we encounter here is the myth of a strong and unique individual. This myth was revived in the era of Enlightenment but has its origins in ancient Greece.[53] The Enlightenment period challenged the "divine right of kings" and substituted it with liberty and equality of individuals who are responsible for their actions and can determine their own fate. The idea of the human being as a creative and unique individual is at the very centre of liberal thinking: "Classical liberalism has a heroic aura of its own: enlightenment demands self-emancipation, and liberty is the work of independent spirits able to resist authority and find their own way out of prejudice."[54] The Mašíns do not succumb to the Communists, they do not even submit to state institutions (U.S. Army). They are romantic heroes in the purest sense. Romanticism developed the idea of a strong individual even further.

The Mašín myth is deeply rooted in these ideological structures. The narrative structure of romance is coherent with the liberal ideological edifice. The "predatory" individualism is at the root of liberal thinking. The Mašíns are strong individuals, being able first to resist communist evil and later to win their struggle in a capitalist society. The USA are a "free" country which created the conditions for developing their skills and abilities. They tried hard and finally succeeded. This also serves as a direct refutation of communist ideology as it effectively proves that if one makes an effort he/she has the chance to make his/her fortune. The Mašíns' story is the embodiment of the American dream and as such it fits into the contemporary liberal ideology. And so whilst the Marxist romance is identified as utopian, the same can be said about the liberal romance. The American dream about strong individuals who can be successful if they work hard has a utopian core. As Žižek put it: "[T]he very notion of capitalism as a neutral social mechanism is ideology (even utopian ideology) at its purest."[55] The liberal discourse is predominant in the texts post-1989 and the Mašín romance is just one example.

Communist ideology in the narratives produced before 1989 in Czechoslovakia is usually easily discernible. The question is whether we really live in a post-ideological world today. Peter Steiner claims that "the ideological battles of today are fought in Czechia on the

---

52 Novák, Zatím dobrý, 708.

53 Petr A. Bílek (Ed.), James Bond a major Zeman. Ideologizující vzorce vyprávění, Prague 2007, 104.

54 Nancy Rosenblum, Another Liberalism: Romanticism and the Reconstruction of Liberal Thought, Cambridge, Mass.; London 1987, 107.

55 Slavoj Žižek, First as Tragedy, Then as Farce, London, New York, 2009, 25.

floor of Parliament rather than in the pages of books."[56] Can we really agree with his observation? This paper can be regarded as an attempt to reassess this opinion. The Mašín brothers' narratives published today are not free from ideology, but one can say that by using the powerful heroic myth which promotes liberal democracy, they seem to be even more universal and "natural" (in Roland Barthes' sense)[57] than the narratives produced in the era of communism. The political change which occurred after the 1989 Velvet Revolution brought about a radical discursive shift. The communist heroes, symbols and slogans were repudiated and substituted by new heroes, new slogans and ideology. The Mašín myth is an excellent example of this process. Josef Mašín Sr. represents the greatest Czech hero of a home resistance in World War II. He was revived along with Masaryk and other iconic figures from the First Republic. The Mašín brothers represent a new phenomenon in the Czech discourse. The inconvenient and ambivalent facts are rather suppressed in order to raise them on a heroic pedestal. Instead of a Marxist romance, we encounter another romance – at this time a liberal one. Although the wine (ideology) is new it tastes as bitter as before because the wineskins (the mental patterns) are the same.

---

56 Steiner, Deserts, 24.

57 Roland Barthes, Mythologies, London 1972.

Europa Orientalis
hrsg. vom Institut für Osteuropäische Geschichte an der Universität Wien

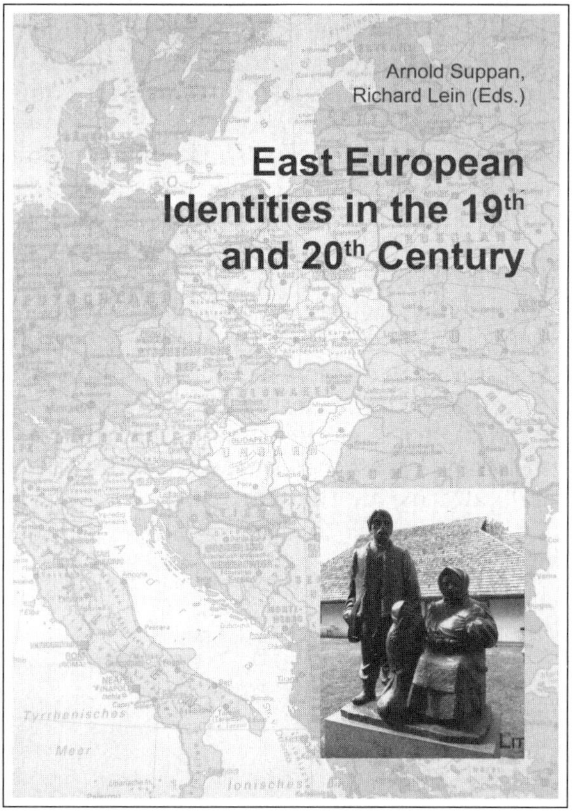

Arnold Suppan; Richard Lein (Eds.)
East European Identities in the 19th and 20th Century
During the 1970s the Austrian Ministry of Science and Research supported the founding of the "Centre for Austrian Studies" at the University of Minnesota in Minneapolis and the Austrian chair at Stanford University in California. Nowadays there are six institutions of this kind operational, besides the U.S.A. also in Canada, Hungary and Israel. Their tasks are to promote Austrian and Central European studies among professors and students of their host nation and to provide Austrian students the possibility to conduct research in a foreign country and to get in touch with the respective national scientific communities. This anthology contains not only a description of the Institution's activities in the academic year 2008/2009, but also the working papers of ten of their present PhD students. Their research, which is for the most part connected to the History of East Central Europe, covers a period from the 19th century to the present.
Bd. 8, 2009, 256 S., 24,90 €, br., ISBN 978-3-643-50102-8

LIT Verlag Berlin – Münster – Wien – Zürich – London
Auslieferung Deutschland / Österreich / Schweiz: siehe Impressumsseite

Impressum

Die Autorin und der Verlag bedanken sich bei folgenden Institutionen für die Unterstützung dieses Buchs:

Heinrich Hössli Stiftung

Kanton St.Gallen Kulturförderung

Kanton Zürich Fachstelle Kultur

KULTUR RAUM.SH
Kanton und Stadt Schaffhausen Kulturförderung

LOS Lesbenorganisation Schweiz
Organisation suisse des lesbiennes
Organizzazione svizzera delle lesbiche

MIGROS Kulturprozent

PINK CROSS

Stadt Zürich Kultur

st.gallen

TRANSGENDER NETWORK SWITZERLAND TGNS

www.rotpunktverlag.ch
in Kooperation mit Saiten Verlag

Gestaltung und Satz:
Dorothee Dähler, Sina Egger
Fotografie: Lea Reutimann
Druck und Bindung:
Friedrich Pustet, Regensburg

ISBN 978-3-85869-981-7
3. Auflage 2024

Dieser Titel ist auch als E-Book erhältlich.

Der Rotpunktverlag wird vom Bundesamt für Kultur mit einem Strukturbeitrag für die Jahre 2021 bis 2024 unterstützt.

Die Autorin

Anna Rosenwasser, 1990 in Schaffhausen geboren, lebt in Zürich. Die LGBTQ-Aktivistin und Politinfluencerin hat Journalismus und Politikwissenschaft studiert und arbeitet seit 2008 als Journalistin. 2017 übernahm sie die Geschäftsführung der Lesbenorganisation Schweiz. In ihrer Heimat Schaffhausen gründete sie den queeren Jugendtreff AnderSH mit und engagierte sich zudem im Vorstand der LGBTQ-Jugendorganisation Milchjugend. Heute spricht und schreibt sie beruflich über Geschlecht und Anziehung. Ihr Kanal auf Instagram gehört zu den meistbeachteten aktivistischen Kanälen der Deutschschweiz. Im Herbst 2023 wurde sie für die SP des Kantons Zürich in den Nationalrat gewählt.